Public Procurement in the European Community: Volume II

A GUIDE TO THE PROCUREMENT CASES OF THE COURT OF JUSTICE

Sue Arrowsmith,
Professor of Law,
University College of Wales,
Aberystwyth

© Sue Arrowsmith

First published in 1992 by
Earlsgate Press,
Earlsgate House, 11 West End,
Winteringham, South Humberside, DN15 9NR
Tel: 0724 733517 Fax: 0724 732676

British Library Cataloguing - in- Publication Data:

A Catalogue record for this book is available from the British Library

ISBN   1-873439-05-9

Printed by M&D Printers, Hull, North Humberside

Other books available in the same series:

PUBLIC PROCUREMENT IN THE EUROPEAN COMMUNITY
Series ISBN   1-873439-30-X

Volume 1:   The Single Market Rules and the Enforcement Regime After 1992
by Prof. Andrew Cox, Contracts and Procurement Research Unit, University of Birmingham
ISBN   1-873439-00-8

Volume 3:   The Texts of the Community Directives, Recommendations, Proposals, Decisions, Resolutions and Communications in Force
edited by Prof Andrew Cox and Frances Lamont, Contracts and Procurement Research Unit, University of Birmingham
ISBN   1-873439-40-7

Volume 4:   The Remedies for Enforcing the Works and Supplies Directives in the 12 Member States
edited by Prof Sue Arrowsmith, Dept of Law, Univeristy College of Wales, Aberystywth
ISBN   1-873439-45-8

Preface

The aim of this book is to make accessible to both lawyers and non-lawyers
the case law of the European Court of Justice on public procurement. The
book deals with nineteen judgments and orders which concern the
Community's open procurement policy. (A twentieth, case C-24/91
Commission v Spain, was handed down on March 18th 1992 and came too
late for inclusion; but it is hoped to deal with this and other future cases in a
supplement in due course). Obviously, the book cannot cover cases raising
issues of a general nature which have a potential application to procurement,
such as the numerous cases on the general principles of free movement of
goods and persons; it deals only with those cases which raise issues special
to procurement, or which throw light on the application of general
principles in the procurement context. For this reason I have not dealt with
case C-113/89 (*Rush Portuguesa*), which, although it involves a public
works contract, does not seem to raise legal issues relating to procurement
specifically.

For each of the nineteen judgments and orders dealt with in the book
there is an explanation of the facts, the legal issues and the ruling, and a
discussion of any important implications of that ruling. I have included
straightforward explanations of basic Community law principles, where
appropriate, in order to make the text accessible to those without a legal
background, and there is also an introductory account of the European Court
and its procedure. The text of the judgments and orders considered is
provided in an Appendix. It seemed useful to include these since not all
libraries have the relevant reports available, and some of the cases have not
yet been reported. At the time the book was compiled there was no official
English translation of the last four cases, and the English text of these cases
is our own unofficial version, translated from French.

I would like to express my thanks to all those who have helped in the
preparation of the book. In particular I am grateful to Laurence Gormley
and Peter-Armin Trepte, who read parts of the manuscript; to Dorothy
Whyte, who helped prepare the unofficial translations; and to Lillian
Stevenson and Meirion Derrick in the UCW law library, who assisted in
numerous ways. My research in this area has been facilitated by a small
grant from the funds of the ESRC, and I am also grateful for that assistance.

Sue Arrowsmith,
Aberystwyth, June 1st 1992

Table of Contents

List of Abbreviations

Legislation

The main Directives on procurement are referred to in the text in abbreviated form. The abbreviations used are as follows:

Compliance Directive: Council Directive 89/665, [1989] OJ L395/33

Supplies Directive: Council Directive 77/62, [1976] OJ L13/1, as amended by Council Directive 80/767, [1980] OJ L215/1 and Council Directive 88/295, [1988] OJ L127/1

1988 Supplies Directive: Council Directive 88/295, above

Utilities Directive: Council Directive 90/531, [1990] OJ L297/1

Utilities Compliance Directive: Council Directive 92/13 [1992], OJ L76/14

1971 Works Directive: Council Directive 71/305, [1971] OJ L185/5

Works Directive: Council Directive 71/305, [1971] OJ L185/5, as amended by Council Directive 89/440, [1989] OJ L210/1

1989 Works Directive: Council Directive 89/440, above

Books

A number of books are also referred to in the text in abbreviated form. The abbreviations used are as follows:

Lasok and Bridge: D.Lasok and J.W.Bridge, *Law and Institutions of the European Community* (5th ed. 1991; Butterworths)

Steiner: J. Steiner, *Textbook on EEC Law* (2nd ed. 1990; Blackstones)

Wyatt and Dashwood: D.Wyatt and A. Dashwood, *The Substantive Law of the EEC* (2nd ed. 1987; Sweet & Maxwell)

Detailed Table of Contents

Table of Cases

European Community - Numerical List

European Community - Alphabetical List

Table of Legislation

European Community - Treaties

European Community - Secondary Legislation

Directives

Rules of Procedure

United Kingdom

1. The European Court of Justice and its Role in the Field of Procurement

1.1. INTRODUCTION

What is commonly referred to in England as the European Community (EC) is in fact three separate Communities. The first is the European Coal and Steel Community (ECSC), set up by the **Treaty of Paris** in 1951 to implement a common European policy in relation to the coal and steel industries. The other two Communities were established under the **first and second Treaties of Rome**, both signed in 1957. The **first Treaty of Rome** set up the European Economic Community (the Common Market or EEC), the main objective of which was at that time the general economic integration of Europe, including the creation of a free market within Europe. The **second Treaty of Rome** established the European Atomic Energy Community (Euratom), designed to put into effect a common policy in the area of atomic energy. The rules on open procurement fall mainly within the province of the European Economic Community, and all cases to date have arisen in the context of the EEC. This chapter will thus be concerned solely with actions in the European Court in the context of the EEC. References to "the Treaty" or "the Treaty of Rome" hereafter refer to the **first Treaty of Rome** - that is, to the EEC Treaty.

Though there remain today three distinct Communities, the three in fact share common governmental institutions. The merger process began with the **Convention on the Merger of Certain Institutions Common to the European Communities**, concluded at the same time as the **Treaties of Rome,** which provided for a single court, and also a single Parliament. (Fusion of the executive authorities of the three Communities occurred later in accordance with a Treaty signed in 1965 and implemented in 1967). Thus a court was established to operate for all three of the Communities, taking over the functions of the court which had already been established for the European Coal and Steel Community, as well as taking on the judicial function in relation to the two new Communities - the EEC and Euratom - created under the Rome Treaties. The full title of the court is the Court of Justice of the European Communities, though it is often referred to simply as the European Court of Justice, or just the European Court.

It is this court which deals with those categories of case in which issues relating to public procurement generally arise, as will be explained below. It may be noted that a second Community court, called the Court of First Instance, has now also been set up, in order to take on some of the load previously carried by the Court of Justice. The new court became operational in 1989, and deals with limited categories of case assigned to it by the Court of Justice, notably staff cases and actions against the Commission concerning the conduct of the latter in relation to the EEC competition rules. It is not of much significance in relation to procurement. References in this work to the European Court, or simply to the court, are references to the Court of Justice of the European Communities.

In relation to the EEC Treaty the function of the European Court is stated in the **Treaty of Rome** as being to "ensure that in the interpretation and application of this Treaty the law is observed" (**Article 164**). This highlights the two main functions of the court, which are, first, to secure the enforcement of the law in certain cases where there has been a breach, and, second, to develop and interpret the rules and principles of Community law. The Court fulfils both functions in relation to procurement.

There are two main ways in which the Court has become involved in public procurement issues. The first is where an action for an alleged infringement of the procurement rules has been brought against a member state by the Commission under the procedure provided for in **Articles 169 of the Treaty of Rome**. Such actions are heard by the European Court. The second way in which the court has come to adjudicate on procurement issues is where national courts have sought a ruling from the European Court on a question of Community law which have arisen in actions before that national courts. The procedure for this is set out in **Article 177** of the Treaty.

Each of these types of proceeding will now be explained.

1.2. ENFORCEMENT ACTIONS (ARTICLES 169-170)

1.2.1. Actions by the Commission under Article 169

1.2.1.1. Introduction
Article 169 of the Treaty of Rome provides for a procedure for the Commission to bring a member state before the Court of Justice where the Commission considers that there has been some infringement of Community law by the institutions of the state concerned. Such an action may be brought for an alleged infringement of the Community rules on public procurement.

A number of 169 actions relating to procurement have already been brought by the Commission. At the time of writing six have proceeded to a full hearing. These are case 10/76 against Italy, discussed at 2. below; case 274/83 against Italy, discussed at 4. below; case 199/85, again against Italy, and discussed at 5. below; case 45/87 against Ireland (*the Dundalk case*), discussed at 7. below; case C-3/88 (*Re Data Processing*), again against Italy, and discussed at 9. below; and case C-247/89 against Portugal (*the Lisbon Airport case*), discussed below at 14.. In all but one of these cases, the state brought before the court was declared to be in breach of its obligations, the exception being the *Lisbon Airport* case, where there was found to have been no breach. In two further cases interim measures have been granted by the court (see case 194/88R, discussed at 12. below; and case C-272/91, at 16.). Actions might be brought for a breach of the **Treaty of Rome** itself; for a breach by awarding authorities of the procurement Directives or of implementing legislation; or for failure by a member state to implement a Directive.

1.2.1.2. Procedure
Before it brings an alleged infringement before the Court of Justice, the Commission must, according to **Article 169**, give the state concerned the opportunity to submit its observations on the alleged breach. This requires that the state be given an adequate and realistic opportunity to reply to the allegations (case 31/69, *EC Commission v Italy* [1970] ECR 25, [1970] CMLR 175). In practice, where a breach is perceived by the Commission, a letter will be sent to the state concerned, setting out the allegations and calling for comments on those allegations. This is generally referred to as a "letter of infringement".

If the Commission is not satisfied with the response received from the member state, it must then deliver a "reasoned opinion" on the matter - that is, an explanation of the breach of Community law which it believes has occurred. This opinion must contain a "coherent statement of the reasons which convinced the Commission that the state in question had failed to fulfil one of its obligations under the Treaty" (case 7/61, *EEC Commission v Italy* [1961] ECR 317, [1962] CMLR 39). **Article 169** provides that if the state concerned does not comply with the reasoned opinion within the period laid down by the Commission, the Commission may bring the state concerned before the Court of Justice.

In relation to certain breaches of the procurement rules, there is a special procedure for Commission intervention at an early stage, which is provided for in **Article 3 of the Compliance Directive**, for public works and supplies contracts, and in **Article 8 of the Utilities Compliance Directive**, for works and supplies contracts in the utilities sector (though note that at the time of writing the latter Directive was not yet required to be implemented. It is proposed also that the procedure will apply to contracts for services when these are brought within the Community's scheme of procurement Directives). This intervention procedure may be invoked by the Commission where it considers that there has been a "clear and manifest infringement of Community provisions in the field of public procurement" (**Compliance Directive, Article 3 (1); Utilities Compliance Directive, Article 8 (1)**). In such an event the Commission must notify both the member state and the relevant contracting authority of the reasons which have led it to conclude that there is a clear and manifest breach of the law, and must request that it be corrected (**Compliance Directive, Article 3 (2); Utilities Compliance Directive, Article 8 (2)**).

Following receipt of such a notice the member state concerned must reply within 21 days, and then confirm to the Commission that the alleged breach has been corrected or give a reasoned submission as to why there has been no correction. It is specifically provided that such a reasoned submission may rely on the fact that review proceedings are on foot: in this case no doubt the Commission will leave the matter to be resolved in the national review forum. In this event, the state has an obligation to inform the Commission of the outcome of the review proceedings as soon as they are known. It is also possible that the contract award procedure may have been suspended, either by the authority itself or by some review body. In this case, the state need simply inform the Commission of this fact. The Commission must be notified when any suspension is lifted and the state must then either confirm that the infringement has been corrected or explain why this has not been done. (The Commission must also be informed if a new award procedure is started in respect of the contested matter). These various rules are set out in **Compliance Directive, Article 3 (3)-(5), and Utilities Compliance Directive, Article 8 (3)-(5)**).

What is the position if a state does not comply with its obligations under the above procedure? No sanctions are specifically stated in either Directive. In practice, the Commission treats the notification of the alleged breach which is given under this special procedure as the equivalent of a "letter of infringement". If there is no response to its notice, or the Commission is not satisfied with the response - for example, with reasons given for a failure to correct an alleged breach - then it is the practice for it to issue a reasoned opinion for the purpose of **Article 169** proceedings *immediately* on the expiry of 21 days from a state's receipt of the notice (that is, immediately on expiry of the period specified for reply under the special procedure). If the reasoned opinion is not complied with, the Commission will commence proceedings under **Article 169**.

It should be noted that, as with other provisions of the two **Compliance Directives**, the special procedure for Commission intervention applies only to award procedures which are within the scope of the relevant Directives (though, with respect to such award procedures, it seems that it applies both to breaches of the Directives and to breaches of the Treaty itself). The special procedure does not apply to breaches of the Treaty occurring in relation to award procedures which are outside the Directives - for example, because the value of the contract to which they relate is below the relevant threshold. It should also be pointed out that the procedure may only be invoked where a contract has not yet been concluded (**Compliance Directive, Article 3 (1); Utilities Compliance Directive, Article 8 (1)**).

Once the matter of an alleged breach does come before the court, the court will examine the question of whether there has been a breach of Community law for which the state can be held responsible. It must be emphasised that ultimately it is for the court itself, and not the Commission, to decide whether there has been a breach of the law. If the court finds the state concerned to be in breach, it will issue a declaration to this effect.

1.2.1.3. Authorities for which a member state is responsible

Actions under **Article 169** are brought against member states, and not against individual authorities within that state. A breach of Community law relating to procurement may occur where there is a failure properly to implement Directives, and in this case the state is clearly held responsible for its actions under **Article 169**. A breach may also arise, however, from the actions of individual awarding authorities which fail to comply with the procurement rules, and in such a case the question may arise as to whether the member state can be held responsible for the actions of these authorities in proceedings brought under **Article 169**.

It is now clear that states may be held responsible for the conduct of authorities which are completely independent from the central executive, such as local authorities (see 7.5. below). This general issue is discussed further below at 8.2. in relation to the *Beentjes* case, where there was some discussion of the scope of a state's responsibility under **Article 169** for independent authorities (and see also 14.3.). It is not clear whether a state's responsibility extends to *all* authorities which are subject to the procurement Directives. It may be argued, for example, that the state cannot be held responsible for some of the entities subject to the **Utilities Directive**, many of which are substantially independent from governmental control and funding; and it may be that this is so even with some entities subject to the **Works Directive** and **Supplies Directive** (see further 14.3.).

It is also not clear how far the test for determining which bodies are subject to the doctrine of direct effect is co-extensive with that for

determining the bodies for which a state is to be held responsible in
Article 169 proceedings.

1.2.1.4. Enforcement

What is the position where a member state is found, in a 169 action, to be
in breach of its obligations under Community law? In such an action the
European Court may not order any specific steps to be taken by the state,
but is confined to issuing a declaration that Community law has been
breached. The obligations of a state in the case where a declaration has been
issued against it are dealt with by **Article 171** of the Treaty. This
provides: "If the Court of Justice finds that a Member State has failed to
fulfil an obligation under this Treaty, the state shall be required to take the
necessary measures to comply with the judgment of the Court of Justice".

There is, however, no provision in the Treaty for the imposition of
sanctions should the member state fail to take "necessary measures". If the
Commission considers that necessary measures have not been taken in
response to a declaration by the court in a 169 action, it may bring the state
concerned before the European Court in a new 169 action. This second
action will be based not on the same breach of Community law as gave rise
to the first action (such an action would not be permitted), but on the state's
failure to fulfil its obligations under **Article 171.** In such an action it
will be for the court to decide what are the "necessary measures" required for
compliance with **Article 171.** If the member state concerned still refuses
to take any action, the only "sanctions" available are political. There is
currently no provision in the Treaty for any sanction - such as a fine - to be
imposed by law. It may be noted, however, that the Maastricht Treaty
proposes an amendment to **Article 171** to provide for the imposition of
sanctions where an action is brought to the Court in respect of a breach of
the obligation to take "necessary measures."

It is an interesting question what are the "necessary measures" required
to be taken under **Article 171** where a declaration has been made that a
state has breached its obligations under the procurement rules. If a contract
has not yet been awarded, it would seem that a member state would be
expected to ensure that the award process is recommenced in a lawful
manner. It is less obvious what should be the position where an award has
already been made, particularly if the contract has already been entered into.
This question has been touched on in some cases, but no answer to the
question has yet been given by the court. (For discussion see 5.2.2. and
16.3. below). It is also an open question whether the court might ever be
willing to find that payment of compensation to a party affected by a breach
of Community rules is a measure necessary to redress the breach under
Article 171: this issue has not yet been put to the court. The court might
perhaps be willing to find that compensation must be provided, at least in

some limited circumstances. (This view is taken by Dashwood and White, (1989) 14 EL Rev 388, at pp.406-7). On the other hand, it may be that the court would consider that those wishing to claim compensation should be left solely to any compensation remedy which they have in the national courts. The question of what remedies are available in the national courts to a party affected by a breach of the procurement rules is touched on further at 1.3. below.

1.2.1.5. Interim measures

There may be some considerable period of time between the lodging of an application under **Article 169** by the Commission and the hearing of the case. (At the present time the average length of the whole **Article 169** procedure is two years: see Millett, (1992) 1 PPLR 70 at 78). Sometimes the Commission may wish to seek interim measures - that is, temporary relief to preserve the *status quo* until the case has been heard. In public procurement cases the Commission will frequently wish to obtain interim relief, with the objective of preventing the procurement from proceeding until the alleged breach of the procurement rules has been adjudicated by the court. It may be felt, in particular, that it is advisable to stop any contract actually being concluded, or to prevent work beginning, since this may make it more difficult for the contract to be re-awarded if it is eventually found to have been awarded in breach of the procurement rules. (On this see further 5.2.2. below).

Article 186 of the Treaty empowers the Court of Justice to give "any interim measures" on an application by the Commission which relates to a case before the court, including proceedings under **Article 169.** The procedure and other matters relating to such applications are governed by **Articles 83-88 of the Rules of Procedure** of the court. Such applications are normally, though not invariably, heard by the President of the court. (The application is made to the President who may hear it himself or assign it to be heard by the court). The application must be served on the other party, and the President is required to prescribe a short period of time in which that other party may submit observations (**Article 84 (1) of the Rules of Procedure**). There is provision, however, for an order to be granted by the President even before the other party is heard, subject to later variation or cancellation: this is referred to as an *ex parte* order.

There is no provision for an application for interim measures to be made until **Article 169** proceedings have actually been instituted before the European Court. This follows from **Article 83 (1) of the Rules of Procedure** which states that interim proceedings must relate to the case, and must be sought by someone who is party to the case. There is obviously some time-lag between commencement of an investigation by the

Commission and the initiation of legal proceedings, since, as explained, the Commission must listen to submissions from the member state concerned, and then deliver a reasoned opinion before proceedings can be instituted (see 1.2.1.4.). The absence of any possibility of interim relief during the investigation period may mean that it is impossible to prevent the conclusion of a contract during this period, and the position has been criticised (see Gormley, (1989) 14 EL Rev 156). In this regard it is interesting to note a proposal made in relation to the **Compliance Directive** - that is, the Directive which regulates the remedies to be given in the case of a breach of the procurement rules in relation to contracts covered by the **Works** and **Supplies Directives**. It was originally proposed that, in cases where the Commission considered there to be a clear breach of the rules, the Commission itself should have a power to order a suspension of the procurement process, without the need first to initiate a 169 action or, indeed, even to seek the authority of the court. However, the suggested provision was ultimately dropped from the Directive because of opposition from the member states. It should be pointed out, however, that the absence of a legal remedy at an earlier stage is not as important now as might once have been thought, since it has now been made clear in the Italian lottery case that interim relief may be given given even after the contract has been concluded (see 16. below).

As indicated above, applications for interim relief are normally heard by the President of the court alone. This means that such applications can generally be heard very quickly. In cases where an application is referred to a the court, it is expressly provided by **Article 85 of the Rules of Procedure** that it shall have priority over all other matters.

The principles which govern the question of whether to grant interim relief and the application of these principles in the context of public procurement are considered below at 7.2, 12.2-3, and 16.2.

1.2.2. Actions by other member states under Article 170

It is not only the Commission which may bring member states before the European Court - other member states may also do so. This is provided for in **Article 170 of the Treaty of Rome**. Before a member state may commence such an action it must bring the matter before the Commission. As before the commencement of 169 proceedings, the Commission must deliver a reasoned opinion on the question of breach, after first giving the state alleged to be in breach an opportunity to submit its observations. If the Commission fails to deliver an opinion within three months, an action may be brought under **Article 170** without an opinion being delivered.

The procedure provided for in **Article 170** has not been important. No cases of this kind have been heard in relation to procurement, and indeed, there has been only one case of any kind which has proceeded to a hearing under **Article 170**. This is because in practice complaints by other member states are often be taken up by the Commission, which will bring an action under **Article 169**.

The principles relating to matters such as enforcement and interim relief are similar to those applying in 169 actions, which were explained above (see 1.2.1.4. and 1.2.1.5.).

1.3. ACTIONS IN THE NATIONAL COURTS

1.3.1. Introduction

The second main way in which procurement issues may come before the European Court is where a question of the interpretation or validity of Community law arises in the course of an action brought in the national courts of one of the member states. The national authority may in such a case refer the question of Community law to the European Court, under a procedure set out in **Article 177 of the Treaty of Rome**. Such a reference is generally referred to as a "preliminary ruling" or "**Article 177** ruling".

Before considering further the preliminary ruling procedure, it is useful to say a few words about the circumstances in which actions relating to the Community procurement rules may arise in the national courts.

1.3.2. Availability of actions in the national courts

Issues relating to the Community rules on procurement may arise in the national courts where a party aggrieved by conduct in the procurement process brings a legal action against the offending authority. Where a private party feels that there has been a breach of Community law by an authority in a member state, it is not open to him to bring an action before the European Court - that option is open only to the Commission and to other states. A complaint to the Commission may, of course, lead the Commission to take up the issue and to institute 169 proceedings; but if a private party wishes himself to bring an action, any such action can be brought only in the courts of the relevant member state.

What principles govern the availability of remedies in the national courts to enforce the Community procurement rules ?

In the case of provisions in the **Treaty of Rome** itself, individuals are able to enforce these in the national courts whenever the relevant provision has *direct effect*. For a provision to have direct effect, it must impose an obligation which is (1) unconditional, and which is (2)

sufficiently precise, to be enforceable by the national courts. The provisions
of the Treaty which are most important in relation to procurement are
Article 30, on the free movement of goods, and **Article 52**   and
Article 59, on freedom of establishment and the freedom to provide
services. These Articles all have direct effect, and so may be relied on before
the national courts.

The general principle is that the remedies and procedures for enforcing
Treaty provisions in the national courts are those which are applicable to
similar actions in domestic law, though this principle is subject to some
important qualifications designed to ensure that remedies are made effective
for the enforcement of Community law. (For further details see Arrowsmith,
Civil Liability and Public Authorities (1992) ch.1 at 1.6.). The question of
remedies for breaches of the Treaty in procurement cases is now also
governed to some extent by the **Compliance Directive**, adopted in
1989, and the **Utilities Compliance Directive**, adopted in 1992, as is
explained further below.

There are, of course, important Directives on procurement which
supplement and reinforce the Treaty provisions. Where rules are contained in
Directives, member states are required to provide for specific measures in
their national legal systems to implement those rules. Where member states
have fulfilled their obligations in this respect, and have properly
implemented the rules in a Directive, any action to enforce the relevant rules
will be based on the national rules implementing the Directive, and not on
the Directive itself. For example, the rules regarding advertising of public
supplies and works contracts and the procedures for the award of such
contracts are contained in the **Works Directive** and the **Supplies
Directive**. In the UK the **Works** and **Supplies Directives** have been
implemented by the **Public Works Contracts Regulations 1991** (SI
1991 No 2680) and the **Public Supply Contracts Regulations
1991** (SI 1991 No 2679). To the extent that these Regulations properly
implement the rules set out in the Directives, any action to enforce the rules
on advertising etc will now be based on the Regulations: there is no need in
an action in the United Kingdom courts to rely on or cite the Directives
themselves.

What, however, is the position where a member state does not
implement a Directive by the time set for implementation? In this case the
rules laid down in the Directive may be enforced in the national courts in
spite of the absence of specific implementing measures, provided that the
provision in question has direct effect - that is, that it imposes obligations
which are unconditional and sufficiently precise to be enforced by the
national courts. The question of whether certain provisions of the
procurement Directives have direct effect has been discussed by the
European Court in several cases, and it seems that the rules in the

Directives on advertising and award procedures generally have direct effect (see 8. and 11.3 below). Thus the fact that a member state fails to adopt national measures implementing these rules within the required time will not prevent a contractor aggrieved by a perceived breach of the rules from bringing an action in the national courts: he may rely in such a case on the Directive itself. In the UK, for example, the rules in the Directives on public works and supplies contracts were not embodied in national legislation, as seemed to be required for implementation, until December 1991, well after the set date. For the period between the implementation date for the rule in question and December 1991 contractors could have enforced that rule in the UK courts by relying on the relevant Directive itself, by virtue of the doctrine of direct effect.

The same applies where a state has purported to implement a Directive but has done so improperly. In such a case a party may enforce the rule as laid down in the Directive itself.

It must be emphasised that it is not generally possible to enforce the rules contained in Directives until the date set for implementation has passed. At the time of writing (March 1992) the date for implementation of the major **Works** and **Supplies Directives** has passed, but the date has not yet passed for any state to implement the **Utilities Directive**. Thus this last Directive cannot generally be enforced. However, if national implementing legislation is made effective by the state concerned before the date for implementation - that is, where a state chooses to implement earlier than actually required - it is possible to bring an action based on that national legislation.

Rules in Directives which have not been implemented in time, or have been improperly implemented, cannot, under the doctrine of direct effect, be enforced against *any* party to whom the rules apply. They may be enforced against the State itself, and also against bodies or persons made responsible by state measures for providing a service under state control, and which have special powers for the purpose (case C-188/ 89, *Foster v British Gas*, [1990] 2 CMLR 833); but they cannot be enforced against most private individuals (see Wyatt and Dashwood, pp. 45-47). It seems probable that all bodies within the scope of the **Works** and **Supplies Directives** are bodies against which directly effective Directives may be enforced; but there is room for argument that some bodies which are within the scope of the **Utilities Directive** are not sufficiently linked to the State for the purpose of the principle of the direct effect of Directives. It may be noted, however, that the courts of member states have certain obligations to interpret national law so as to ensure that Community law is complied with. This means that in some cases the obligations provided for by Community Directives are effectively made to apply to private individuals and authorities, even though the relevant Directive has not been properly implemented by legislation, because of the interpretation of the law adopted by the courts. (For discussion of the scope of this principle, over which there is much uncertainty, and of other aspects of enforcing Directives see further Howells, (1991) 54 MLR 456; de Burca, (1992) 55 MLR 215).

The general principles which apply in relation to remedies and procedure for enforcing the rules in Directives are the same as those which apply to actions for enforcing directly effective Treaty provisions. Thus the applicable remedies and procedures are generally those which govern comparable actions under national law. Thus, for example, remedies and time limits which apply to contractors suing for a breach of domestic rules on procurement will apply to actions for breach of the Community procurement rules.

In addition, the question of remedies in the national courts is also subject in some cases to specific requirements laid down in the **Compliance Directive** and the **Utilities Compliance Directive**. The former applies to actions to enforce the rules in the **Works** and **Supplies Directives**, and also to conduct in relation to contracts within the scope of those Directives, which is in breach of some other Community law rule - for example, of the Treaty itself (**Compliance Directive, Article 1**). It also applies to actions for enforcing national measures which implement the relevant Community rules. The **Utilities Compliance Directive** applies, similarly, to actions to enforce the **Utilities Directive** or to enforce other Community rules in relation to award procedures covered by that Directive, and also to national measures implementing these rules. Neither of these **Compliance Directives** applies to actions which concern award procedures not covered by the three substantive Directives - for example, actions concerning a breach of the Treaty in awarding contracts of too low a value to be caught by the Directives.

The Directives provide generally for *effective* remedies to be made available for breach of Community law, and also certain specific forms of relief, including damages for disappointed contractors.

1.3.3. The Article 177 ruling procedure

Questions concerning the interpretation of Community law may sometimes arise where it is sought to enforce directly effective rules in the national courts. For example, in an action based on a breach of the Treaty, there may be a dispute over the meaning and scope of the relevant Treaty provisions, as in *Du Pont de Nemours* (see 9. below). Questions may also be raised concerning the interpretation of the procurement Directives, either where a member state has failed to implement a Directive at all or where there is some argument as to whether national measures purporting to implement the Directive have properly done so - several cases have involved requests for a ruling concerning the interpretation of the procurement Directives (see below, at 3., 8., 10., 13., and 15.). Procurement cases have also raised the question of whether particular provisions have direct effect (see 8. and 11. below). Issues might also potentially arise as to the validity of Community measures on procurement.

It has been thought unsatisfactory that questions regarding the interpretation of Community law which arise in the course of proceedings in the national courts should be left solely to those courts: this might lead to unacceptable differences of approach to Community law as between the different member states. To achieve some uniformity in the way Community law is applied, a procedure has been established which gives the European Court the primary role in interpreting Community law, even where the question of interpretation arises in the context of an action in the national courts. This is the procedure set out in **Article 177 of the Treaty of Rome.** Essentially it provides a method by which the national courts may seek authoritative guidance from the European Court when questions of Community law are raised in actions before them.

Article 177 states that the court may give guidance on, *inter alia*, the interpretation of the Treaty itself, and on the validity and interpretation of acts of the institutions of the Community, which of course includes Directives. When any such question arises in an action in the national courts, and that court considers that resolution of the question is necessary for it to make a decision, it may always, if it chooses, refer the question to the European Court. When the national court is a body "against whose decision there is no remedy under national law" - that is, whose decisions are not subject to appeal or review - **Article 177** states that there is a *duty* to refer any relevant question of Community law to the European Court. The court has, however, accepted that there are exceptions to this duty, first, when an interpretation of the same point has already been given by the European Court and, second, where, even though no previous ruling has been given, the correct application of Community law is so obvious as to leave no room for reasonable doubt.

Even where a ruling has already been given on a particular point, it is open to a national court to seek a further ruling on the same point in a different case, in the hope that the European Court may change its mind, at least where the interpretation as opposed to the validity of a Community measure is in issue. (This was done in *Donà Alfonso,* discussed at 13. below). This is possible, since the court is not bound to follow its own previous decisions - though it normally does so.

When a national court seeks guidance under the **Article 177** procedure, the proceedings before the national court are suspended whilst the question of European law is put to the European Court. The European

Court answers the question put, and the national court then decides the matter before it on the basis of the view of European law taken by the European Court. The national court is bound to apply the ruling in relation to the facts of the case before it.

It must be emphasised that the European Court does not itself decide the case brought in the national court; it simply enlightens the national court as to the relevant rules of European law, which the national court must itself apply in disposing of the case. The European Court answers the question put to it in an abstract form, leaving the national court to apply the principle which the European Court has formulated to the facts of the particular case. This is why the ruling given under **Article 177** is sometimes referred to as a "preliminary" ruling. As it has been explained, "The ruling is preliminary in the sense that it does not form part of the decision which disposes of the case. The proceedings in the European Court represent a stage in proceedings which begin and end in another court." (Wyatt and Dashwood, p.78). This contrasts with the position in respect of actions under **Article 169** and **Article 170**, when the whole case is heard by the European Court.

A ruling is sought, as indicated, through the means of questions to the European Court which are formulated by the national court. The European Court takes an informal approach in answering these questions, and attempts to give rulings in the form which it feels will be most helpful to the national court. In order to do this it sometimes reformulates questions which it considers to have been worded by the national court in an inappropriate way, or it may give a ruling which does not strictly relate to the terms of the question put, but which addresses what the European Court thinks the national court really wishes to know.

A reference to the European Court may be made by any national body which is a "court or tribunal", terms which are quite wide but exclude, for example, private arbitrators. It may be noted that under the **Compliance Directive** and the **Utilities Compliance Directive** it is effectively provided that bodies responsible for the review of procurement decisions covered by the Directives must be themselves capable of making a request for an **Article 177** ruling, or must be subject to review by an authority which is capable of making such a request (see **Compliance Directive, Article 2 (8); Utilities Compliance Directive, Article 2 (9)**).

1.3.4. Interim measures and actions in the national courts

When an aggrieved party sues in the national courts for an alleged breach of the Community procurement rules, or for national measures implementing those rules, that party may, like the Commission in an action under **Article 169 of the Treaty of Rome,** wish to seek interim measures to prevent the award process from continuing until the legal dispute has been resolved. It may be particularly important to obtain interim measures when there is a point of European law in issue, since the time needed to obtain a ruling from the European Court is likely considerably to lengthen the time taken to dispose of the proceedings in the national court.

Any application for interim measures which relates to national court proceedings is made to the national court itself. Such relief must be made available where it is available in actions for review of procurement under domestic law. In the case of decisions which are subject to the **Compliance Directive**, the Directive specifically provides that the review body must be given the power to award interim measures (**Article 2**). Under the **Utilities Compliance Directive** states have a choice as to whether to apply to particular utilities a remedies regime which is similar to that provided under the public sector **Compliance Directive**. Where this is done interim relief must be made available (**Article 2 (1)**). Alternatively, states may choose a regime which relies instead on financial penalties against defaulting utilities, and in this case there is no need for interim relief to be made available (**Article 2 (1)**).

When a dispute concerns the interpretation of Community law, or of domestic measures implementing Community law, the principles governing the circumstances in which interim relief will be granted are a matter for national law (case 213/89, *R v Secretary of State for Transport, ex parte Factortame (No. 2)* [1990] ECR 2433; **Compliance Directive, Article 2; Utilities Compliance Directive, Article 2 (4)**). This is the situation which will generally apply in procurement actions. However, it should be pointed out that the provision of relief in the national courts, certainly under the **Compliance Directives**, is subject to an overriding requirement that an *effective* system of remedies should be provided, which may impose constraints on the discretion left to national law. This is particularly so where national law does not provide for a power to set aside concluded contracts: in this case a readiness to award interim relief may be required in order to ensure the effectiveness of the remedies system.

Should an action in the national courts involve a challenge to the *validity* of a Community measure, as opposed to its interpretation, the principles governing the exercise of the discretion to grant interim relief by the national courts are prescribed by the European Court itself (cases C-143/88 and C-92/89, *Zuckerfabrik Suderdith Marscher AG v Hauptzollant Itzehoe*, February 1st 1991.

1.4. PROCEDURE

1.4.1. Actions under Articles 169 and 170

In actions under **Article 169** and **170** the action begins with the filing of an application with the court registry by the Commission, or the member state bringing the action. This application sets out the grounds of the claim.

There then follows the first stage of the procedure - the written stage. The defendant state must put in a written reply to the allegations made in the application, normally within a month. The plaintiff may then respond to the reply of the defendant; and the defendant may make a further response (called the rejoinder). The detailed arguments of the parties and the evidence on which their submissions are based are all set out in these written submissions.

Following this stage there may be what is termed a preparatory enquiry. This is held where there are disputed questions of fact, and is concerned to establish the true facts of the case. It may involve the examination of witnesses and of documents.

Following these procedures a report on the case is presented to the court by the Judge Rapporteur. The Judge Rapporteur is one of the judges who will decide the case: one of these judges is designated Judge Rapporteur by the President of the court. The main formal function of the Judge Rapporteur is to prepare a report which sets out the facts of the case and summarises the submissions of the parties. It is also the Judge Rapporteur who decides whether any preparatory inquiry is necessary, and in some cases he alone will conduct the preparatory inquiry.

Following the written stage, the preparatory enquiry and the presentation of the report by the Judge Rapporteur, an oral hearing is held. During the first stage of this hearing the parties may make oral representations to the court, and may be asked questions by the members of the court who are sitting on the case, and also by the Advocate General. Parties are required to be legally represented.

Opportunities for submission of argument are not confined to those who are plaintiff and defendant in the case. In the case of an action under **Article 169** it is also possible for other member states and Community institutions other than the Commission to submit arguments to the court. The procedure for such intervention is governed by **Article 37 of the Statute of the Court.**

Following the submission of oral argument and questions, there is the second stage of the oral procedure, which consists of the oral presentation of an opinion on the case by the Advocate General. The Advocates General are individuals attached to the Court of Justice whose task is to act as independent advocates of the legal interests of the Community - that is, to ensure the proper development of European Community law. Advocates General have the same status and protection as judges themselves, and the same qualifications for office apply. The office of the Advocate General of the Court of Justice has an equivalent in the courts of most of the Civil Law systems, and it is modelled very closely on that of the *Commissaire du gouvernement* of the French *Conseil d'Etat* (the supreme French administrative court). It has, however, no close counterpart in the English common law system.

An Advocate General is assigned to each case before the Court of Justice. He must prepare an opinion on the case, setting out his view on how the case should be decided. The purpose of the opinion is to assist the court in making the best decision possible. The opinion will contain discussion of the facts of the case and of the arguments put forward by the parties, will analyse previous decisions of the Court of Justice which might assist it in resolving the case before it, and will also discuss questions of policy. The Advocate General may, in considering how the law should develop, also put forward arguments and opinions not raised by the parties themselves.

As indicated, the opinion is delivered as part of the oral stage of proceedings. Normally it is not delivered immediately following the submissions of the parties, but there is a delay of two or three weeks whilst the Advocate General considers the case.

Once the opinion of the Advocate General has been delivered, the judges begin deliberation. This is done in private. It is possible at this stage for the judges to reopen the proceedings to hear further oral argument. A final decision on the disposition of the case is determined on the basis of a majority vote. The form and style of the judgment given by the court are considered in section 1.5. below. In the vast majority of cases the court follows the solution put forward by the Advocate General.

In actions against a member state the language in which proceedings are conducted ("the procedural language") is the official language of the defendant state. Both oral and written submissions must be made in the procedural language, and supporting documents which are not in that language must be accompanied by a translation. The court may permit another language to be used for the whole proceedings or for limited purposes if a party requests, except that such a request cannot be made by the Commission or other Community institutions. The report of the Judge Rapporteur and the questions and opinions of the Advocate General may be put in that individual's own language, but will then be translated into the procedural language.

1.4.2. Preliminary rulings

The above description of European Court procedure has been concerned with actions under **Articles 169** and **170**. Obviously the procedure is slightly different where an **Article 177** ruling is sought, because of the different nature of the proceedings. The procedure begins when the national court submits the relevant question(s) of law to the Court of Justice. The Court then notifies this to the parties to the proceedings before the national court. It also notifies other member states and the Commission, and where the act in issue in the reference originates from the Council, the Council is also notified. All these parties may submit written observations on the questions put by the national court. As with 169 actions, one member of the court is designated Judge Rapporteur, and once written observations have been submitted makes a report on the case. There will be no need for any preparatory inquiry, since on an application for an **Article 177** ruling the Court of Justice is not responsible for making any findings of fact.

Once the Judge Rapporteur has made his report there follows an oral hearing stage. The first stage involves oral argument from the parties entitled to be notified of the case (and such parties may make oral argument even though they have chosen not to submit written observations). The second stage involves delivery of an opinion from the Advocate General.

In contrast with proceedings in connection with actions under **Articles 169** and **170** parties need not always be legally represented before the European Court: since the proceedings are regarded simply as an extension of proceedings before the national court, no rigid rules on representation are laid down, but it is provided that the Court of Justice shall itself decide the issue of representation having regard to the position which applies before the national court seeking the ruling (**Rules of Procedure, Article 104 (2)**). If legal representation is not required before the national court, then it will generally not be required before the European Court either.

The procedural language in **Article 177** proceedings is that of the national court requesting the ruling.

1.5 UNDERSTANDING THE REPORT AND JUDGMENT

1.5.1. The judgment

The first draft of a judgment of the Court of Justice is in practice prepared by the Judge Rapporteur for the case. The draft is then discussed with the other judges sitting on the case, and a final draft agreed.

There is only one single judgment, given on behalf of the court as a whole. This applies even in a case where not all judges agree with the majority view: there are no dissenting judgments, and, indeed, it is not even indicated whether or not any judge did dissent. In this the European Court follows the practice generally adopted in the courts in Civil Law jurisdictions. It contrasts with the position in the English system where each judge gives a judgment in his own name, and may give a separate substantial statement of reasons, whether agreeing with or dissenting from the majority view on the disposition of the case. Because the judgment of the Court of Justice is not the work of a sole individual, "the resulting judgment may perhaps have the look of a "committee" document, lacking in elegance and occasionally even in coherence" (Wyatt and Dashwood, p.87).

The judgment is divided into numbered paragraphs for ease of reference. Today, judgments are divided into two main parts - the reasons *(motifs)*, and the ruling *(dispositif)*.

In the first part the court sets out its conclusions on the facts and law in a very brief form. It does not discuss in detail the specific arguments of the parties nor the policy which led it to adopt a particular conclusion, and nor does it attempt to explain the intended scope and implications of its decision. Further, it does not deal with previous decisions of its own relating to the matter in issue, except that where the court states a legal principle in a form taken from a previous judgment it now tends to acknowledge the source. Where it appears to take a different view of the law from that adopted in an apparently similar previous case it does not indicate this or explain why it is doing so, nor does it explain whether it thinks a distinction between the two cases may exist. This style of judgment is modelled on that normally found in Civil Law jurisdictions, and is very different from that of English judgments, which set out the reasons for the court's conclusion in much more detail.

In order to understand what may have motivated the court to take a particular view, and thus to appreciate the way in which future cases may be resolved, it is often helpful to look at the opinion delivered by the Advocate General, which is likely to have had considerable influence on the court's thinking about the case. This may also assist an understanding of how the case relates to others in the field. The opinion of the Advocate General is published alongside the judgment in the official report of European Court cases (see 1.5.2. below).

The question of the language to be used in proceedings before the court (the "procedural language") was explained at 1.4. above. In practice the language generally used in the deliberations of the judges is French, and judgments are generally also drafted in French. Excepting the case where the procedural language is French, however, the authentic version is not that of the original French draft, but the version later produced in the language of the case.

1.5.2. Reports of European Court decisions

The texts of all judgments of the court, as well as a summary of the facts
and arguments and the opinion of the Advocate General, are published by
the court itself in each of the official languages of the Community. The
reports appear in periodical parts. The English language version of the
official reports is the European Court Reports (referred to by the
abbreviation ECR). Judgments are also published in some private
collections (for example, the Common Market Law Reports).

The official report in the ECR begins with a very brief summary of the
issues raised and decided, and then outlines the main legal principles which
can be extracted from the judgment, in order to provide a quick reference
guide to the case. There then follows, under the heading "Report for the
hearing" the Report of the Judge Rapporteur, in which the facts, issues and
arguments are summarised (On the role of the Judge Rapporteur see 1.4.1.
above). Next comes the opinion of the Advocate General, and after that the
judgment of the court - first the reasons, and then the ruling.

The above is the format of reports published since the mid-1980s.
Before that time the report took a slightly different form, with the summary
of facts and submissions appearing not in the form of a separate report, but
as part of the judgment itself, under the heading "Facts and Issues".
However, in practice the summary was generally taken directly from the
report of the Judge Rapporteur. The part of the judgment referred to as the
reasons *(motifs)* is in older judgments set out after the "Facts and Issues"
under the heading "Decision".

The cases on procurement which are discussed in this book are attached
in the Appendix at the back. There is provided in all cases the judgment of
the court in so far as it deals with questions of law. In the case of more
recent judgments this means the whole judgment; with older cases it means
the second part of the judgment, omitting that part which summarises the
facts and issues. The opinions of the Advocate General have not been
included.

1.6. BIBLIOGRAPHY

Further useful reading on the European Court is found in the following
English language works:

L.N.Brown and F.G.Jacobs, *The Court of Justice of the European
Communities* (3rd ed. 1989)
Butterworth's Guide to European Court Practice (looseleaf)

U. Everling, "The Member States of the European Community before their Court of Justice" (1984) 9 EL Rev 125

W.Feld, *The Court of the European Communities: new dimension in international adjudication* (1964)

K.P.E.Lasok, *The European Court of Justice: Practice and Procedure* (1984)

D.Lasok and J.W.Bridge, *Law and Institutions of the European Communities* (5th ed. 1991) at pp.160- 204, and chs. 9 and 10

C.Lenz, "The Court of Justice of the European Communities" (1989) 14 EL Rev 127

T.Millett, *The Court of First Instance of the European Communities* (1990)

T.Millett, The Court of Justice, law of the European Communities "in *Halsbury's Laws of England* (4th ed) Vol. 51 at p.344 *et seq*

T.Millett, "The Role of the European Court of Justice in relation to Public Procurement" (1992) 1 PPLR 70

H.Schermers, "The ECJ, Promoter of European Integration" (1974) 22 AJCL 279

G.Slynn, "The Court of Justice of the European Communities" (1984) 33 ICLQ 409

J.Usher, *European Court Practice* (1983)

J-P.Warner, *The Evolution of the Work of the Court of Justice* (1976)

D.Wyatt and A.Dashwood, *The Substantive Law of the EEC* (2nd ed. 1987), at pp. 72-94

A.Arnull, "References to the European Court" (1990) 15 EL Rev 375

A.Barav, "Some Aspects of the Preliminary Ruling Procedure in EEC Law" (1977) 2 EL Rev 3

E.Bebr, "Article 177 of the EEC Treaty in the Practice of National Courts" (1977) ICLQ 241

G Borchardt, "The Award of Interim Measures by the European Court of Justice" (1985) 22 CML Rev 203

A.Breidmas, *Methods of Interpretation and Community Law* (1978)

A.Dashwood and R.White, "Enforcement Actions under Articles 169 and 170 EEC" (1989) 14 EL Rev 388

F.G.Jacobs and A.Durand, *References to the European Court* (1975)

T.G.Koopmans, "Stare Decisis in European Law" in O'Keefe and Schermers eds., *Essays in European Law and Integration* (1982) p.11

K.Kutschner, *Methods of Interpretation as Seen by a Judge at the Court of Justice* (1976)

P.Oliver, "Interim Measures: Some Recent Developments" (1992) 29 CML Rev 7

A.J.Pavlopoulos, *The Advocate General's Office and Its Contribution to the Development of the Law and the Justice Machinery of the European Communities* (1986)

2. Case 10/76, Commission of the European Communities v Italy

22nd September 1986; [1976] ECR 1359

SUMMARY

This case concerned proceedings under Article 169 of the Treaty of Rome.
The court ruled that Italy was in breach of Community law for failing to take the measures necessary to implement Directive 71/305 within the period prescribed for implementation of that Directive.

FACTS AND RULING

This case concerned an action brought by the Commission against Italy, under the procedure laid down in **Article 169 of the Treaty of Rome**. This procedure is explained at 1.2. above.

The Commission alleged that Italy had failed to implement the **Works Directive**, and was thus in breach of **Article 189 of the Treaty of Rome**, which places on member states the obligation to take measures in national law to implement Directives. First, it was argued that measures necessary for the implementation of the provisions in the original **1971 Works Directive** had not been enacted until 2nd February 1973, whilst the date by which implementation was required by Community law was 29th July 1972. Second, it was alleged that the measures enacted did not implement the Directive completely and properly, and hence that there was a still-continuing failure by the Italian government to implement certain aspects of the Directive. At the time of the judgment a draft Bill had been conveyed to the Italian Parliament which contained provisions considered by the Commission to be "in large measure satisfactory" in bringing Italian law in line with the Directive's requirements; but the Bill had not yet been enacted.

Italy did not dispute the Commission's contention that measures to implement the Directive had not been taken in time, nor that Italian law still contained deficiencies with regard to the Directive's implementation, and neither the court nor the Advocate General addressed the question of whether deficiencies existed. The only matter raised by the Italian government in its defence was that a Bill to remedy the continuing deficiencies was before Parliament, and that the government hoped that it would be enacted as soon as possible. The Commission seemed to take the view that there had been adequate time for a law to be enacted by Italy already, a point accepted by the Advocate General. In any case, it should be pointed out that it is now established that even if for some reason enactment has not been possible because of delays in the constitutional process this provides no defence. The state will be held responsible for failure to implement a Directive even if delays are caused by the actions of independent organs of government and the Executive branch has done all it possibly can to ensure implementation (see, for example, case 77/69, *Commission v Belgium* [1970] ECR 237; case 254/83, *Commission v Italy* [1984] ECR 3395), and it is also responsible for any inherent deficiencies in the legislative process which hold up implementation.

The court thus declared that Italy was in breach of its obligations under Community law.

3. Case 76/81, S.A.Transporoute v Minister of Public Works ("Transporoute")

10th February 1982; [1982] ECR 417; [1982] CMLR 382

SUMMARY

This case concerned a request for a preliminary ruling under Article 177 of the Treaty of Rome.

The court ruled that a contracting authority may not, in relation to a contract covered by the Works Directive, call for an establishment permit issued by the state of the awarding authority as proof of a contractor's good standing and qualifications. This is because the means of proof which may be called for in relation to matters covered by Articles 23-26 of the Directive are laid down in the Directive, and an establishment permit is not a stipulated means of proof.

The court noted that under Article 25 of the Works Directive an authority may stipulate any means of proof of financial and economic standing; but with other matters in Articles 23-26 only those means of proof laid down may be called for.

The court discussed the status of qualification lists.

The court also stated that a requirement for an establishment permit from the state of the awarding authority contravenes Article 59 of the Treaty of Rome.

Finally, the court ruled that under Article 29 (5) of the Works Directive (as it then stood) the exclusion of a contractor as a low bidder was only ever permitted after first seeking explanations from the contractor and giving the contractor a reasonable time to reply.

3.1. INTRODUCTION AND FACTS

The *Transporoute* case concerned a request for a preliminary ruling from the European Court, made by a judicial authority in Luxembourg, the Judicial Committee of the Council of the Council of State (*Comité du Contentieux du Conseil d'Etat*, hereafter "the Committee"). The preliminary ruling procedure is explained at 1.3.3. above.

The proceedings before the Committee arose out of a decision by the Minister of Public Works to reject Transporoute's tender for a works contract, though it was the lowest tender submitted. One reason given for rejecting the bid was that Transporoute was not in possession of an "establishment permit" issued by the Luxembourg government, which was generally required of contractors as confirmation of their professional good standing. Transporoute sought to have the decision annulled by the Committee, on the basis that it was not permissible under the **Works Directive** for the government to call for such a permit. One question referred to the European Court by the Committee concerned this issue.

A second reason given for rejecting the tender was that it was "abnormally low". Transporoute contended that in rejecting the bid on this ground the Minister had breached **Article 29 (5) of the Works Directive**, since the firm had not been given an opportunity to furnish explanations, as was claimed was required by the Article. The second question referred by the Committee concerned this issue.

3.2. REQUIREMENT OF AN ESTABLISHMENT PERMIT AS PROOF OF PROFESSIONAL STANDING

3.2.1. Application of the Works Directive

3.2.1.1. Introduction
The first question put to the European Court, asked, *inter alia*, whether it is contrary to the **Works Directive** to require a contractor from another EC state to hold an establishment permit issued by the awarding state.

The court's treatment of this question must be considered in the light of the purpose of the permit, which was to serve as proof that the contractor was of general "good standing" in the relevant trade or profession. The concept seemed to embrace, *inter alia*, the questions of honesty and integrity, and solvency. An establishment permit thus served as a *means of proof* that the contractor satisfied certain *substantive criteria* relating to such matters, which had been laid down by the Luxembourg government.

3.2.1.2. The scope of Articles 23-28
The provisions of the Works Directive relevant to the question asked were those in **Articles 23-28.** These Articles are concerned with two things. The first is the substantive criteria and standards which member states may lay down for contractors ("substantive criteria"). The second is the requirements which member states may lay down as to the methods by which contractors are to prove compliance with those standards ("means of proof"). These two issues are not always clearly separated in the Directive.

A number of cases before the European Court have considered what exactly are the requirements of these Articles with respect to the two issues. *Transporoute* is the first of these cases.

Before considering the establishment permit point it is necessary to outline the scheme of **Articles 23-28.**

Article 23: This Article states certain very specific *substantive criteria* which member states may require contractors to meet. For example, it is stated that authorities may exclude from participation contractors who have been guilty of grave professional misconduct, who are subject to proceedings for a declaration of bankruptcy, or who have been guilty of serious misrepresentation regarding certain information which they are required to provide to authorities.

The Article also prescribes certain *means of proof* of the criteria listed above, which it is stated contracting authorities must accept as "sufficient evidence". For example, as proof of the fact that a contractor is not the subject of bankruptcy proceedings (as well as of certain other matters specified in the Article), the authority must accept an extract from the "judicial record" of the contractor's state, or an "equivalent document" issued by a "competent judicial or administrative authority" (or, where no relevant documents are issued, a declaration on oath made by certain specified persons in the contractor's state). In the case of grave professional misconduct, proof may be by any means which the awarding authority can justify. In the case of misrepresentation of information, no *means of proof* is specified.

Article 24: This Article provides that an authority may require enrolment in certain professional or trade registers *of the contractor's home state*, the relevant registers being specified in the Article. This Article can be seen to be concerned with both substantive criteria and methods of proof, authorities being permitted to exclude contractors on the basis of *criteria* which must be met for registration, and being permitted to request registration as a means of proof of any of the criteria on which registration is based.

Article 25: Article 20 makes it clear that the *substantive criteria* of financial and economic standing of contractors may be taken account of in excluding contractors from participation. **Article 25** contains a list of certain *means of proof* which may be called for by an authority in relation to the contractor's financial and economic standing (for example, statements from bankers). It also states that authorities are to state in the tender documents which of the references in the list, and which other references are to be called for. This allusion to other references suggests that with respect to financial and economic standing an authority is not limited to the means of proof stated in **Article 25**, as indeed the court has confirmed (see 3.2.2.3.). However, even if other means are called for, the Article provides that contractors who for a "valid reason" cannot supply the means of proof requested have a right to substitute any other documents which the authority considers appropriate.

Article 26: Article 20 makes it clear that the *substantive criteria* of technical knowledge and ability may also be taken into account. **Article 26** contains a list of *means of proof* of such knowledge and ability which may be called for by authorities.

Article 27: This Article states that authorities may invite contractors to supplement or clarify the documents provided *within the limits of Articles 23-26.*

Article 28: This Article deals with certain matters relating to official lists of contractors maintained by member states, and is considered further below.

3.2.1.3. Permissible means of proof

As indicated, the requirement of an establishment permit is, at the very least, a *means of proof* that a contractor is of good standing. Is it, however, a means of proof of good standing which is permissible in accordance with the terms of the **Works Directive**? What are the permissible means of proof of good standing which are permitted under the Directive?

The notion of "good standing" as it was used by the Luxembourg government comprised at least satisfaction of some of the substantive criteria for exclusion which are listed in **Article 23**, and for which specific methods of proof are prescribed in that Article - for example, solvency. In addition to the methods of proof of those criteria contemplated in **Article 23**, it seems that registration in the relevant trade or professional register of the contractor's home state, in so far as that register provides proof of good standing, is also a permissible means of proof of that matter: this is one consequence of **Article 24** providing specifically that evidence of such registration may generally be called for. The question for the court in *Transporoute* was whether an establishment permit is also a permissible means of proof of such good standing, even though not expressly specified by the Directive as such.

The view of the court was that, with respect to the substantive criteria referred to in **Articles 23-26** (as outlined above), only those means of proof specified in the Directive may permissibly be called for by contracting authorities. According to the court the Directive "must be interpreted as precluding a Member State from requiring a tenderer established in another Member State to furnish proof by any means, for example by an establishment permit, other than those prescribed in **Articles 23 to 26** of that directive, that he satisifies the criteria laid down in those provisions and relating to his good standing and qualifications" (para. 15 of the judgment). According to the court the specific mention in **Article 25** of references other than those listed means that the authority is free to call for any other references in relation to the substantive criteria mentioned in **Article 25**, that is, financial and economic standing (a view confirmed by the court in its later decision in CEI: see 6.2. below). However, with respect to the other substantive criteria mentioned in **Articles 23-26** the means of proof listed in the Articles were stated to be exhaustive of those which may be called for; and since the establishment permit requirement was, as explained above, concerned with proof of criteria other than financial and economic standing the court considered that it was impermissible (para. 10).

One argument for the view that an establishment permit is a permissible means of proof of good standing even though the means of proof set out in the Directive are exhaustive was put forward on the basis of **Article 28**. This Article is concerned with certain matters relating to official lists of contractors in member states. It was argued in *Transporoute* that one effect of this Article is to permit member states to require registration in a list of contractors maintained by that state as proof of satisfaction of criteria which must be met; that an establishment permit is equivalent to registration in a list for the purpose of this Article; and that therefore an establishment permit is a means of proof specifically authorised by the Directive. This argument was rejected by the court, on the grounds that **Article 28** does not anywhere provide that registration in a list of the awarding authority is a permissible means of proof which may be *called for* by an authority. Rather, in so far as it is concerned with means of proof, the Article merely makes registration in a list (of the contractor's own state) a means of proof which a contractor can *choose* to use for certain matters instead of those means of proof called for by the authority (see paras. 11-13 of the judgment).

3.2.1.4. The status of qualification lists

Prior to the adoption of the **Works Directive** it was common for authorities to maintain lists of contractors qualified to carry out certain types of work with respect to matters such as the contractor's technical competence or financial status, and to limit participation in public works contracts to those registered on such lists. The court in the *Transporoute* case, however, makes it clear, as explained at 3.2.1.3., that under the terms of the **Works Directive** awarding authorities may not restrict access to contracts to persons on official lists, in so far as these lists are used as means of proof of the substantive criteria referred to in **Articles 23-26**, except where this is permitted under the terms of these Articles.

This precludes the use of such lists in relation to technical competence, since, as explained, only references specifically contemplated by **Article 26** may be called for in relation to this matter.

In principle their use seems permissible under the terms of the Directive in relation to financial and economic standing, since under **Article 25** other references may be *called for* in regard to these matters. However, it seems that contractors unable to show registration in a list must be permitted to use other suitable documents as means of proof, since this is allowed where for a "valid reason" the contractor cannot provide the references called for (see 3.2.2. above).

3.2.1.5. The effect and scope of Article 28

The court's conclusion that means of proof other than those specified in the Directive may not be required, and that an establishment permit is not a specified means of proof, was sufficient to show that a permit could not legitimately be required. Advocate General Reischl also went on to note that to require such a permit might be impermissible in any case under the terms of the Directive, even if it had been specified as a means of proof in **Articles 23-26**. This was because of the effect of **Article 28 (3)**. This provides that registration in an official list of contractors is conclusive evidence of facts which can be deduced from registration. It seemed that in this case the contractor was registered on a Belgian list, inclusion on which required proof that the contractor met the criteria set out in **Article 23** (dealing with integrity, solvency etc). If so, the Luxembourg authorities were required to accept that the contractor complied with the criteria in **Article 23** without calling for other means of proof, even means specified in the Directive.

Article 28 applies in this way to information which can be deduced from "official lists of recognised contractors", and it is pertinent to note that the Advocate General also makes some comments on what is an official list of contractors. These were made in response to Luxembourg's argument that Article 28 authorises authorities to *require* registration on official lists, an argument which it has been explained was rejected; but the question of what counts as an official list under **Article 28**, is still, of course, relevant for other purposes.

In the Advocate General's view an establishment permit could not be treated as equivalent to an official list. This was, first, because "a number of establishment permits simultaneously can hardly be described as a list" and, second, because an establishment permit was required for all Luxembourg firms operating in the state and not just those wishing to bid on government contracts. The first reason given is perhaps open to criticism: **Article 28** should surely operate wherever information is collected from a contractor and officially accepted for the specific purpose of access to the government market, regardless of whether the authorisation takes the form of the issue of a permit or inclusion on a list. The issue is one of form only - no doubt in all states official lists are in any case kept of all those contractors issued with any form of permit.

3.2.1.6. Secondary factors in contractor selection
One further point to note concerning the Articles discussed above is that the
court seemed to assume that the only substantive criteria by which
contractors can be excluded from the award process are those listed in
Articles 23-29, and that, apart from this, the contract must be awarded in
accordance with the factors stated in **Article 29** - that is, lowest price or
economically most advantageous tender. (This was most certainly the view
of Advocate General Reischl: see [1982] ECR 417 at p.433). This view has
now been rejected by the court in CEI and, more clearly, in *Beentjes* (see
6.3.3. and 8.3. below). These cases make it clear that secondary factors
wholly unrelated to the sort of economic considerations dealt with in
Articles 23-29 may be taken into account, provided they do not operate
in a discriminatory manner and comply in all other respects with the Treaty.
Obviously authorities are free in principle to prescribe any means of proof
relating to this type of criteria, subject to **Article 28,** provided, however,
that the means specified are themselves consistent with the Treaty.

3.2.2. Application of Article 59 of the Treaty of Rome

In relation to the legality of a requirement of an establishment permit the
court also stated the view that, regardless of the provisions of the Directive
itself, such a requirement would be unlawful as a breach of **Article 59 of
the Treaty of Rome** (para. 14 of the judgment). This Article guarantees
the freedom of entities and individuals to provide services in other member
states. Conduct which is discriminatory against contractors from other states
wishing to provide services, whether because it applies only to such
contractors or because in practice it hinders wholly or primarily such
contractors, is generally unlawful under **Article 59.** (On this Article see
further 9.2.1. below). The fact that the establishment permit requirement
was applied to contractors established in Luxembourg as well as other states
thus did not prevent the requirement from being caught by **Article 59** - it
appeared to hinder principally contractors from outside Luxembourg. As the
Advocate General explained, Luxembourg contractors would always have
such permits anyway, since they were required for carrying on business,
whilst foreign contractors often would not and would therefore have to take
special steps to participate in a government contract. The court noted this
point regarding the Treaty in support of its conclusion that **Article 28 of
the Works Directive** could not be read as authorising the use of
establishment permits as means of proof of good standing: the court will
generally not construe provisions in a Directive as contravening the Treaty.
(If this should be the case, the relevant provision in the Directive will, of
course, be invalid).

3.3. PROCEDURE FOR REJECTING ABNORMALLY LOW BIDS

3.3.1. Article 29 (5)

A question was also put to the European Court regarding the procedure which must be followed before a bid can be rejected by a contracting authority as abnormally low. At the time of the conduct which was in issue in *Transporoute*, the provision in the **Works Directive** dealing with this question, **Article 29 (5)**, read as follows:

"If, for a given contract, tenders are obviously abnormally low in relation to the transaction, the authority awarding the contract shall examine the details of the tenders before deciding to whom it will award the contract. The result of this examination shall be taken into account.

For this purpose it shall request the tenderer to furnish the necessary explanations and, where appropriate, it shall indicate which parts it finds unacceptable".

3.3.2. An exception to the requirement of a hearing?

The question referred for a preliminary ruling by the Judicial Committee of the Council of State concerned the issue of whether there was any exception to the procedure stated in **Article 29 (5)**. The question put was as follows:

"Do the provisions of Article 29 (5) of Directive 71/305/EEC require the authority awarding the contract to request the tenderer whose tenders, in the authority's opinion are obviously abnormally low in relation to the transaction, to furnish explanations for those prices before investigating their composition and deciding to whom it will award the contract, or do they in such circumstances allow the authority awarding the contract to decide whether it is necessary to request such explanations ?"

Luxembourg argued that it was permissible to reject a tender without seeking explanations where the tender was so low that it bore no relation to reality. On the face of it, the Article clearly appeared to require explanations in every case of an abnormally low tender, and any exception would have had to be based on the spirit and intention of the provision. An argument in favour of an exception might be that automatic rejection of tenders which are not merely abnormally low, but quite exceptionally low, saves the delay and effort of a verification procedure where the outcome must inevitably be the rejection of the bid.

The court rejected the argument that such an exception should be made, ruling in terms which suggests that the verification procedure must be applied in every case:

"....when in the opinion of the authority awarding a public works contract a tenderer's offer is obviously abnormally low in relation to the transaction Article 29 (5) of Directive 71/ 305 requires the authority to seek from the tenderer, before coming to a decision as to the award of the contract, an explanation of his prices or to inform of the tenderer which of his tenders appear to be abnormal, and to allow him a reasonable time within which to submit further details".

In this conclusion the court agreed with Advocate General Reichsl, who emphasised a number of factors. First, he noted the dangers of refusing a hearing when the outcome *appears* to be obvious: the very point of a hearing is to allow a party to correct the apparent but possibly mistaken, perception of a case. As he explained, "it should be remembered that a situation which appears at first sight to be abnormal may create a different impression once the actual circumstances in which it is made, known often only to the tenderer, come to light" ([1982] ECR 417 at 437). For example, a low bid may reflect the fact that a bidder has been able to acquire materials at much less than market price, and there will then be no reason to doubt his ability successfully to complete the contract. Such factors cannot be known without investigation, and it is therefore desirable that a hearing should be given however low the bid.

The Advocate General also stressed that the provision was designed to protect bidders, and he considered that such protective provisions must generally be construed in favour of the bidder. In addition, he pointed out that recognition of the alleged exception to the verification requirement would produce great uncertainty, depending as it does on a nebulous distinction between two types of abnormally low bid - those which are simply abnormally low, and those which are so low they bear no relation to reality.

The application of the general principle that a hearing must be given in *all* cases of abnormally low tenders has been affirmed in another context, in *Costanzo* and *Donà Alfonso*, where the European Court rejected the argument that a verification procedure could be denied where an objective mathematical formula was used to identify low bids (see 11.2. and 13. below)

3.3.3. Subsequent amendments to Article 29 (5)

Since *Transporoute* **Article 29 (5)** has, under **Article 1 (20) of the 1989 Works Directive**, been replaced by a new **Article 29 (5)** which reads as follows:

"If, for a given contract, tenders appear to be abnormally low in relation to the transaction, before it may reject those tenders the contracting authority shall request, in writing, details of the constituent elements of the tender which it considers relevant and shall verify those constituent elements taking account of the explanations received...."

There are no reasons to think that the court's conclusion in *Transporoute*, that no exception to the hearing procedure should be made for tenders which bear no relation to reality, would not generally apply also in relation to this new version of **Article 29 (5)**. It may be noted, however, that a limited exception to the verification procedure has been included in the new version of of **Article 29 (5)**: rejection of abnormally low bids is permitted without following the usual procedure if the number of tenders for a particular contract is so high that the verification procedure would lead to a considerable delay and jeopardise the public interest attaching to the execution of the contract in question. This exception may be invoked only until the end of 1992.

4. Case 274/83, Commission of the European Communities v Italy

28th March 1985; [1985] ECR 1085; [1987] 1 CMLR 345

SUMMARY

*This case concerned proceedings under **Article 169** of the Treaty of Rome.*

*The court held that a legislativre provision for contracts to be awarded to the contractor whose tender equals the average tender or, failing that, whose tender is the tender below the average which is closest to the average, is incompatible with the criteria for contract awards laid down in **Article 29** of the **Works Directive**.*

*The court also ruled that Italy was in breach of its obligation under **Article 33** of the **1971 Works Directive** in failing officially to notify the Commission of a Law adopted to implement that Directive. This applied even though the Commission was aware of the implementing law.*

4.1. INTRODUCTION AND FACTS

This case concerned proceedings by the Commission against Italy, brought under the procedure laid down in **Article 169 of the Treaty of Rome**. This procedure is explained at 1.2. above.

The Commission alleged that a number of the provisions of an Italian procurement Law infringed the **1971 Works Directive**. Most of the complaints were either withdrawn in the course of the hearing, or were not disputed. The only complaint specifically addressed related to the criteria for contract awards provided by the Law. The court upheld the Commission's contention that certain provisions of the Law on award criteria were incompatible with the Directive. This issue is considered at 4.2. below.

The Commission further complained that Italy was in breach of **Article 33 of the 1971 Works Directive** in failing to notify the Commission of the relevant Law. This complaint was also upheld. It is considered at 4.3 below.

4.2. DID THE ITALIAN PROCEDURES INFRINGE THE 1971 WORKS DIRECTIVE?

The Commission made a number of complaints concerning the content of an Italian Law, Law No. 741 of 10th December 1981, various provisions of which it was claimed infringed the **1971 Works Directive.**

Four of the Commission's complaints were dropped in the course of the hearing, two because of submissions made by Italy (see paras. 10-12 and 31-32 of the judgment), and two because Italy adopted amending legislation (see paras. 13-15 and 36-39).

Three of the remaining complaints were not disputed by the Italian government, and the court declared Italy to be in breach of the Directive in respect of these matters without specifically considering the issues raised (see paras. 26-28, 29-30 and 34-35).

This left only one complaint for the court to consider relating to the content of the Italian legislation. This was a complaint by the Commission that a certain provision in the law was incompatible with the rules in the Directive concerning the criteria for the award of works contracts. The **1971 Directive** provided, as it does still in its amended form, that contracts must be awarded on the basis of one of two criteria - lowest price, or most economically advantageous tender (see **Article 20; Article 29**). The Italian law made provision for contracts to be awarded to the contractor whose tender equalled the average tender, or, failing that, the contractor whose tender was the closest to the average out of those tenders below the average. The Italian government contended that this provision was compatible with the Directive in that the application of this formula was a method of identifying which of the tenders was economically the most advantageous. Not surprisingly, this argument was rejected by the court. It was stated that the identification of the most advantageous bid requires the authority to exercise its discretion with regard to the various qualitative factors considered relevant in each case (para. 25 of the judgment). It seems absolutely clear that a formula which makes reference solely to price cannot possibly be used to identify which tender is the most advantageous in the light of factors other than price.

4.3. FAILURE TO NOTIFY IMPLEMENTING MEASURES

Article 33 of the 1971 Works Directive required member states to notify the Commission of national measures designed to implement the Directive. The Commission claimed that Italy was in breach of its obligations under the Directive in failing officially to notify the Commission of Law No. 741.

Italy contended that this complaint ceased to be material once the Commission was aware of the legislation in question, which was the case at the time that its reasoned opinion was delivered.

The court considered that the obligation to notify was not affected by this fact - the Commission was required to be officially notified of implementing measures in accordance with the express terms of the Directive. Hence the court declared Italy to be in breach of its Community law obligations for failing to give this notification.

5. Case 199/85, Commission of the European Communities v Italy

10th March 1987; [1987] ECR 1039

SUMMARY

This case concerned proceedings under Article 169 of the Treaty of Rome.

The court ruled that failure by the municipality of Milan to advertise the award of a works contract in the Official Journal constituted a breach of the Works Directive, and declared that Italy was thus in breach of its obligations under Community law. Derogations from the advertising requirements which related to exclusive rights and to urgency could not be invoked in this case. The court stated that such derogations must be strictly interpreted, and that the burden of proving their application lies on the party wishing to invoke them.

The Advocate General discussed whether Article 171 of the Treaty of Rome may require a state to take steps to set aside a concluded contract which has been declared in Article 169 proceedings to have been made in breach of Community law.

5.1. INTRODUCTION AND FACTS

This case concerned proceedings by the Commission against Italy, brought in the European Court under the procedure laid down in **Article 169 of the Treaty of Rome**. This procedure is explained at 1.2. above.

The case concerned conduct of the Council of Milan in awarding, in 1979, a contract for the construction of a waste recycling plant to a consortium of three Italian undertakings. It was not disputed that the contract had not been advertised in the Official Journal. The Commission alleged that this failure to advertise constituted a breach of the **Works Directive** and also of the Italian legislation implementing that Directive, which generally required the advertisement of all works contracts above a certain threshold. Milan, however, contended that it was not necessary to advertise the contract, even though its value was above the threshold, since it fell within one of the exceptions to the advertising requirements. In a reasoned opinion, delivered in 1984, the Commission rejected this contention, and demanded that measures be taken to comply with the law.

Since the Commission believed that the works had already been completed - five years having elapsed between the award and the reasoned opinion - the Commission's sole specific demand was for a written undertaking by Milan that Milan would comply with the Directive in the future. In fact, the works had not been completed because of new Italian laws governing recycling plants, which had required considerable alterations to the original plans. Instead a fresh contract, for the construction of the works in accordance with new plans, had been awarded to the Italian consortium - again without advertisement in the Official Journal.

In response to the reasoned opinion of the Commission regarding the 1979 award, the relevant Italian Minister ordered Milan to make a declaration as required by the Commission, and a declaration was made. The Commission, however, considered that the form of the declaration was unsatisfactory and that, consequently, its reasoned opinion had not been complied with. These **Article 169** proceedings were therefore instituted.

The court considered, first, whether there had been compliance with the reasoned opinion: if there had, the action could not be entertained. It was concluded that there had not been compliance. Consideration of this question raised some interesting questions concerning the steps which must be taken under **Article 171 of the Treaty of Rome** to redress a breach of the procurement rules. These are considered at 5.2. below.

Second, the court considered whether there had in fact been a breach of the relevant advertising requirements. It concluded that there had, and thus granted a declaration that Italy had failed to comply with its Community law obligations under the Treaty. This question is considered below at 5.3.

It should be pointed out that the conduct of Milan regarding the award of the *second* contract without advertisement was not in issue in these proceedings. **Article 169** proceedings may only be instituted following a reasoned opinion relating to the breach in issue. Since, as Advocate General Lenz pointed out, no opinion had been delivered in relation to this separate, second, award, proceedings relating to that award would not have been admissible before the court.

5.2. STEPS REQUIRED TO REDRESS A BREACH

5.2.1. Form of the declaration

The first question considered was whether there had been compliance with the Commission's reasoned opinion. As explained at 1.2. above it is a condition of **Article 169** proceedings that a reasoned opinion has been delivered by the Commission, and that there has been a failure to comply with that opinion. If these conditions are not satisfied, the action is said to be inadmissible. In its opinion, the Commission may order a member state to take specific steps to redress a perceived breach of the law, provided that these are "necessary steps" for redress, in accordance with the principle stated in **Article 171** of the Treaty (see 1.2.1.4. above).

In its opinion in this case the Commission asserted that there had been a breach of legal requirements to advertise the contract, and that the Italian government should adopt the measures necessary to comply with the opinion within thirty days of notification. More specifically, the opinion stated:

"By necessary measures is meant above all a written undertaking by the Municipality of Milan that it will comply with all the provisions of Directive 71/305/EEC in future."

This statement seems to have been made on the assumption that the works in question had already been completed - in fact, as mentioned, above, this was not the case.

One issue raised was whether the declaration given was in compliance with this demand. A declaration had been issued by the Mayor of Milan which stated that "....although convinced that the Municipal Administration acted in a lawful manner.... I hereby declare ... that the Municipality of Milan will ensure that, in the future, too, its administrative action is in conformity with the principles of primary and secondary legislation." The Commission argued that compliance with its demands required in this case an admission of the breach, and that the declaration was unsatisfactory since it contained no such admission.

The court agreed, stating that the declaration was unsatisfactory in view of the fact that there had been neither specific steps to correct the breach, nor an acknowledgement that the breach had occurred (para. 8 of the judgment). Clearly the court thought, as the Advocate General expressly stated, that an express admission of a breach is implicitly required by a general demand for redress of a breach of the law, at least in those cases where no concrete steps are taken which might themselves be treated as an admission of the authority's legal obligations.

An alternative basis put forward by the Advocate General for finding that Italy had failed to comply with the reasoned opinion was that the declaration given did not give a clear assurance for the future. On the contrary, he considered that it could possibly be construed as meaning that the Municipality would act in the future in the same manner as in the past - a manner which the court and Advocate General considered unlawful. This point was not considered by the court.

5.2.2. Reopening the award procedure

The Commission seemed to have decided to call specifically for a declaration only, because of an assumption that the works in question had already been completed. It seems clear that in such circumstances the award procedure should not be reopened. However, it transpired that the works had not in fact been completed in this case since, as noted above, the plans for the plant had had to be significantly revised to comply with new legislation.

In such cases, where the contract has not yet been performed, an important question is whether a reopening of the procedure might be required where the European Court finds a breach of the procurement rules, by virtue of **Article 171 of the Treaty of Rome**, which provides that states must take "necessary measures" to comply with a decision of the court under **Article 169**. (On this see 1.2.1.4. above). If no award has yet been made, then probably the procedure must be reopened although there may arguably be exceptions - for example, for cases of urgency not due to the fault of the state concerned. When, on the other hand, the procedure has progressed to the award stage or beyond, it might be argued that a reopening of the procedure should not be considered a "necessary measure" under **Article 171,** particularly since this may cause hardship to the party to whom the contract has been awarded. There may be some dispute as to the exact point at which the possibility of a re-award should be precluded. Should this be when the award has been made? When the contract itself has been concluded? Or only when the work is substantially underway? It may also be considered appropriate to take account of the particular circumstances of a case, of course, such as whether the successful contractor or the authority knew of the possible illegality when the contract was made.

When a contractor brings an action in the national courts, the question of whether the procedure should be re-opened is a matter for national law (both under the **Compliance Directives,** where applicable, and also under general principles of Community law), although this discretion is always subject to the overriding principle that an effective remedy must be available to enforce Community rights. Probably the principle of effectiveness does not require the setting aside of a concluded contract, however - this is expressly stated in **Article 2 of the Compliance Directive** and **Article 2 of the Utilities Compliance Directive**, which provide that where the agreement has actually been made national law may always limit a contractor to a damages remedy.

What is the position in relation to proceedings brought by the Commission under **Article 169**? The court in the present case did not deal with this issue of the reopening of the award procedure, confining itself to a finding of illegality based on the failure to issue an adequate declaration.

However, the problem was considered by the Advocate General, in the course of giving his views on whether Italy had complied with the reasoned opinion of the Commission. He took the view that since the works had not been completed, the Italian government ought to have directed, or at least urged, the municipality to rescind the contract which had been made: this was required by the reasoned opinion delivered in this case, in which the Commission had directed that the authority should take necessary measures to comply with its obligations (see para. 24 of the opinion). The fact that one measure - a declaration - was specified, was not intended by the Commission to preclude other, more concrete, measures, if also necessary in the circumstances (para. 24). It seems that the Commission could not order something which is not a "necessary measure" for compliance with Community law, and it therefore assumed that action to set aside a contract could be required under **Article 171**. The Advocate General likewise seems to assume that this is a measure which could lawfully be required.

The Advocate General does not state that measures must be taken to actually achieve a setting aside of the contract in a national legal system. He merely suggests that the municipality should be directed to set aside the award, or in a case where the state has no direct control over the actions of the municipality but it is subject instead to regional supervision, should be urged to set the award aside. This may suggest that what is required in relation to the contract depends to a degree on what is possible under domestic constitutional arrangements. However, it is clearly established that such internal arrangements cannot affect a state's responsibility to ensure that domestic measures comply with Community law. The position must be the same in principle for all unlawful contracts made by authorities for which the state has responsibility under **Article 169**: if a state can be directed to set aside any such contracts, then this must apply to all comparable contracts, regardless of the apparent power of the state to achieve this result under domestic law. No doubt the Advocate General was merely intending to indicate that the Italian government would be required to put in motion the process for achieving a set aside which ordinarily would be followed in Italy, given the constitutional set-up. However, if a municipality failed to respond to any urging of the Italian government to set aside the contract, this should not excuse the government from its obligation to ensure the required result is achieved.

The view that measures may be required to be taken for a concluded contract to be set aside now finds further support in the *Italian lottery* case, in which the President of the court awarded interim measures to prevent the Italian government from acting on a concluded contract. This case is discussed at 16. below. If indeed it may be required that a contract be set aside, a disappointed contractor who cannot obtain an annulment of the agreement in the national courts because this is precluded by national law, may be able to achieve this by persuading the Commission to act under **Article 169.** This will make complaint to the Commission a particularly attractive option in those cases where the contract in issue has already been awarded.

5.3. EXCEPTIONS TO THE ADVERTISING REQUIREMENTS OF THE WORKS DIRECTIVE

The court's having declared the action admissible, the question of the merits of the case then fell to be considered. In this regard, it was argued by Italy that there had been no breach of the advertising requirements imposed by the law for works contracts, since the case before the court fell within one or more exceptions to these requirements.

The municipality relied first on the "sole contractor" exception, then contained in **Article 9 (b) of the Works Directive**, which provides that a tender notice need not be published "when, for technical or artistic reasons or for reasons connected with the protection of exclusive rights, the works may only be carried out by a particular contractor". (This exception is now found in **Article 5 (3) of the Works Directive:** see the **1989 Works Directive, Articles 1 (8) and 1 (9)).**

It was argued that both for technical reasons and reasons connected with the protection of exclusive rights no other entity in the Community was capable of constructing the plant.

Reliance was also placed on **Article 9 (d)** which stated that contracts could be placed without compliance with the procedures of the Directive "in so far as is strictly necessary when, for reasons of extreme urgency brought by events unforeseen by the authorities awarding contracts, the time limit laid down in other procedures cannot be kept ." (The "urgency" derogation, with very slightly different wording but identical in substance, is now found in **Article 5 (3) (c) of the Works Directive:** see the **1989 Works Directive Articles 1 (8) and (9)).**

In response to these arguments, the court made two important points concerning the exceptions to the general rules in the Directives (see para. 14 of the judgment). First, it stated that such exceptions (or "derogations") must be strictly interpreted. Second, it was said that the burden of proof that the circumstances justifying the derogation are met is on the party seeking to invoke that derogation.

The court then briefly concluded that in this case the existence of conditions for invoking the above derogations had not been proven.

With regard to the argument that there was only one possible contractor for technical reasons, the Advocate General noted that the Commission in its investigations had concluded that other firms could have undertaken the construction, and no evidence had been put forward to contradict this view. Evidence had been put forward to show that the chosen firms would produce the most *efficient* plant; but as the Advocate General pointed out, this is not sufficient to invoke the derogation which was relied on. With regard to the question of exclusive rights, he considered that specific evidence - for example, of particular patents - must offered by the authority, and none was put forward here. In relation to urgency he noted that events so far belied this claim, the award process having already been delayed for several years for various reasons.

6. Joined cases 27-29/86 S.A. Construction et Entreprises Industrielles (CEI) and others v Societé Co-operative "Association Intercommunales pour les Autoroutes des Ardennes" and others ("CEI" and "Bellini")

9th July 1987; [1987] ECR 3347; [1989] 2 CMLR 224

SUMMARY

*These cases concerned requests for a preliminary ruling under **Article 177** of the **Treaty of Rome**.*

*The court ruled that the references listed in **Article 25 of the Works Directive** which may be called for by contracting authorities to establish a contractor's financial and economic standing are not exhaustive: others may also be called for.*

*It was stated that levels of financial and economic standing and of technical expertise required of contractors are matters for national law. Thus, where a requirement that contractors' total work should not exceed a set limit is designed to ensure adequate financial of standing of contractors, it is not precluded by the **Works Directive**.*

*The principle that levels of financial standing and technical competence are for national law is not affected by **Article 28 of the Works Directive** concerning registration in an official list in the contractor's home state. This Article is concerned only with the means of proving that standards set by national law are met, and does not restrict the freedom of states to set their own standards.*

6.1. INTRODUCTION AND FACTS: CASE 27/86 ("CEI")

The above cases all concerned requests for a preliminary ruling from the European Court, made by the Belgian Council of State (*Conseil d'Etat*) under the procedure laid down in **Article 177 of the Treaty of Rome**. The Article 177 ruling procedure is explained at 1.3.3. above. It is convenient to consider, first, case 27/86 (*CEI*), and, second, cases 28 and 29/86 *(Bellini)*. The last two may be examined together since both involved the same question to the court.

Case 27/86 arose out of a decision by a Belgian authority to reject a tender put in by CEI for a contract for works on the Ardennes motorway. A Royal Decree provided for rejection of bids where the total value of the contractor's work in hand plus the value of the contract sought exceeded a prescribed maximum, and bidders for the contract were thus asked to state the value of all current work in hand. The bid of CEI was rejected in accordance with the above Decree because the level of its current work exceeded the stated limit. The purpose of the limit was, according to the Council of State, twofold - first, to prevent a monopoly on works contracts by certain firms, and, second, to prevent individual contractors from overstretching themselves.

The decision to reject the bid was challenged by CEI before the Council of State. CEI alleged that rejection for this reason was contrary to the **Works Directive**, on the basis that that Directive regulated the factors which could be taken into account in determining the eligibility of contractors, and did not specify the total value of a contractor's work as a relevant criterion.

Two questions relating to this matter were referred by the Council of State to the European Court. The first concerned the means of proof of financial and economic standing which can be required of contractors. The second was intended to establish whether the total value of work undertaken by a contractor may be a ground for excluding a contractor from an award procedure.

6.2. MEANS OF PROOF OF FINANCIAL AND ECONOMIC STANDING

The first question related to the means by which a contractor may be required to prove to contracting authorities the contractor's financial and economic standing. The question of financial and economic standing is referred to in **Article 25 of the Works Directive**. As explained in the discussion of *Transporoute* at 3.2. above, an authority may always take into account a contractor's financial and economic standing as substantive criteria for his exclusion from the award process. (This is implied by **Article 20**). **Article 25** deals with the methods by which the authority may require a contractor to prove his financial and economic standing. It provides that proof may "as a general rule, be furnished by one or more of the following references", namely, bankers statements, balance sheets and statements of turnover. The Article then goes on to state that authorities shall specify in the notice or invitation to tender which references are to be supplied, and also which references "other than those mentioned" are to be produced. Finally, it states that if "for any valid" reason a contractor cannot provide those requested, he may prove his financial and economic standing by other documents which the authority considers appropriate.

The first question put to the European Court in *CEI* asked:

"Are the references enabling a contractor's financial and economic standing to be determined exhaustively enumerated in Article 25?"

The court, agreeing with the opinion of Advocate General Mishco, ruled that such references are not exhaustively enumerated in **Article 25** (see paras. 8-10 of the judgment). The court noted, in particular, the provision in **Article 25** requiring authorities to state what references *other than those mentioned in the Article* are to be provided. This clearly assumes that references other than those listed may be required. In this ruling the court confirmed the view which it had already stated in its previous judgment in *Transporoute* (see 3.2.1. above); and indeed the point was not seriously disputed before the court.

6.3. MAXIMUM TOTAL WORK AS AN ELIGIBILITY CRITERION

6.3.1. The question before the court

Through its second question to the European Court it seems that the Belgian Council of State wished to ascertain whether it is permissible to exclude contractors from an award on the basis of a "maximum work" criterion and to call for contractors to provide information on this matter, as had been done in the case which was before the Council of State. This was the way in which the Council's intention was interpreted by the European Court.

The question as actually framed by the Council of State, however, did not appear apt for its intended purpose. The question asked whether the value of works which may be carried out at one time could be regarded as a "reference enabling a contractor's financial and economic standing to be determined within the meaning of Article 25 of the directive". The point of the question was that if the value of the work *is* a reference relating to financial and economic standing, then in the light of the court's ruling, discussed at 6.2. above, that an authority may specify *any* references in relation to these matters, the value of work being undertaken would be a permissible "reference".

The problem with the question as put, however, is that the "value of work undertaken" cannot possibly constitute a "reference" at all, as was pointed out by Advocate General Mishco. A reference is a *means of proof* by which a contractor's compliance with certain *substantive criteria* is demonstrated. A bank statement, for example, is a *means of proof*, by which a contractor may demonstrate that he has a certain amount of capital available, the availability of a certain amount of capital being itself a *substantive criterion* of eligibility which a contractor may sometimes be required to meet. The requirement that a contractor's current value of work should be below a certain amount is not a reference - a means of proof of something - but a substantive criterion. Hence the "value of work" referred to in the question put by the Council of State could not be a reference relating to financial and economic standing under **Article 25** since it could not be a reference at all.

If the court had confined itself to the question submitted the answer would thus have been in the negative on the basis just explained. This answer would simply have told the Council of State that the "value of work" requirement was a substantive criterion for evaluation, and not a "reference" at all. Clearly this would have been unhelpful: what the Council really wished to know was whether the value of work being undertaken is a criterion which may permissibly be taken into account by a contracting authority, and whether the authority may call for a statement of a contractor's position in this regard as a reference in relation to this criterion. The court therefore decided to address these issues. As was explained at 1.3. above, when the court addresses a request for an **Article 177** ruling it will attempt to address the issues which it considers are the concern of the national court, regardless of the formal wording of the question put to it.

6.3.2. The criteria of financial and economic standing

The court concluded that specification of a maximum level of current work for contractors wishing to participate in a public works contract may be permissible.

As indicated earlier, one purpose of the "value of work" requirement was to prevent individual contractors from overstretching themselves. This obviously relates to - it is one aspect of - the general concept of "financial and economic standing". As explained, the combined effect of **Articles 20 and 25 of the Works Directive** is to make it clear that financial and economic standing are relevant criteria in choosing a contractor, so to the extent that the "value of work" is an aspect of financial and economic standing, it seems clear that it may *prima facie* be taken into account. An issue considered by the court, however, was whether **Article 25** imposes any limits on an authority's discretion regarding the nature and level of the economic and financial criteria to be considered, which might have precluded the "value of work" standard set in this case.

The view of the court was that **Article 25** is not concerned at all to limit the authority's discretion to set *levels* of financial and economic standing for contractors: it is merely concerned with the *means of proving* that the contractor meets the standards which the authority has decided to set. Since there is nothing dealing with this question of the appropriate levels of standing elsewhere in the **Works Directive**, it follows that the determination of the appropriate levels remains a matter for national law. Thus it is permissible to specify compliance with any standards which relate to financial and economic standing, including a condition relating to the total value of a contractor's commitments (see paras. 12-18 of the judgment). Eligibility conditions such as a minimum annual turnover or a minimum amount of existing capital are also matters which generally relate to financial and economic standing and so, under this principle, are established as matters for national law. This view of the law has been repeated by the court in the later case of *Beentjes* (see 8.3.2. below).

6.3.3. Secondary factors in contractor selection

The "value of works" requirement was imposed not only in order to ensure adequate financial and economic standing, but also to prevent the concentration of works contracts amongst a limited number of contractors. This may be referred to as a "secondary" policy in contractor selection - that is, one which does not relate to the primary objective of procurement of securing the goods or services required on the best possible terms. The question of whether such secondary criteria may be taken into account in selecting a contractor is not expressly dealt with in the procurement Directives. The court did not specifically discuss whether the provisions on contractor selection in the Directive preclude consideration of such criteria. However, the view that consideration of secondary matters is not precluded is arguably implicit in the court's conclusion that the "value of work" requirement was permissible, since one of the purposes of the requirement was the secondary purpose of preventing monopolies. On the other hand, it may be that the court considered the level set would have been the same even had its sole purpose been to ensure the adequate economic standing of contractors, and that on this basis it would be permissible whether or not its second purpose was a lawful one.

In any case, it may be noted that the whole question of "secondary" factors in contractor selection has now been expressly considered by the court in the *Beentjes* case, in which the court ruled that consideration of such factors is not forbidden by the **Works Directive**. This issue is discussed further at 7.3.2. below.

6.3.4. The requirement of a statement of the value of current works

The court also considered whether an authority may require a statement from a contractor of the value of his current works. It concluded that this was permissible, since this was a method of proving financial and economic standing, and the court had already concluded that *any* references relating to the proof of financial and economic standing could be called for (see para. 11 of the judgment).

6.4. INTRODUCTION AND FACTS: CASES 28-29/86 ("Bellini")

As mentioned earlier, these two cases concerned references made to the European Court by the Belgian Council of State under the procedure in **Article 177 of the Treaty of Rome**. They arose out of the rejection by the Belgian authorities of two tenders for works contracts submitted by a firm called Bellini. The reason for the rejection was the same in both cases. This was that Bellini did not meet minimum manpower and capital requirements which were prescribed by legislation for firms bidding on contracts of a certain value.

Bellini challenged the decisions alleging, *inter alia*, a breach of the **Works Directive**. The company's argument was based on the fact that it was able to produce a certificate of registration in an official list of contractors maintained by the government of Italy. Registration in this list qualified it to bid on contracts of the same type and value from which it had been disqualified in Belgium. It was contended that the effect of **Article 28 of the Works Directive** was to require the Belgian authorities to recognise its competence to undertake for the Belgian government work for which it was recognised as qualified in Italy by virtue of registration on this list. The question referred by the Council of State to the European Court concerned this issue, and was identically worded in the two cases.

6.5. THE EFFECT OF ARTICLE 28

As has been explained at 6.3.3. above, the court stated in considering the first question posed in *CEI* that it is for national law to prescribe the qualifications relating to financial and economic standing. Thus it is in principle for national law to decide the level of capital which may be demanded of contractors, one of the matters in issue in *Bellini*, since this is a matter which relates to economic standing.

The other matter in contention in *Bellini* was the level of the firm's manpower, a matter generally considered as relating to technical competence. The question of technical competence, like financial and economic standing is one which may always be taken into account by authorities in deciding the eligibility of a contractor for an award. (This can be deduced from the combined effect of **Article 20** and **Article 26**). **Article 26** lists the references which may be called for as proof a contractor's technical expertise. It would seem that if **Article 25** is concerned only with the means of proof of the criteria to which it refers, and does not limit the freedom of states to prescribe their own standards of financial eligibility, then the same is true of **Article 26** in relation to technical competence: states may set their own standards in relation to this question also. It is clearly the view of the court in *Bellini* that this is the case, although this issue is not explicitly discussed. Thus in principle it is open to states to determine the minimum manpower levels for contractors, as well as the minimum capital requirements.

The question effectively put to the court in the two *Bellini* cases asked whether this freedom of member states to determine levels of financial standing and technical competence is ever ousted when a contractor is recognised in his home state as eligible for a contract of the relevant type and value. Must other EC states then also recognise the contractor as qualified to perform such contracts, regardless of the usual requirements of domestic law?

Bellini argued that this is sometimes the case, basing its argument on **Article 28 of the Works Directive**. **Article 28 (3)** provides that registration in an official list of contractors maintained by another EC state shall "constitute a presumption of suitability for works corresponding to the classification" in respect of certain of the provisions in **Article 23-26** of the Directive. These provisions include **Article 26 (d)**, which says that a contractor's technical ability may be proved by a statement of its manpower, and **Article 25 (b)**, which states that financial and economic standing may generally be proven by calling for evidence from a firm's balance sheets. Bellini argued that the effect of **Article 28 (3)** is that where inclusion in a "qualification list" for a certain type of contract in the contractor's state requires him to satisfy requirements relating to manpower and capital, registration in that list requires that he be presumed by all other member states to possess adequate capital and manpower to carry out that type of contract.

This argument was rejected by the court, which considered that **Article 28 (3)** does not interfere at all with a member state's freedom to set its own qualification standards and criteria. This clearly seems correct. To accept Bellini's argument would effectively mean that the standards required of contractors to compete for public works contracts would for all EC states be those prescribed by the least stringent of the member states, which surely cannot have been an intended consequence of the **Works Directive.**

What, then, is the effect of **Article 28 (3)**? According to the court it is simply concerned with the *means of proof* which may be used by a contractor to show that the contractor meets any standard set. Its effect is that registration in the official list of another state may be used by contractors as "an alternative means of proving before the authority of another member state awarding the contract that they satisfy the qualitative criteria listed in **Articles 23-26...**" (para. 25 of the judgment). Thus, if registration is based on satisfying standards relating to matters such as manpower or capital, the contractor need not produce a specific statement of manpower or his balance sheets, but may instead point to his registration in the list as evidence of his position in relation to these matters. It may be noted that it is also provided by **Article 28 (3)** that "information which can be deduced from registration in official lists may not be questioned". This seems to mean that where registration presupposes that certain *factual* matters have been proven - for example, that a contractor's turnover exceeded a certain level - the correctness of these facts cannot be challenged by another state.

The purpose of these provisions in **Article 28** is to minimise the procedural burdens placed on foreign as opposed to domestic contractors. Obviously a domestic is more likely than a foreign contractor to be registered in a list maintained by the awarding authority, which will exempt him from being required to prove that he satisfies various eligibility conditions: a foreign contractor who has to produce specific documentation relating to these conditions is under a heavier burden and the paperwork may discourage him from bidding. To allow him to use registration in his own state as evidence of these matters may help reduce this burden and so produce more open competition.

7. Case 45/87R, Commission of the European Communities V Ireland; Case 45/87, Commission of the European Communities V Ireland ("the Dundalk cases")

i) 16th February 1987; [1987] ECR 783; [1987] 2 CMLR 197 (Order on *ex parte* application for interim relief)
ii) 13th March 1987; [1987] ECR 1369; [1987] 2 CMLR 563 (Order on hearing of application for interim relief)
iii) 22nd September 1988; [1988] ECR 4929; [1989] 1 CMLR 225 (Judgment of the court)

SUMMARY

These cases concerned proceedings under Article 169 of the Treaty of Rome.

Interim relief: *Interim relief was granted on an application made ex parte by the Commission in connection with the main proceedings. However, it was refused at the hearing on interim relief, because of the danger to public health and safety which might result from a delay in the procurement.*

Merits: *The court concluded that where an award procedure is not expressly covered by the requirements of the Works Directive, the requirements are not binding in relation to the procedure simply because a notice has been published in the Official Journal by reference to the requirement for obligatory publication which is stated in the Directive.*
Regarding the application of Article 30 of the Treaty of Rome to public works contracts, the court ruled that a stipulation relating to goods provided under such a contract is to be assessed under Article 30, notwithstanding that a works contract may fall within the services provisions of the Treaty. The court concluded that a stipulation in this case that certain goods used in performing a works contract should comply with an Irish national specification was a measure equivalent to a restriction on imports under Article 30. The restriction could not here be justified under

Article 36 of the Treaty of Rome nor by reference to mandatory requirements.

The court made it clear that in proceedings under *Article 169* member states may be held responsible for the actions of local authorities.

7.1. INTRODUCTION AND FACTS

The *Dundalk* cases concerned proceedings by the Commission against Ireland, brought in the European Court under the procedure in **Article 169 of the Treaty of Rome.** This procedure is explained at 1.2. above.

The conduct in issue related to an open call for tenders for the construction of a water main, which had been issued by Dundalk Urban District Council. The contract specifications provided that certain pipes to be used in the construction should be asbestos cement pipes which had been certified as complying with a certain Irish standard specification. This certification had to be made in accordance with the certification procedure laid down under the auspices of the Irish Standard Mark Licensing Scheme of the Institute for Industrial Research and Standards. Pipes made to this specification were at that time produced by only one firm - an Irish firm. There was no provision to allow bidders to use pipes of an equivalent standard which did not meet the detailed specification. The authority rejected one tender on the basis that the pipes that the bidder proposed to use did not comply.

The Commission contended that both the inclusion of this specification in the contract documents and the subsequent refusal of the authority to accept tenders which did not comply was conduct which a) constituted a breach of **Article 10 of the Works Directive**, which sets out specific rules on contract specifications and b) amounted to a breach of **Article 30 of the Treaty of Rome.**

The European Court rejected the argument based on **Article 10 of the Works Directive**, since the Directive had no application to a contract of this type. However, it found that the relevant conduct was a breach of **Article 30 of the Treaty of Rome**, and consequently ruled that Ireland was in breach of its obligations under Community law.

Three stages of the litigation are reported:

i) First, there was an application by the Commission for interim measures, made *ex parte* (that is, without Ireland's being given a hearing). The purpose of this application was to prevent the authority's taking any action, pending the court's full consideration of whether the *status quo* should be maintained until the trial or whether Ireland should be allowed to proceed with the award nevertheless. This *ex parte* application was successful. The order made on this application is reported in [1987] ECR 783 and [1987] 2 CMLR 197. This stage of the litigation will be referred to as "*Dundalk 1*".

ii) Second, there followed a hearing on the question of whether there should be interim measures to secure postponement of the project pending final resolution of the dispute over whether Ireland was in breach of its obligations under Community law. Such measures were in fact refused, and the municipality thus became free to go ahead with the project again, even though the dispute had not yet been resolved. The order made here is reported at [1987] ECR 1369 and [1987] 1 CMLR 563. This stage of proceedings will be referred to as "*Dundalk 2*".

iii) Finally, the court considered whether there had been a breach by Ireland of its Community law obligations. As indicated, the court took the view that there was a breach of **Article 30 of the Treaty of Rome**. The court's judgment is reported at [1988] ECR 4929 and [1989] 1 CMLR 225. This stage will be referred to as "*Dundalk 3*."

7.2. INTERIM MEASURES

7.2.1. General

As was explained in the introduction at 1.2.1.3., when proceedings are brought under **Article 169 of the Treaty of Rome**, there is provision for the European Court to order any necessary interim measures. In the *Dundalk* litigation the Commission sought interim relief to order Ireland either 1) to take such steps as were necessary to prevent the award of the contract until judgment was given by the court or, alternatively, a settlement agreed; or 2), in the event that the contract had already been concluded, to take the measures necessary to cancel the contract. During the run-up to the proceedings under **Article 169**, the Irish government had agreed to postpone further action on the intended award until a specified date, but at the time of the application this date was imminent. Ireland had indicated that it would not contemplate further postponement unless this was ordered by the court - hence the need for this application for interim relief.

The case raised the important issue of the circumstances in which the European Court will be willing to grant interim measures in relation to procurement awards challenged by the Commission under **Article 169** (and doubtless the same principles would apply in the context of an action by another member state under **Article 170**). When an infringement of the procurement rules is alleged, a party bringing any sort of legal proceedings will often wish to obtain interim measures, either to prevent the award decision being made, or, if it has been made, to prevent a contract actually being concluded. If the contract has already been entered into, the objective of seeking interim measures may be to stop any work from being done. Generally, the further the process had gone, the more difficult it is to unscramble should there ultimately prove to have been some illegality, and the more reluctant the court will then be to reopen the award procedure.

The importance of interim measures will, of course, depend on what *is* the legal position following a successful challenge. Particularly important are the questions of whether the court will indeed refuse to order a reopening of the procedure (a matter discussed at 5.2.2. above and 16.3 below), and, where this is the case, what compensation is available to anyone suffering loss.

A successful application for interim relief made by the Commission may benefit individual contractors prejudiced by a breach of the procurement rules. Alternatively, such contractors may protect their own interests by applying for interim relief in the national courts. In relation to contract procedures falling within the **Works Directive** and **Supplies Directive**, interim measures must be available in national law, under **Article 2 of the Compliance Directive**; and, in the case where a "classic" remedies system is in place in relation to authorities subject to the **Utilities Directive**, interim relief must be available in those cases also, under **Article 2 of the Utilities Compliance Directive**, once the date for implementation of that Directive has passed. When such relief will be granted is a matter for the discretion of national courts, so that the applicable principles may vary as between different states - though it must be remembered that national discretion is limited by the general requirement that an *effective* system of remedies should be provided (as stated in **Article 1** of both **Compliance Directives**). Where a breach of Community law is alleged in relation to contracts falling outside the Directives (for example, because their value is too low), interim measures must always be available when they would be available in a "comparable" case in domestic law, by virtue of the general Community law principle of non-discrimination. Arguably they might also be required to be made available in other cases also, when this is necessary to provide an *effective* remedy for contractors (for example, where domestic law does not provide adequate damages for contractors as an alternative). Under these principles it may be that contractors can use the national courts to obtain interim relief, though it would not be given by the European Court; and likewise they may gain from a successful application for interim relief by the Commission, though they could not obtain such relief themselves in national law.

7.2.2. Interim relief: *ex parte* proceedings

Dundalk 1 concerned the Commission's request for interim relief in an application made *ex parte*. (On *ex parte* proceedings see further 1.2.1.3. above).

The application was granted by the President, who indicated that this was necessary to prevent the court's being presented with a *fait accompli* - that is, a situation where the contract, and possibly even the work under the contract, had been completed. He also noted that a delay in awarding this contract might not affect the municipality's ultimate objective of improving the water supply since, the Commission contended, other phases of the project were not planned for completion until much later. The prospect of delay if the *ex parte* application is granted is, of course, a relevant factor to consider, and it may in principle lead to the conclusion that relief should be refused. However, in practice interim measures granted on an *ex parte* application will be very temporary, in effect only until a hearing can be held on the matter of interim relief. Usually such a hearing is quickly arranged - in *Dundalk* this hearing was held about a month later - and the fact that any delay will only be a short one suggests that an *ex parte* application will rarely be refused for this reason. It is submitted that there is in fact a strong presumption in favour of the grant of such an application. *Dundalk 1* is consistent with this view, and it is also supported by the order made in case 194/88R, discussed at 12. below.

7.2.3. Principles governing interim relief

In *Dundalk 2* the President was faced with the more difficult decision of whether to postpone the award process pending a final resolution of the dispute. Having listened to Ireland's arguments against postponement, the President decided to allow the process to proceed.

A number of matters must be considered by the court in deciding whether to grant or refuse interim relief:

<u>Legal and factual grounds for relief</u>: First, it is necessary, as specified in the **Rules of Procedure, Article 83 (2)**, that the applicant for interim measures should demonstrate legal and factual grounds which justify interim measures. In other words, he must show a *prima facie* case. This was found in *Dundalk* on the basis of the allegation of a breach of **Article 30** of the Treaty (a claim eventually upheld at the trial).

<u>Circumstances of urgency</u>: According to **Article 83 (2) of the Rules of Procedure** the court must then consider whether there are circumstances of urgency. It has been held that this requires the applicant to demonstrate that without interim measures he would suffer serious and irreparable damage.

In the case of an alleged breach of the procurement rules, this will consist of the damage to the Community's open procurement policy from allowing the specific infringement to go uncorrected, and also the damage which may be caused more generally to this policy if breaches of the procurement rules are not deterred by the imposition of effective sanctions. The President of the court clearly accepted in *Dundalk* that damage to Community procurement policy constitutes damage to the Commission, as "guardian of the Community interest" (see para. 82 of the order), and he specifically rejected an argument that the Commission must demonstrate the precise nature and extent of the damage which might occur.

It seems that it will generally be assumed that damage to this interest will occur if no interim relief is given, on the basis that the court may well be presented at trial with a situation in which it is not possible to reopen the award procedure. This was assumed in *Dundalk 2* and also in case 194/88R (see 12. below) and the *Italian lottery* case. (see 16.2)

In the context of **Article 169** actions it is arguable that the interests of other affected individuals may also be taken into account in deciding if there is serious and irreparable damage. Thus the interests of affected contractors can perhaps be considered here. This was argued by the Commission but disputed by Ireland on the basis that contractors could obtain compensation in the national courts, a matter considered below. The President did not comment on this point.

Balance of interests: Once serious and irreparable damage has been shown, the court must proceed to a "weighing" exercise, to decide whether interim relief should be granted on the facts. On the one hand, it must consider the damage which would occur if interim relief were refused and a breach of the rules were shown. On the other, it must consider the adverse consequences of granting interim relief.

Damage if relief is refused will include, of course, damage to the Community's open procurement policy, as mentioned above. How serious this damage will be will depend to some extent on how willing the court will be to require the set aside of any contract which has been concluded in breach of the rules, a question which has not been resolved. This is discussed at 5.2.2. above, and at 16.3. below in considering the *Italian lottery* case. It seems likely now that the court will be prepared to require a set-aside, in some circumstances at least. Even if a set-aside is sometimes required, however, it may be argued that this should not preclude interim relief, since if relief is refused there is still the possibility that the work will have been substantially completed by the time of trial, which will probably preclude any new award's being made.

In addition to damage to Community policy, the court may also, arguably, take into account damage to suppliers prejudiced by a breach of the rules.

Contractors will be able to obtain compensation where there is a breach of Community law in relation to award procedures covered by the **Works and Supplies Directives** and the **Utilities Directive**, since this is provided for in the **Compliance Directives**. It is possible also that they are entitled to compensation for breaches in relation to other award procedures, following the decision in *Francovich* (joined cases C-6/90 and C-9/90, *Francovich v Italy*, 19th November 1991), in which the court ruled that in some circumstances at least national law must provide compensation for loss resulting from a breach of Community law. Even if compensation is available in principle, however, this may often be an inadequate remedy because of the difficulty of proving loss. For example, where the complaint is that the contractor has been excluded because there has been no advertisement, or where, although the contractor has participated, the award is to be made on the basis of very subjective factors, it may be impossible for that contractor to show he would have won the contract. Whether damages are adequate will depend, of course, on how they are to be calculated and measured. This is a matter which is in principle for national law, and this makes it difficult for the European Court to make a judgment about the need for interim relief to protect contractors. It might thus be argued that a rule of convenience should be adopted. One such rule might be that the protection of contractors is for the national courts alone, and that their interests should not be taken into account in deciding whether to grant interim relief in an action under **Article 169 of the Treaty of Rome.** Alternatively, it might be suggested that, on the contrary, damages are not generally adequate in this kind of case, and a rule of convenience should be adopted which presumes damage to contractors.

The President in *Dundalk* did not specifically comment on the relevance of the interests of disappointed suppliers and how these should be taken into account. It may be noted, however, that in the later case 199/88R the possible damage to other contractors was specifically given as one reason in favour of granting interim relief (see 12.2. below) though it is not entirely clear whether it relates to the "balance of interests" or "irreparable damage" stage. If it relates to balance of interests, then this suggests either that the European Court should examine the position of contractors in national law on the facts of each case, or that damage should be presumed. However, this case, which concerned a contract alleged to be subject to the **Works Directive,** was decided when it was considered that damages were generally *not* required to be provided as a remedy for contractors - that is, before the **Compliance Directive** was required to be implemented and prior to the decision in *Francovich*. In cases where damages are now provided for, it seems at least arguable that the rule of convenience should be adopted that contractors are adequately protected by national law.

Whatever the significance of the interests of individual contractors, it seems unlikely to make much difference to the balance of convenience in any given case. As will be explained below, it seems that interim relief will normally be granted by the court in view of the importance of upholding the open procurement policy; and in those exceptional cases where other public interests are sufficient to override this it seems likely that those public interests would also override the interests of individual contractors.

On the other side, the main argument *against* interim relief is the delay which this might cause to the project to which the procurement relates. The importance of the consequences of delay will, of course, vary - a delay to a contract for the repair of a busy highway will no doubt be considered more urgent than delay to a contract for the construction of a monument of purely aesthetic value. The severity of the consequences in each case must be considered in determining whether the arguments in favour of relief outweigh those against.

In *Dundalk* itself the Commission argued that there would be no delay at all. This was because it was contended that a delay to the particular contract would not affect the ultimate objective of improving local water supply, since other phases of the project were not scheduled for completion until much later. Ireland, on the other hand, argued that delay would occur, on the basis that progress on the other phases would be held up by late completion of this contract. By refusing to grant the measures requested the President seems to have accepted Ireland's argument, since if interim measures would not result in any delay or other adverse consequences there is obviously no reason to refuse them. (The President's view of the facts has been criticised by Gormley, who suggests that there was in fact no real evidence that the project as a whole would be delayed: see (1989) 14 EL Rev 156 at 160).

The President considered that the objective of the project in question was sufficiently important to warrant the refusal of relief. He accepted that there was a shortage of water in the area, and that this posed dangers to health and safety, for example, because the supply might be inadequate for fire fighting. The President seems, however, to indicate that the case before him, in which public safety was threatened, should perhaps be regarded as exceptional. He states: "It should be emphasised that this assessment may be entirely different for public works contracts with other objectives, where a delay in awarding the contract would not involve such dangers to the health and safety of a population." (para. 83 of the order). The view that there is quite a strong presumption on favour of interim relief also finds strong support in two later cases - case 199/84R and the *Italian lottery* case, discussed at 12. and 16. below.

7.3. APPLICATION OF THE WORKS DIRECTIVE

In *Dundalk 3* the European Court considered the merits of the case. The first allegation was that there had been a breach of the **Works Directive**. The Commission contended that the provisions of the Directive governed the award procedure, and that Dundalk had failed to comply with these provisions, in particular with **Article 10** on specifications.

On the face of the Directive it seemed that the award procedure was not covered, and so it was contended by Ireland: although the contract was a public works contract of the requisite value, it appeared to be excluded by **Article 3 (5)**. This provided, at that time, that the Directive did not apply to "public works contracts awarded by the production, distribution, transmission or transportation services for water or energy". In considering the application for interim relief in *Dundalk 2* the President had taken the view that, because of this exclusion, there was no *prima facie* case made out for a breach of the Directive; but the Commission nevertheless persisted in arguing this point. Although it was accepted that the contract fell within the terms of the exclusion, the Commission argued that the Directive should nevertheless be applied. This was because a notice calling for tenders had been placed in the Official Journal in the form stipulated for those awards subject to the Directive, and had been requested by Dundalk by reference to the obligatory requirements of the Directive. It was contended that in such circumstances, all the provisions of the Directive must be applied, particularly since contractors who read the notice will assume the Directive is to be followed, and may rely on this belief in deciding whether to put in a bid - a type of estoppel argument.

The court rejected the argument and ruled that the Directive had no application, governing only those contracts expressly within its terms (see paras. 10-11 of the judgment). This applied whether the reason for publication was an error, or whether publication had occurred because the municipality had originally intended to seek Community funding for the project (in which case advertisement would have been a condition of funding).

It may be noted that, since the relevant events, the wording of the "utilities" exclusion, which was relied on in *Dundalk,* has been slightly amended (see **Directive 89/440/EEC, Article 2**). Many of the award procedures covered by the exclusion are now, of course, subject to regulation in any case, under the **Utilities Directive**.

7.4. ARTICLE 30 OF THE TREATY OF ROME

7.4.1. General Principles

As explained at 7.3. the **Works Directive** was found to have no application in *Dundalk*, and at that time no other Directive applied. The Commission argued that the conduct in question was still unlawful, however, since it infringed **Article 30 of the Treaty of Rome**.

This Article is concerned to ensure the free movement of goods between the states of the European Communities. To this end it prohibits generally "quantitive restrictions" on imports - for example, quotas - and also all measures having "equivalent effect" to quantitive restrictions, a concept which includes a wide variety of measures which make the import of goods more difficult or cut down the market for such goods. For an outline of the scope of Article 30 and related provisions the reader is referred to Steiner, ch.8; Wyatt and Dashwood, ch.6; N. Green, T. Hartley and J. Usher, *The Legal Foundations of the Single European Market* (1991) chs. 5 and 6; and for a detailed account to L.W.Gormley, *Prohibiting Restrictions on Trade within the EEC* (1985) and P.Oliver, *The Free Movement of Goods within the EEC* (2nd ed. 1988).

It is well recognised that the Treaty principles on the free movement of goods have an application to the procurement process. In *Dundalk* the European Court considered several issues relating to the application of these principles to procurement. Ultimately the court concluded that the municipality's conduct in *Dundalk* constituted a breach of **Article 30** .

7.4.2. Relationship between Article 30 and the Articles on services

One argument made by Ireland was that **Article 30** has no relevance to the award of a works contract since such a contract is a contract for services and as such is the province solely of the Treaty provisions on services. The key services provisions are **Article 59**, concerned with the freedom to provide services in another member state on a temporary basis, and **Article 52**, concerned with freedom of establishment - that is, the freedom to set up permanent business in another state (see Steiner, ch.19; Wyatt and Dashwood, chs. 8 and 9; and 9.2.1. below). A public works contract is normally a contract primarily for the provision of services. However, such a contract does generally involve the provision of goods, as well as services, since a contractor normally supplies all or most of the materials, as well as labour, as it did in *Dundalk*. It would seem, *prima facie*, that to the extent that such a contract involves a supply of goods, it would be subject to the provisions contained in **Article 30** on the free movement of goods.

It was argued in *Dundalk*, however, that since conduct relating to a works contract falls within the services Articles because of the services element, it cannot also fall within **Article 30**. In support of this argument Ireland referred to cases in which the court has declined to apply **Article 30** to measures caught by other Articles of the Treaty, such as **Article 95**, which prohibits discriminatory taxation.

The court rejected the argument (see paras. 14-17 of the judgment), and held **Article 30** applicable. It seems that the court considered the application of **Article 30** is precluded only by other Articles of the Treaty *which are directed specifically at the problem of the free movement of goods* (see para. 16 of the judgment). Articles which have been held to oust **Article 30**, such as **Article 95**, are all concerned specifically with the movement of goods problem like **Article 30**, but in a more limited context. Where the problem of free movement of goods has been specifically addressed by provisions concerned with a particular context, it is considered that different rules of a more general nature contained in **Article 30** should not be applied where this would undermine the principles laid down in the more specific provisions. The Articles on services are not, however, directed specifically at the movement of goods problem, and thus cannot be taken to supply rules on the provision of goods which override those in **Article 30** (see para. 17).

It seems that any stipulations relating to goods ought to be assessed under **Article 30**, and any stipulation on services under the services provisions. Specifications for products to be used in a works contract should not be assessed under the services provisions simply because the contract to which they relate is partly, or even primarily, one for services.

The Articles on services should, however, be relevant to a measure relating to the supply of goods to the extent that that measure actually affects the freedom to provide services. Restrictive specifications concerning a product to be used will often affect a contractor's ability to participate in a services contract, and may thus infringe **Article 52** or **Article 59** as well as **Article 30**. For example, if the products specified for use in a works contract are more difficult for foreign contractors to obtain, the specification will have the effect of discriminating against foreign contractors in relation to the provision of the services under the contract.

7.4.3. Application of Article 30

7.4.3.1. Scope of Article 30: general
Having concluded that **Article 30** was capable of applying to a public works contract, the court then considered whether Dundalk's conduct amounted to a measure having an "equivalent effect" to a restriction on

imports under **Article 30.** A very broad definition of measures of equivalent effect was put forward by the European Court in *Dassonville* (case 8/74, *Procureur du Roi v Dassonville* [1974] ECR 837, [1974] 2 CMLR 436): this concept includes, said the court, all "trading rules " enacted by member states "which are capable of hindering, directly or indirectly, actually or potentially, intra-Community trade". The definition is subject to a number of qualifications and exceptions, some of which are touched on below, but in principle it is very wide indeed. It covers, *prima facie*, any conditions imposed as to the standard or quality of goods in the market place, since such conditions prevent access to the market for goods which do not meet those standards, and hence potentially reduce imports of these goods from other member states. A long line of case law has established that it is immaterial that the conditions imposed apply equally to domestic as to imported goods, and this was confirmed in *Dundalk*. Ireland had argued that the specification did not infringe **Article 30** because it set a standard which was required to be met by both domestic and foreign manufacturers; but the court found that nevertheless there was a breach.

Member states must, of course, be able to regulate for some standards, in order to protect interests such as consumer health and safety. Hence, exceptions are made to the principle set out above in order to allow such regulation, though within limits controlled by the European Court. Some of these are set out expressly in **Article 36**, and certain others are also recognised by the court. Ireland argued in *Dundalk* that the restrictive specifications were justified on these kind of grounds, but this contention was rejected by the court. This matter is considered below at 7.4.4.

A number of other issues were also raised regarding the application of the *Dassonville* test in the context of procurement, and these are considered next.

7.4.3.2. Does a restrictive specification impede imports?
One argument made by Ireland was that the use of the specification in issue was not a measure which concerned imports since such conduct did not prevent manufacturers from *importing* products which did not comply with the specification, but merely restricted access to the government market. The argument was expressly rejected by Advocate General Darmon, who said that it is sufficient that a measure impedes imports indirectly by reducing the market for the goods. The court did not specifically address the Irish argument on this point, but obviously rejected it since it found there was a breach of **Article 30**.

7.4.3.3. Is there a de minimis rule?
Another question raised was whether any *de minimis* rule might be applied in this type of case. In other words, may certain conduct relating to

procurement be disregarded for the purposes of **Article 30** on the basis that any potential impact on imports will be negligible? It seemed to be assumed in argument in *Dundalk* that this might be so. The Advocate General considered this question, but concluded that the potential effect of the conduct in this case was significant: he noted that public works contracts were the main "if not exclusive" outlet for the type of pipes in question. The court did not specifically consider this issue.

It is now considered that there is generally no *de minimis* rule under **Article 30** (see, for example, L.W.Gormley, *Prohibiting Restrictions on Trade within the EEC* (1985) at p.3, esp. note 5; P.Oliver, *Free Movement of Goods in the EEC* (2nd ed. 1985) at p.74). At the very least, this is clearly the case where the measures in question are concerned to control the content and nature of the goods themselves (as opposed, for example, to the manner of their marketing and use), as was the case in *Dundalk*. Most measures considered under **Article 30**, however, have been binding regulatory provisions, whilst the measure in *Dundalk* was merely a practice of government. Might it be argued that no *de minimis* rule applies in the former case, where a significant impact on the market may be presumed because of the nature of the measures, but it does in the latter? It is suggested that there is no justification for any such distinction, and that it would be unsatisfactory, since any *de minimis* rule is uncertain and difficult of application. Certainly there is no express support for it in the judgment. Indeed, the existence of any *de minimis* rule was not expressly addressed at all. Conduct relating to procurement should be within **Article 30** without any need to show any particular effect on the market as a whole. It may be noted that no limiting rule of this kind applies in relation to the operation of the procurement Directives.

7.4.3.4. Meaning of "measure"
Article 30 applies only to "measures" of government. A number of previous cases had stated that ephemeral or isolated acts do not constitute "measures" and it was argued by Ireland in *Dundalk* that a restrictive specification in a procurement contract does not have the necessary consistency and generality to be a "measure". Whether some element of generality is required for conduct to fall under **Article 30** is a question distinct from that of the existence of a *de minimis* rule, though obviously they tend to merge in that the less "general" the government's conduct the less likely it is to have a significant impact on imports.

The Advocate General, whilst accepting that isolated acts do not fall within **Article 30**, concluded that this particular case was covered, since the inclusion of Irish standard specifications in government contracts was "usual practice" and the conduct here was thus not an isolated act but a "specific manifestation of a general practice". He also notes that works contracts are the main outlet for the type of pipes in question, and that a major individual contract may have significant and immediate consequences for imports, and also that the use of such specifications in one case may discourage contractors from including foreign products in their tenders in future. He appeared to take the view that in these circumstances an act relating to a single contract could amount to a measure under **Article 30** even if it were not part of a more general practice.

The court itself, since it concluded that there had been a breach of **Article 30**, obviously accepted that the conduct here amounted to a "measure". The matter was not specifically discussed in the judgment, except that the court did expressly make the point at the start of its discussion of **Article 30** that the inclusion of a requirement of compliance with Irish standards was the usual practice in relation to public works contracts in Ireland (see para. 13 of the judgment).

A distinction between isolated decisions and those which exemplify a general practice obviously produces uncertainty in the application of **Article 30**, particularly if something done by different government bodies can be a general practice though not ordered or encouraged by a single central authority. Likewise the Advocate General's suggested additional criteria for qualification as a measure, which relate to the quantitive impact of the conduct on the market, are difficult to apply (and, indeed for this reason it was suggested that a general *de minimis* rule should not be applied). The most that can be said is that generally the court has taken a generous view of what constitutes a measure and it seems likely to do so in this context also. It is hard to see any justification for the supposed "isolated act" rule: it simply creates unnecessary uncertainty and should be jettisoned.

7.4.3.5. A requirement of discrimination?
Another interesting question is whether a procurement measure must be discriminatory to be caught by **Article 30**. It has already been explained that the application of the Article is not precluded because a restriction applies to both imported and domestic products (ie. is "equally" or "indistinctly" applicable). Many such measures are clearly objectionable because, although formally applicable to all products, their effect in restricting access to the market is more significant in relation to imported than domestic products. The measure in *Dundalk* was of this type: although both Irish and imported products were required to meet the same specification, it was more likely that Irish products would do so, since manufacturing processes in Ireland were likely to be set up already to comply with the standard, whilst foreign manufacturers would generally have to modify their products. (As explained, only one firm, an Irish firm, made pipes to the requisite standard at that time). In this sort of case the measure, though indistinctly applicable, is said to be "discriminatory".

Generally, a measure relating to the nature and quality of goods need not be discriminatory to be caught by **Article 30** (Gormley, above, at pp. 262-264; Oliver, above, at p.89; Wyatt and Dashwood, at p.144), although discrimination may be relevant to some aspects of the article's application (for example, mandatory requirements probably cannot be invoked to justify a discriminatory measure, as explained at 7.4.4. below). In other words, for the article to apply, *prima facie*, it need be shown only that the measure hinders imports, and it is irrelevant that it hinders equally the sale and production of domestic products. Thus, for example, restrictions on safety standards which are equally burdensome to both imported and domestic products are caught by **Article 30**. The consequence is that regulation of products by member states is permitted only if justified before the European Court under the rules on mandatory requirements and **Article 36**, which are discussed at 7.4.4.

It has been suggested, however, that conduct in relation to the award of public contracts will not be within the Article unless there is discrimination. Thus Oliver has asserted that "with certain categories of measures of equivalent effect, discrimination is an inherent element. Examples are discrimination in the award of public supply contracts or measures inciting the purchase of national products. In these cases, discrimination is the very essence of the measure, and if it were removed, there would be no restriction on imports left". (Oliver, above, at p.90).

The court does specifically mention the fact that only one undertaking, which was located in Ireland, manufactured pipes complying with the standard set (para. 20). This might be thought to suggest that discrimination was an element of the claim.

It is suggested, however, that discrimination is not required: it is not true that without discrimination no restriction on imports would exist. This is indeed the case with the "buy national" policy referred to by Oliver. However, it is not the case with procurement. The size of the market is fixed once the government has made its decision to purchase a product to fulfil certain objectives, and any specification which eliminates products which are capable of satisfying those objectives may potentially hinder the access of imports to that market. This is no different in principle from a restriction on access to the domestic market as a whole. Thus, specifications for products supplied to the government, as well as conditions laid down for goods sold in the general market place, should be open to review by the European Court even though not discriminatory.

Of course, the decision *what* to buy - the nature of the product and the quality of the product - remains within the discretion of member states. There may in fact be some difficulty in separating the decision on what is needed from the separate process of specifying the purchase. For example, the government may wish to purchase pipes to take hot materials, and for this reason require a certain degree of heat resistance. Clearly the decision to buy pipes which may safely carry this material is in principle one for the member states. However, it may be that different pipes are available for this purpose but some involve slightly more risk of some damage than others. It should be for the member state to determine the quality which is preferred. What, however, if in the opinion of the court the state has "over specified"- for example, has demanded a certain degree of thickness to guarantee safety when it is generally considered that pipes of a lesser thickness can provide an equivalent guarantee. In this case it seems that thinner pipes must be accepted if they can meet the *objectives* of the purchase. In practice, there will be no room for consideration of specifications by the European Court where a contracting authority indicates that is is prepared to consider products which are *equivalent* to those meeting the specifications.

It should also be emphasised that the objectives which it is sought to achieve through the specification of products - whether related to performance, safety, the environment or anything else - should not be limited to those recognised under **Article 36 of the Treaty of Rome** or as mandatory requirements (on this see 7.4.4. below), although in practice they will generally fall within these recognised interests. This is because of the fact that the taking account of these interests is an element of the decision to buy - the creation of the market - rather than a restriction on an existing market. As explained, this question of *what* to buy is a matter solely for the discretion of member states. The sole question for the European Court is whether products which are excluded are or are not capable of meeting the objectives set by the authority, regardless of what these objectives are.

7.4.4. Justifying restrictions in the public interest

As indicated earlier, measures restricting Community trade which fall, *prima facie*, within the *Dassonville* principle, are permissible where necessary to protect certain legitimate interests.

First, **Article 36 of the Treaty of Rome**, permits restrictive measures on a number of specified grounds including, *inter alia*, "public morality, public policy and public security" and "the protection of health and life of humans, animals and plants". Second, certain restrictions may be justified where necessary to protect certain interests, referred to as "mandatory requirements", which have been laid down by the European Court. The list of recognised mandatory requirements is not closed and may be added to by the court. These cover many interests also covered by **Article 36**, but also certain others which are not within the closed list of legitimate interests recognised by the Article - for example, defence of consumers and protection of the environment. Measures are permissible only when they go no further than necessary to achieve the relevant objective. For further details of these derogations from **Article 30** readers are referred to the works cited at 7.4.1.

In *Dundalk* it was argued that the restrictive specification was necessary to protect legitimate interests. First, it was argued that it was necessary to ensure pipes used were compatible with the existing network, and was thus justified by the need to protect the "general interest", a recognised mandatory requirement. Second, it was contended that it was needed to protect health, including by ensuring the asbestos fibres used in the pipes did not come into contact with drinking water, protection of health being recognised both under **Article 36** and as a mandatory requirement.

The court rejected these arguments (see paras. 21-25 of the judgment).

On compatibility, the court pointed out that this could be achieved without such a restrictive specification, by specifying compliance with the Irish standard *or equivalent*. This same argument can be made with any restrictive standard: it seems the government must be prepared to accept any product which achieves the required level of performance, safety etc, and cannot impose restrictions on the precise way in which this achieved. Since the restriction went further than necessary to achieve its objective, it was not necessary for the court to consider whether the objective mentioned was capable of falling within the "general interest" category of mandatory requirements.

In relation to the protection of health, the court considered that another specification in the contract already dealt with the objective noted above, and that the Irish standard could therefore not be justified on this basis. Even had there been no other such specification, obviously again the point could be made that the quality required could be obtained by using a specification which allowed "equivalent" products.

Another method of securing both the above objectives was noted by the Advocate General in considering the compatibility point: he pointed out that these factors can be considered in evaluating the technical merits of individual tenders and taken into account in deciding which is the most advantageous. In practice, of course, it is more economical to deal with these matters through precise minimum specifications, to cut out at an early stage bids which are unsuitable.

As far as mandatory requirements are concerned, it is generally considered that they may, anyway, not be invoked in relation to measures which are discriminatory, and for this reason could not have been invoked in *Dundalk*. The same appears not be true of the derogations in **Article 36** which can be invoked provided there is no arbitrary discrimination, so that indirectly discriminatory measures may be permissible if justified to achieve **Article 36** objectives.

In fact, as explained at 7.4.3.5., there was probably no need for **Article 36** and mandatory requirements to have been relied on in this case. Where the government determines that it wishes a product to meet certain compatibility or health criteria, this is part of the definition of the product, and as such is solely within the discretion of the contracting authority, regardless of the scope of Article 36 or mandatory requirements. The only question for the European Court is whether the specification used excludes products which are capable of meeting the government's determined objectives.

7.5. RESPONSIBILITY OF THE STATE FOR LOCAL AUTHORITIES

Dundalk was the first case to make it clear that a member state may be held responsible under **Article 30** for the conduct of a local authority. In *Dundalk* the central government in fact had some direct control over local authority procurement, including through a requirement for central approval of certain award decisions, but both the Advocate General and the court (see para. 12 of the judgment) seemed to consider that responsibility would exist even without such direct control. This has been assumed to be so in a number of later decisions of the court.

8. Case 31/87, Gebroeders Beentjes BV v The Netherlands ("Beentjes")

20th September 1988; [1988] ECR 4635; [1990] 1 CMLR 287

SUMMARY

This case concerned a request for a preliminary ruling under Article 177 of the Treaty of Rome.

The court ruled that under Article 1 (b) of the Works Directive, as it stood before amendment in 1989, "the State" includes a body whose composition and functions are laid down by legislation and which depends on the authorities for the appointment of its members, the observance of obligations arising out of its measures and the financing of its public works contracts, even though that body is not formally part of the administration.

A condition relating to the employment by contractors of the long term unemployed was ruled not to be precluded by the terms of the Works Directive, though to be lawful it must be compatible with the Treaties and any other relevant provisions of Community law. Such a condition must be stated in the contract notice.

The court also ruled that a requirement for contractors to have experience of the kind of work in question was permissible in relation to contracts covered by the Works Directive, as a factor relating to technical ability, which is a matter for member states. Such a requirement need not specifically be stated in the contract notice.

It was ruled that Articles 20, 26, and 29 of the Works Directive are capable of having direct effect.

8.1. INTRODUCTION AND FACTS

Beentjes concerned a request for a preliminary ruling from the European Court under the **Article 177** ruling procedure, made by the District Court of the Hague in the Netherlands. The preliminary ruling procedure is explained at 1.3.3. above.

The proceedings before the Dutch court concerned a decision taken by the Waterland Local Land Consolidation Committee, concerning the award of a public works contract. Beentjes had submitted the lowest bid, but the contract had been awarded to another undertaking. Three reasons were given for preferring the other bid: first, that Beentjes lacked sufficient experience of the type of work in question; second, that Beentjes' tender appeared to be less acceptable; and, third, that Beentjes was not in a position to employ long term unemployed persons, which the authority had stated as a necessary qualification. Beentjes challenged the decision, contending that the **Works Directive** precluded the Committee from taking account of these three considerations.

The Dutch court referred three questions to the European Court. The first concerned the question of which authorities are within the scope of the **Works Directive**. The second raised various issues concerning the factors which may be taken into account in selecting a contractor, and also the publicity which must be given to the intended criteria. The third sought to establish whether the relevant provisions of the Directive had direct effect.

8.2. AUTHORITIES COVERED BY THE WORKS DIRECTIVE

At the relevant time the obligations under the **Works Directive** applied, under **Article 1 (b)**, to "the State, regional or local authorities and the legal persons governed by public law specified in Annex I ". The Land Consolidation Committee was not mentioned in the Annex, and would therefore be bound by the Directive only if part of the State or a regional or local authority. The Committee was financed, and its members appointed by, the relevant Provincial Executive, it was bound to follow rules laid down by a central committee appointed by the Crown, its functions and composition were laid out in legislation, and the Executive was responsible for ensuring the enforcement of its obligations; but it was not an integral part of the Executive, but functionally independent. The first question put to the European Court asked whether a body with the characteristics of the Committee satisfied this requirement that it should be part of the State or a regional or local authority.

The court took the view that it should be considered part of the State (see paras. 7-13 of the judgment). The court felt that if a narrow view of "the State" were adopted to exclude an authority simply because it were not an integral part of the central administration, this would jeopardise the effectiveness of the Directive. The court stated that a body would be considered part of the State "whose composition and functions are laid down by legislation and which depends on the authorities for the appointment of its members, the observance of the obligations arising out of its measures and the financing of the public works contracts which it is its task to award" (para. 12). Thus relevant factors are the sources of an authority's powers; the manner of appointment of its members; and the source of its finance for the functions which are subject to the Directive. It is open to debate how far an authority is part of the State when it exhibits only some of the characteristics mentioned by the court or, where, for example, only some of its members are state appointed, or it is mainly but not wholly state financed. It is also not clear how far the definition of "the State" in this context corresponds with the definition of "the State" for other purposes in European Community law - for example, for the purpose of determining whether a member state can be held accountable for the actions of an authority under **Article 169 of the Treaty of Rome** (as to which see 1.2.1. above), and whether Directives have direct effect against an authority. It may be noted that a decision concerned with the problem in the context of **Article 169** was mentioned by Advocate Darmon in his opinion as a relevant analogy. In relation to the direct effect of Directives, it appears now that direct effect is not confined to bodies considered *part of* the State, but extends at least to those entrusted by the State with responsibility for providing a service and which are subject to state control and have special powers (see case C-188/89, *Foster v British Gas* [1992] 2 CMLR 833). In many cases disputes on direct effect may be resolved by considering whether this test in *Foster v British Gas* is satisfied, rather than whether a body is actually part of the State. It seems unlikely that the definition of "the State" under the **Works Directive** extends so far as to cover *all* authorities against which Directives may be invoked.

At the time relevant in *Beentjes* the **Works Directive** applied, as indicated, to the State, regional and local authorities, and bodies governed by public law which were listed in an Annex to the Directive. Most bodies on the fringes of "the State" were listed in the Annex, and so within the Directive whether or not they were regarded as part of the State. It was only necessary to consider this matter in relation to the Land Consolidation Committee because it appeared to have been overlooked in drawing up the Annex. Since *Beentjes* the provision referred to above outlining the authorities to which the Directive applies has been replaced by a new **Article 1 (b)** (see **1989 Works Directive, Article 1 (1)**). According to this provision the Directive now applies to all "authorities or bodies governed by public law" whether or not listed in Annex 1. A definition of "bodies governed by public law" is stated in the Article: it covers bodies established to meet needs in the general interest (provided they are not of an industrial or commercial character) and which have legal personality, and which *either* i) are financed for the most part by bodies covered by the Directive *or* ii) are subject to managerial supervision by such bodies *or* iii) have at least half their members appointed by such bodies. A list of bodies considered to be within this definition is contained in the Annex but is for guidance only: if an authority is omitted but falls within the general definition of a "body governed by public law" it is subject to the Directive. Thus the question of whether a body is part of the State is less likely to arise: where this is arguable, it is likely that that body will fall clearly within the definition of a "body governed by public law", and the Directive will thus apply whether or not the authority is regarded as part of the State.

As far as the **Supplies Directive** is concerned, it applies still only to "the State, regional or local authorities and the legal persons governed by public law or, in member states where the latter are unknown, bodies corresponding thereto as specified in Annex 1" **(Article 1 (b))**. Thus in States where the concept of bodies governed by public law is not known (as, for example, in the United Kingdom), bodies which are not either part of the State or local or regional authorities are not covered, unless specifically listed. Where an authority is omitted from the Annex the definition of "the State" thus remains important. No doubt the guidance as to the meaning of "the State" for the purpose of the **Works Directive** which was given in *Beentjes* will be relevant in deciding which bodies are part of the State for the purpose of the **Supplies Directive**. It may be noted that it is currently planned to adopt a consolidated version of all the current EC Directives on public supplies, and when this is done it is likely that an amendment will be made to bring the provisions concerning the authorities covered by the Supplies provisions into line with those covered by the **Works Directive**.

8.3. CRITERIA FOR CONTRACTOR SELECTION

8.3.1. Introduction

The second question put to the European Court was as follows: "Does Directive 71/305 allow a tenderer to be excluded from a tendering procedure on the basis of considerations such as those mentioned in paragraph 6.2. of [the national court's judgment] if in the invitation itself no qualitative criteria are laid down in this regard (but reference is simply made to general conditions containing a general reservation..."

The "considerations" referred to are those on which the national court based its decision, namely:

i) that Beentjes lacked sufficient experience;

ii) that Beentjes' tender appeared "less acceptable" than that of the winner; and

iii) that Beentjes was not in a position to give work to the long term unemployed.

This second question was interpreted by the court as concerned with two distinct questions. The first was whether the three criteria listed above could lawfully be taken into account. The second was whether, if these criteria could be taken into account, they were required to be notified to bidders in advance. The first of these matters is considered next, the second at 8.4. below.

8.3.2. The principles governing contractor selection

In considering whether the three factors mentioned above could be taken into account, the court began by outlining in general terms its view of the scope of the **Works Directive** in relation to contractor selection.

Article 20 of the Directive provides that "contracts shall be awarded on the basis of the criteria laid down in chapter 2" after authorities have considered, in accordance with **Articles 25-28**, the suitability of contractors not excluded by **Article 23**. (For further details of these Articles see 3.2.1. above). Chapter 2 provides in **Article 29** that, with some limited qualifications, the contract shall be awarded to the contractor submitting either the lowest or the most economically advantageous tender. According to the court the above Articles of the Directive regulate two distinct aspects of contractor selection.

The first is that of determining the *suitability* of potential contractors. This is done in accordance with the criteria stated in **Articles 25 and 26** - that is, financial and economic standing (**Article 25**) and technical ability (**Article 26**) (see para. 16 of the judgment). Although the court did not expressly state this, it seemed to consider that the concept of "suitability" relates to the question of whether the contractor will be able to complete the project as specified, in a satisfactory manner. The court stated that in determining suitability an authority is limited to considering only the general matters referred to in **Articles 25 and 26** - that is, financial standing and technical ability (para. 16). The court confirmed the view it stated in *CEI* (see 6.3.2.), that the *levels* of financial standing and technical ability which must be met for a contractor to be considered suitable for a project are for the national authorities themselves (para. 16). It may be noted that an authority may also, of course, eliminate a contractor on the basis of the matters stated in **Article 23**, as is indicated in **Article 20**.

The second aspect of contractor selection regulated by the Directive is that of making the contract award to one of those contractors considered suitable, and not eliminated on the basis of matters mentioned in **Article 23**. As indicated, this must be done according to the criteria of lowest price or most advantageous tender, as stated in **Article 29**.

These two aspects, which may be called respectively the "suitability" and "best value" aspects, were regarded by the court as relating to two distinct stages of the award process (see para. 15). This was seen as implicit in **Article 20**. The recognition of this two-fold division does not imply, however, that the two processes must be carried out at different times or in any particular order: for example, it is possible to exclude a contractor as unsuitable at any stage of the process, even though a formal suitability check might already have been completed, and the "award" process have commenced (see para. 16). It simply means that there are two distinct stages which are to some degree governed by different rules (see para. 16).

What is the position, however, in relation to factors which are not concerned either with suitability or with value for money? Public bodies often take into account in selecting contractor factors which do not relate to either of these matters. These are often referred to as "secondary" factors, or secondary policies. For example, authorities may decide, in order to promote equal opportunities, to award contracts only to firms employing a certain percentage of women or ethnic minorities. One of the matters in issue in *Beentjes*, a contractor's ability to give work to the long term unemployed, was such a secondary policy.

There are two possible views on the effect of the **Works Directive** on a contracting authority's ability to take secondary factors into account.

The first is that the Directive regulates exhaustively the factors which may be taken into account in selecting a contractor - in other words, that **Article 20** lists comprehensively the grounds on which selection may be made. Thus elimination of contractors is permitted on the basis of suitability or under **Article 23,** as provided for in **Article 20,** but once this has been done selection must be made on the basis only of the criteria stated in **Article 29** - namely, lowest price or most economically advantageous tender. This interpretation would leave no room for authorities to take account of secondary considerations, except to the extent specifically authorised by the Directives. This interpretation seemed to be the one favoured by Advocate General Darmon in *Beentjes* (see paras. 32, 39 and 43 of his opinion). The second view is that the Directive is not concerned with the factors used to select contractors except in so far as they relate to the two areas mentioned - that is, suitability and value for money. In other words, in deciding if contractors are suitable in the sense of being able to complete the work, and in deciding which of the tenders submitted offers the best deal, the provisions of the Directive must be followed, but if an authority wishes to eliminate a contractor for reasons unconnected with his suitability or the nature of the product tendered, it may do so in its discretion. In other words, the Directive does not limit the authority's existing discretion to take into account secondary factors.

The European Court in *Beentjes* favoured the second approach. It emphasised that the Directives are not intended to regulate exhaustively procurement in the member states (see para. 18 of the judgment), and on this basis appeared to take the view that secondary policies may still be pursued by individual states. This seems clear from the conclusion the court, which was that the condition relating to long term unemployed persons was not precluded by the rules in the Directive on contractor selection. However, any action must be consistent with the Treaties, and this obviously applies to the adoption of secondary policies, as was emphasised by the court. Thus the court stated that the policy in *Beentjes*, though not precluded by the terms of the **Works Directive**, would be valid only if consistent with the Treaties as well.

The approach in *Beentjes* seems correct. In so far as the use of procurement for secondary purposes does not prejudice the opening up of the procurement market, there is no reason why the discretion to use procurement in this way should not be retained by member states.

A more restrictive view is that *Beentjes* involved a contractual *condition* relating to the long term unemployed, and that the decision merely indicates that a contractor's ability to comply with such conditions is a relevant factor (see Commission Communication of 22 September 1989 COM (89) 400 para. 47). On this view the factors mentioned in the Directive concerning suitability and best value are exhaustive apart from this. Thus "secondary" factors are not permissible *per se* but are relevant only in so far as embodied in contractual conditions. There is, however, little express support for this view in the judgment and it seems unsustainable on policy grounds: why should secondary policies be permissable only if implemented through express contractual guarantees? The wider view of *Beentjes* stated above is to be preferred.

Secondary policies which are discriminatory are, of course, generally impermissible under the **Treaty of Rome.** An example is a policy of reserving a percentage of purchases for firms with operations in a particular region of the awarding state, which has been ruled to be in breach of the **Treaty of Rome** provisions on freedom of establishment and the freedom to provide services (see the discussion of *Du Pont de Nemours* at 10.2. below). Some policies may also be unlawful even though they are not discriminatory. For example, **Article 30 of the Treaty of Rome,** which is concerned with the free movement of goods, covers a wide range of restrictions on free movement which are not discriminatory, and it is arguable that non-discriminatory secondary policies might sometimes be caught. This possibility is discussed further at 10.2.1.3. below.

8.3.3. Application of the general principles

Having set out these principles, the court considered their application in the light of the three factors relevant in this case.

i)The first was that Beentjes lacked experience. The court concluded that this related to technical ability and was permissible, since, the authority is free to set its own standards on this (see para. 24).

ii) The second was that Beentjes' tender appeared "less acceptable". Dutch law required that a contract be awarded to the "most acceptable" bidder. The compatibility of this with Community law was said to depend on its interpretation. If it conferred unrestricted freedom of choice on authorities in selecting between bids, it would be incompatible with **Article 29**. However, if it merely allowed authorities to make a choice based on the objective criteria referred to in **Article 29**, it would be lawful (see paras. 26 and 27).

iii) Finally, the court stated that the condition on the long term unemployed was acceptable provided that it was not in breach of the Treaties. Whether it was discriminatory in all the circumstances was a matter for the national courts (see paras. 28- 30).

8.4. ADVANCE NOTIFICATION OF SELECTION CRITERIA

As explained, the court interpreted the second question as asking how far selection criteria must be made known in advance.

The court considered this first in relation to technical competence. This arose since no mention had been made in the notice in *Beentjes* of the need for relevant experience. It is specifically stated in **Article 26** that authorities must state either in the contract notice or in the invitation to tender which of the references mentioned in the article are to be produced by contractors. However, it is not expressly required for authorities to indicate the aspects of suitability which are to be taken into account. Of course, to some extent this will be apparent from the references mentioned - for example, if a statement of technical equipment available is required (as expressly permitted under **Article 26 (c)**), it is clear the authority is intending to take some account of of such equipment.

The Advocate General considered that the aspects of suitability to be taken into account must be indicated, both in relation to technical competence and to financial standing, and that only those indicated can be taken into account (see para. 39 of the opinion). Although this is not expressly stated in **Article 26**, which requires merely that *references* required are to be stated, it was said to follow from the fact that the purpose of the notice requirement relating to references is to enable contractors to know if they are interested, and an indication of the relevant aspects of suitability is necessary for this purpose. As indicated, the relevant aspects of suitability will normally be obvious from the references listed.

The view of the court on the point is, unfortunately, not entirely clear. It stated that "in order for the notice to fulfil its role of enabling contractors in the Community to determine whether a contract is of interest to them, it must contain at least some mention of the specific conditions which a contractor must meet in order to be considered suitable to tender for the contract in question" (para. 34). However, the court then went on to indicate that the requirement of experience was not such a "specific condition" as to need mention in the notice: it was "not a specific condition of suitability but a criterion which is inseparable from the very notion of suitability" (para. 34). Hence it was not necessary to state in the notice that experience would be taken into account.

It is not clear what is meant by a "specific condition" of suitability as opposed to a criterion inseparable from it. It may be that matters such as possession of necessary equipment and manpower levels would also be considered criteria inseparable from the very concept of suitability, and so would not be required to be stated in the notice. On this view, "specific conditions" might refer, on the other hand, to conditions relating to *specified* levels of manpower or equipment, which have already been settled by the contracting authority; indeed it is hard on this view to see what else it could refer to, given that it is probably only those criteria which can be deduced from the references listed in **Article 26** which can be taken into account. However, it could be, on the other hand, that the very criteria of manpower or equipment levels might be regarded as "specific conditions".

The court also considered the question of advance information in relation to the "most acceptable tender" criterion, which it had said would be permissible if it meant that authorities must choose the most economically advantageous tender (see 8.3.3. above). Where the choice of tender is to be made on the basis of any factors other than lowest price, it is provided expressly by **Article 29** that these factors must be listed in the contract documents or contract notice. This had not been done in this case, but the relevant documents made reference to the application of the Dutch legislation requiring the acceptance of the "most acceptable tender". The court considered that this reference could not satisfy the publicity requirement in **Article 29** (see para. 35). On the basis of this ruling it might be argued that a cross reference to other measures or documents setting out the relevant award criteria can never suffice, and that the criteria must always be specifically listed in the contract documents or notice. On the other hand, it might be considered that this ruling was based on the fact that the legislation referred to did not appear to list the relevant criteria specifically. Might it then be argued that if another document did list the criteria other than price a reference to such a document would be sufficient? Probably it should not be, since this creates unnecessary difficulties for contractors in accessing the relevant information.

Finally, the court concluded that the condition relating to a contractor's ability to provide work for the long term unemployed was required to be stated in the contract notice (or, presumably, the invitation to tender where appropriate) (see para. 36). This is nowhere expressly stated in the Directive, which does not regulate the use of secondary factors in contractor selection. However, the court concluded that it was necessary in order "that contractors may become aware of its existence" (para. 36). The objective of ensuring that contractors know in advance whether they will be interested in a contract would certainly be jeopardised if advance publication of secondary factors were not required.

8.5. THE DIRECT EFFECT OF ARTICLES 20, 26 AND 29

The third question before the European Court in *Beentjes* sought to establish whether **Articles 20, 26** and **29 of the Works Directive** have direct effect (on direct effect see 1.3.2. above). The court concluded that these Articles do have direct effect (paras. 39-44 of the judgment). Thus these provisions can be relied upon by individuals before the national courts where they have not been properly implemented by member states.

9. Case C-3/88, Commission of the European Communities v Italy ("Re Data Processing")

5th December 1989; [1989] ECR 4035; [1991] 2 CMLR 115

SUMMARY

*This case concerned proceedings under **Article 169 of the Treaty of Rome**.*

*The court ruled that a requirement that certain data processing contracts be awarded only to firms in Italian public ownership breached **Articles 52 and 59 of the Treaty of Rome**.*

*The need to protect the confidentiality of the data processed could not justify invoking the derogations in **Articles 56 (1) and 66 of the Treaty of Rome** since confidentiality could be protected by means less restrictive of the freedoms protected by these Articles. Further, the provision of data processing systems was not an activity connected with the exercise of official authority under **Article 55 or 66**.*

*The court also ruled that the **Supplies Directive** governs the award of contracts which are partly for goods and partly for services even when the value of the services exceeds that of the goods. This is so at least in cases where the goods and services can be purchased separately. The Advocate General considered that the Directive applies to such contracts even where the goods and services can not be purchased separately.*

The Advocate General also suggested that in the case of a contract for both goods and services only the value of the goods is to be considered for the purpose of determining whether the value of the contract exceeds the threshold for the application of the Directive.

*Certain derogations from the **Supplies Directive** were held inapplicable in this case.*

9.1. INTRODUCTION AND FACTS

This case concerned proceedings brought by the Commission against Italy in the European Court, under the procedure laid down in **Article 169 of the Treaty of Rome.** This procedure is explained at 1.2. above.

The case concerned Italian legislation which provided that agreements for the development of certain data processing systems for the Italian government could be concluded only with firms of which all or the majority of their shares were, directly or indirectly, in Italian public ownership. The Commission alleged that this legislation breached **Articles 52 and 59 of the Treaty of Rome**, which are concerned with the freedom to establish and the freedom to provide services.

The Commission claimed also that the legislation infringed the **Supplies Directive** by authorising award procedures which were incompatible with the Directive, in particular with the Directive's advertising rules. On this question Italy argued that the **Supplies Directive** was inapplicable because the contracts in question were not contracts for supplies but contracts for services. Further, it was contended by Italy that even if the Directive did apply to these contracts, there was no breach since this case fell within certain derogations and exceptions.

The European Court concluded that there was a breach of both the Treaty provisions and the **Supplies Directive**, and consequently declared Italy to be in breach of its obligations under Community law.

9.2. ARTICLES 52 AND 59 OF THE TREATY OF ROME

9.2.1. Articles 52 and 59: general principles

The Commission's first argument was that the legislation requiring suppliers of certain data processing systems to be in Italian public ownership was contrary to the provisions in the **Treaty of Rome** concerned with the freedom to provide services. The main provisions are **Article 52-58** and **Articles 59-66**. These articles essentially prohibit discrimination on grounds of nationality against companies or individuals who wish to provide services in another member state on a self employed or professional basis. (The right to work in other states as an *employee* is dealt with by other Articles of the Treaty).

Article 52 and the following Articles are concerned with what is called "freedom of establishment" - the freedom to set up and pursue a business or other activity in another member state. **Article 59** and the following Articles are concerned with the freedom of nationals of a member state or companies formed in accordance with the law of a member state to provide services in another member state, including on a temporary basis. Both sets of provisions are concerned with preventing discrimination against those involved in the provision of services, and the difference between them is one of degree rather than kind. As explained by Steiner: "A right of establishment is a right to install oneself, "to set up shop" in another member state, permanently or semi-permanently, whether as an individual, a partnership or a company, for the purpose of performing a particular activity there. The right to provide services, on the other hand, connotes the provision of services in one state, on a temporary or spasmodic basis, by a person established in another state". (Steiner, at pp.185-186). Measures taken by a member state which limit the freedom of persons from other member states to provide a type of service in the first state often infringe both sets of provisions: in practice such measures often affect both the ability of foreign firms and individuals to set themselves up on a permanent basis to provide the service in question, and the ability of such firms and individuals to provide services on a temporary basis. This was assumed to be the case in *Re Data Processing*, as explained below.

Both freedoms are subject to important limitations. For present purposes it is relevant to note that both are subject to derogation on the grounds of "public policy, public security or public health" (**Article 55 (establishment); Article 66 (services)**). In addition, neither applies to activities which are "connected, even occasionally, with the exercise of official authority" (**Article 55; Article 66**).

For a further account of these provisions readers are referred to Steiner, chapter 19, and Wyatt and Dashwood, chapter 9.

9.2.2. Application of Articles 52 and 59

The Commission contended that the legislation in issue in *Re Data Processing* was in breach of the above Articles of the Treaty, since it limited access to the Italian government market in a manner which was discriminatory in favour of Italian firms. The restrictions applied both to firms wishing to set up in Italy to supply the government market, and those wishing to provide systems for the Italian government from a base elsewhere in the Community, and thus were capable of infringing both the freedom to establish **Article 52** and the freedom to provide services under **Article 59**.

It was argued by Italy that these measures did not infringe these provisions of the Treaty since they did not involve any direct discrimination on grounds of nationality - for example, by restricting government contracts to Italian firms. Rather, they merely imposed a condition for participation which was required to be met by both Italian and non-Italian firms in the same way.

The court, however, concluded that direct discrimination was not necessary. The provisions on freedom to establish and freedom to provide services prohibit "not only overt discrimination by reason of nationality but also covert forms of discrimination which, by the application of other criteria of discrimination, lead to the same result" (para. 8 of the judgment).

In stating this principle the court was following the view which it had put forward in a number of previous cases.

The court concluded that the measures in the *Re Data Processing* case were in breach of the Treaty provisions as indirectly discriminatory. It pointed out that at that time there were no data processing firms in other member states which satisfied the condition on Italian public ownership (para. 9 of the judgment). A measure will probably also be invalid if its effect is to "hinder or disadvantage *primarily* nationals of other member states" (Advocate General Mishco, at para. 13 of his opinion, emphasis added). Thus, as the Advocate General pointed out (para. 20 of his opinion) the measures would no doubt have been unlawful even if there had been *some* qualifying firms from other states, since the legislation would still benefit mainly Italian companies.

9.2.3. Derogations

It was argued by Italy that even if the measures in question were *prima facie* within **Articles 52 and 59**, they were covered by certain derogations and exceptions to the provisions.

First, Italy contended that, since many of the data processing systems required concerned matters such as taxation, organised crime and public health, the measures in issue could be justified by reference to the derogations provided for in **Article 56 (1)** and **Article 66**, which permit special treatment for foreign nationals on grounds of public policy, public security and health. It seemed to be argued that measures may provide for such special treatment simply because they relate to one of these sectors of activity. This argument was rejected. As the Advocate General pointed out, to justify special treatment it must be shown that the participation of foreign nationals would *actually prejudice* public policy security or health (para. 33 of his opinion). The court agreed with this approach (para. 19 of the judgment).

It was argued in addition, however, that the participation of firms not in Italian ownership *would* prejudice these interests, since those responsible for the data processing systems in these "strategic" areas might have access to confidential information, and there was a need to ensure it was kept confidential, and also to prevent its misuse. However, measures which restrict the freedom of establishment and the freedom to provide services are only permitted to the extent that they are proportionate to the objective to be achieved. If this objective can reasonably be achieved by means which are not so restrictive of these freedoms, then these alternative means must be employed. In this case, the court concluded that the objective could be achieved by imposing on those with access to confidential data a duty of secrecy, with criminal sanctions for breach, and there was no evidence to indicate that this would be any less effective in relation to the staff of companies not in Italian public ownership than in relation to those which are (para. 11 of the judgment). It was also contended that public ownership of companies involved in the relevant data processing work was necessary so that public authorities could adapt the work to unforeseeable circumstances; but again the court considered that the government had other sufficient legal powers to ensure adaption of the work where appropriate (para. 11). Hence it was concluded that the requirement of Italian public ownership could not be justified under the above derogations.

As indicated at 9.2.1. above, the provisions on freedom of establishment and the freedom to provide services are also inapplicable to activities "connected with the exercise of official authority", and it was also argued by Italy that this derogation covered the measures in this case. The concept of the exercise of official authority is probably confined to activities involving the exercise of the special prerogatives of government, though it is unclear whether it covers all such activities. Certainly it seems to cover at least legislative and judicial powers, and certain administrative powers such as powers of coercion (see Wyatt and Dashwood, pp.207-209). The performance of many of the functions to which the data processing systems related, such as the investigation of crime, thus obviously involved the exercise of official authority.

However, an activity is not connected with the exercise of official authority unless the party performing it is "directly and specifically" involved in the exercise of that authority; and it seems clear that a contractor cannot be regarded as directly and specifically involved in the performance of a function simply because he supplies goods and services needed for that function to be carried out. Further, even if the involvement of a contractor in an activity is direct and specific, the derogation will not apply where the performance of the activity is subject to control and supervision by public authorities. For both these reasons the Advocate General considered that the provision of data processing systems fell outside the derogation. The court also found the derogation inapplicable (para. 31 of the judgment). The court based its conclusion on this point on the lack of *direct* involvement in the exercise of official authority by contractors: it took the view that provision and operation of the data processing systems was merely ancillary to the activities involving an exercise of official authority, and not part of those activities themselves.

The scope of the "official authority" derrogation has now been considered further by the President of the court in the *Italian lottery* case: see 16.4. below.

9.3. APPLICATION OF THE SUPPLIES DIRECTIVE

The Commission argued that as well as breaching the Treaty provisions on services, the Italian legislation on data processing systems was in breach of the **Supplies Directive** in authorising contract award procedures which were incompatible with that Directive. In particular, it was contended that contracts awarded pursuant to the legislation had been awarded in breach of the advertising requirements of the Directive.

9.3.1. Application to the purchase of data processing systems

9.3.1.1. Application to contracts for both supplies and services
The first matter considered was whether award procedures for contracts for the supply of data processing systems to government are subject to the **Supplies Directive** at all. The provisions in the Directive apply only to "public supply contracts". These are defined in **Article 1 (a)** of the Directive as contracts for the purchase, lease, rental or hire purchase of "products". The Italian government argued that a contract for the supply of a data processing system is not a contract for the supply of a "product". Data processing systems may comprise hardware which is, by itself a product; off-the-shelf software, which is also generally considered to be a product; and also software related services, such as the design of bespoke software and software maintenance, which are not products but services. These services generally represent, in practice, the greater part of the value of contracts for the supply of data processing systems. It was argued that in these circumstances the hardware involved in such a contract must be treated as merely ancillary to the services offered, and the contract as a whole cannot be considered a contract for the supply of a product for the purpose of the **Supplies Directive.** In other words, it was suggested that where a contract involves the supply of both products and services, it will only generally be considered a supply contract where the major part of the contract is for the supply of products.

This argument was rejected by the court, which held that the **Supplies Directive** did apply in relation to the hardware element of the systems contracts (see paras. 17-19 of the judgment). Hence, any contract for the purchase of hardware, which is a product, might have to be advertised under the Directive, even though the contract is mainly for the supply of services.

In reaching this conclusion the court observed that "The purchase of the equipment required for the establishment of a data-processing system can be separated from the activities involved in its design and operation", and that hardware and software can generally be purchased separately (para. 19). By splitting the purchase of the supplies from the purchase of the services the authority may, of course, avoid the need to advertise under the **Supplies Directive** the services element of the project. If it decides not to split the two then effectively the services element must be advertised along with the supplies element.

This raises the question of what the position would be if it were not feasible to split the supplies and services elements of a project, but were necessary to obtain both from a single supplier. An argument that splitting is not feasible might be based, for example, on the extra cost of splitting, or on the technical impossibility of doing so. The problem might arise not only in relation to data processing contracts, but also with other types of procurement. The effect of holding in this case that any purchase of products must be advertised under the **Supplies Directive** would be, of course, that the purchasing authority would have no choice but to advertise the services element in accordance with the same rules. If, on the other hand, a "mixed" contract which could not be split were outside the Directive where predominantly a contract for services, it would not have to be advertised at all, since there is as yet no Directive on the award of services contracts in the public sector (though on the Proposal for such a Directive see 9.3.2. below).

The main argument against applying the **Supplies Directive** in such a case is that the rules on advertising and award of contracts which apply to supplies are not necessarily appropriate for services. This is recognised in the Commission's Proposal for a Directive on services contracts, and the Common Position on the Proposal now adopted by the Council, which envisage more flexible procedures than those which govern supplies contracts (see COM (91) 322 Final, August 30, 1991; Common Position adopted by the Council 25th February 1992). However, these rules must inevitably be applied to services to some extent, since many contracts which are *predominantly* for supplies contain some services element, and it surely cannot be argued that a such a contract would be exempt from the rules of the **Supplies Directive** because of a small services element. Given that this is so, there seems no objection in principle to subjecting a contract to the Directive though the services element is greater than the supplies. Further, to recognise that the Directive need not apply because a contract is predominantly one for services would encourage authorities to try and evade its provisions by invoking the exception, and would also produce uncertainty, since there is much room for argument over when it is "feasible" to split a contract and when it is not.

It was in fact the view of Advocate General Mishco in *Re Data Processing* that such a "mixed" contract should be treated as within the **Supplies Directive** even where the value of the services exceeds the value of the products (see para. 45 of his opinion): he considered that had it been intended to exempt products from the Directive in these circumstances this would have been expressly stated. It seems likely that this view would be taken by the European Court. If not, the court will certainly be very reluctant in practice to find that the products and services elements of a project cannot be split. It seems that an argument that splitting was not possible was in fact put by Italy in the *Re Data Processing* case, but the court considered that it was generally possible with a data processing system first to purchase the software services, and then advertise for hardware in accordance with the specifications set by the software supplier.

9.3.1.2. *Valuing the contract for threshold purposes*
A final important question is that of the threshold for advertising. Where a contract comprises both products and services, is the relevant value that of the products, or is it that of the products and services taken together? The Advocate General considered that it is that of the products alone (see para. 47 of the opinion). Thus if the hardware in a data processing system exceeds the threshold the contract would have to be advertised, but if not there need be no advertisement, even though the value of the hardware and software together exceeds the threshold level.

This seems to be the correct approach in light of the objective of the **Supplies Directive**, which is concerned only to secure the advertising etc of *supply* contracts, and is not in principle concerned with services. In fact, any other interpretation of the threshold provisions would have the consequence that any services contract above the threshold value which involves the provision of products, however small the product element, would have to be advertised. For example, if the Advocate General's view were not followed a contract worth 210 000 ECUs would have to be advertised where it is almost exclusively a contract for services but involves the provision of products worth only 100 ECUs. Clearly it was not intended that such a contract should be covered by the **Supplies Directive**.

Further, as the Advocate General pointed out, in some cases it is specifically provided by the Directive that the provision of services is to be treated as part of the delivery of a product, suggesting that in this case the value of the services is to be added in in fixing the value of the contract for threshold purposes. Thus Article 1 (a) states that the delivery of products may include siting and installation operations. The Advocate General was of the view that if it had been intended to treat the provision of software services ancillary to hardware in the same way, this would also have been stated expressly.

It is true that the view of the Advocate General does not fit easily with the literal wording of the Directive. As explained, the Directive provides for the advertisement of public supply contracts, and *Re Data Processing* indicates that a contract for the supply of both products and services is such a supply contract. **Article 2** then provides that the Directive is to apply to "public supply contracts" the value of which exceeds the threshold, which suggests that it is the value of the "supply contract" and not the value of the product element of that contract which is relevant. However, as just explained, an interpretation which takes the contract value rather than the product value seems to bring within the **Supplies Directive** contracts which clearly were not intended to be covered, and it is submitted therefore that Advocate General Mishco is còrrect to suggest that it is the product value which is relevant.

9.3.2. Position under the proposed Directive on services

As indicated above, there is currently no Directive regulating the award of services contracts. However, the Commission has produced a proposal for a Directive covering services (see COM (19) 322 Final, August 30 1991), on which a Common Position was adopted by the Council on 25th February 1992; and it is expected that a Directive will be adopted in the very near future.

9.3.2.1. Coverage of contracts for both supplies and services
Article 2 of the Common Position deals expressly with the question of contracts which are for both products and services. It states that such contracts shall fall within the scope of the proposed Directive on services "if the value of the services in question exceeds that of the products covered by the contract". If it were not for this express provision such contracts would continue to fall within the *Supplies Directive*, as is currently the case under the principle in *Re Data Processing*. This is because the proposed Directive covering services includes within the definition of "public service contract" to which the provision of the proposed Directive apply only those contracts which are not already caught by the **Supplies Directive** (see **Article 1 (a) (i)** of the Common Position). The effect of the proposed **Article 2** will be to lift a mixed contract with a predominantly services element out of the **Supplies Directive** and place this type of contract instead under the proposed Directive on services. Presumably such a mixed contract then becomes a "public service contract" under the definition in **Article 1** of the proposal, since, because of proposed **Article 2**, it is no longer excluded from that definition by virtue of the fact that the **Supplies Directive** applies.

9.3.2.2. Valuing the contract for threshold purposes
An interesting question again arises over the thresholds for the application of the proposed Directive on services. Is the value taken for the purpose of the thresholds that of the services alone, or is it that of the services and any products taken together? Under the Common Position the proposed **Article**

7, dealing with the question of thresholds, simply states that the proposed Directive is to apply to any "public service contracts" of a value above the threshold (**Article 7 (1)**). It is also provided that the estimated total remuneration of the service provider shall be taken into account (**Article 7 (2)**). The literal wording of the provision in **Article 7(1)** indicates that it is the total value of the contract, including both goods and services elements, which is relevant, and not simply the total value of the services, and this is reaffirmed by **Article 7(2)**, which has no parallel in the **Supplies Directive.**

This literal interpretation here corresponds with what is intended. Once the proposed Directive on services is adopted, the award of both goods and services contracts will be subject to regulation and the only issue is which regulatory regime - that for goods, or that for services - is to apply to a particular contract. Where a "mixed" contract covered by the Services Directive exceeds the threshold of the Directives, but the value of the services alone does not do so, this does not affect the conclusion that regulation is in principle appropriate: the point is that the contract as a whole is sufficiently important for the regulatory procedures to apply.

Of course, the same reasoning should apply where a "mixed" contract is predominantly one for supplies, and thus falls in principle within the scope of the **Supplies Directive.** Once the services sector is in principle subject to regulation, it would seem appropriate in applying the **Supplies Directive** to take account of both the goods and services element in determining the value of the contract for threshold purposes. Thus, where the value of supplies alone does not exceed the threshold, but the contract as a whole does so, the Directive ought to apply.

However, as was explained at 9.3.1.2. above, it is arguable that this is not currently the position under the **Supplies Directive.** It seems that it is the value of the products alone which were intended to be taken into account under that Directive when it was adopted. This was because at the time of adoption of the **Supplies Directive** provisions it was not intended that services should generally be subject to regulation. This will clearly be an anomaly, however, once a Directive on services comes into force.

It seems that an amendment to the **Supplies Directive** is probably required to deal with this problem. The Commission is currently considering the adoption of a new Directive on supplies, which will contain all the rules on supplies in a single consolidated text, and will also make some small changes to the rules, in particular to make for more consistency as between the provisions on supplies, and those on works and services. It is to be hoped that an amendment to address and clarify the threshold issue might be included.

9.3.3. Derogations

As explained at 9.3.2. the court concluded that the **Supplies Directive** governed contracts for the supply of data processing systems. Italy further argued, however, that even if the Directive applied in principle, the contracts in this case were not subject to the rules on advertising since they fell within derogations to the advertising requirements.

One argument was that the contracts fell within the exemption from the rules which applies where exemption is required by the need for secrecy or by state security (at that time contained in **Article 6 (1) (g)**; and now in **Article 2 (c)**, as inserted by **Article 3** of the **1988 Supplies Directive**). This exemption was argued to apply because of the confidential nature of the data to be dealt with by these systems. The argument was rejected by the court on the basis that confidentiality could be protected by other means (para. 24 of the judgment), a point already made by the court in considering whether the contracts in question fell within the derogations relating to **Articles 52 and 59 of the Treaty of Rome** (as to which see 9.2.3. above).

Italy also argued that in relation to particular deliveries to the Finance Ministry the derogation in **Article 6 (1) (e)**, relating to the need for compatibility with existing equipment, applied. The court rejected this argument briefly, unable to see how a requirement for Italian public ownership related to this problem (para. 28 of the judgment). It also rejected a contention that the provision of data processing equipment constituted an engagement in a "public services activity", to which the rules in the Directive had no application (see the former **Article 2 (3)**). Finally, the court rejected arguments based on the application of a temporary exemption for certain data processing contracts, an exemption no longer of relevance since it has long been repealed (see paras. 26 and 20-22 of the judgment).

10. Case C-21/88, Du Pont de Nemours Italiana SpA v Unità Sanitaria Locale No. 2 Di Carrara ("Du Pont de Nemours")

20th March 1990; [1990] ECR 889; [1991] 3 CMLR 25

SUMMARY

*This case concerned a request for a preliminary ruling under **Article 177** of the Treaty of **Rome**.*

*The court ruled that a policy of reserving a certain proportion of public supplies contracts for firms in a particular region of the state of the awarding authority was a measure equivalent to a restriction on imports under **Article 30** of the Treaty of **Rome**. The policy was considered discriminatory even though it favoured only part of national production and adversely affected the other part, as well as adversely affecting imports.*

*The court considered that even if the policy constituted a state aid for the purpose of **Articles 92-93** of the Treaty, this would not exempt it from the scope of **Article 30**. The Advocate General discussed whether it was in fact an aid for this purpose.*

*The policy was not legitimised by **Article 26 of the Supplies Directive** which, as it stood before amendment in 1988, expressly permitted certain preference policies, since the Article was stated to apply only to policies compatible with the Treaty, and in any case could not be interpreted as authorising action in breach of the Treaty.*

10.1. INTRODUCTION AND FACTS

This case concerned a request for a preliminary ruling from the European Court made by an Italian authority, the *Tribunale Amministrativo Regionale della Toscana* ("the tribunal"). The preliminary ruling procedure is explained at 1.3.3. above.

The proceedings before the tribunal concerned certain decisions made by the *Unità Sanitaria*, the local health authority, pursuant to Italian legislation. The relevant legislation required the health authority, along with certain other public authorities, to reserve 30% of its supplies purchases for undertakings which had establishments and fixed plant in Southern Italy, and which offered products which had been processed at least partly in that region. The objective of the legislation was to promote the industrial development of that region of Italy. The health authority had thus divided its requirements for the purchase of radiological films and liquids into two lots, reserving 30% for undertakings in Southern Italy, and awarding a separate contract for the remaining 70%. These measures were challenged by Du Pont de Nemours before the tribunal.

The tribunal referred to the European Court questions regarding the application of **Article 30 of the Treaty of Rome** to the Italian regional preference policy, and the extent to which assistance to industry through this type of preference constitutes a state aid under **Article 92** of the Treaty.

10.2. ARTICLE 30 OF THE TREATY OF ROME

10.2.1. Was the preference legislation a measure of equivalent effect?

10.2.1.1. Existence of discrimination
The first question put by the Italian tribunal sought to establish whether the legislation giving preference to firms in Southern Italy in the award of certain public supply contracts was a measure which fell within the scope of **Article 30 of the Treaty of Rome. Article 30** is concerned with ensuring the free movement of goods in the Community. As explained earlier, it prohibits states from imposing restrictions on imports from other member states, and also prohibits all measures "having equivalent effect" to restrictions on imports. Measures of equivalent effect have been defined very broadly as including, *prima facie*, all measures which are capable of restricting Community trade, actually or potentially (see further 7.4.1. and 7.4.3. above). All such measures which operate in a discriminatory manner - that is, which favour wholly or mainly domestic goods as against imported products - are *prima facie* caught by **Article 30.** Where measures impose restrictions relating to the characteristics of goods, it is not even necessary for the measures to be discriminatory to be caught by **Article 30**: all such measures are prohibited unless considered by the European Court to be justified on public interest grounds (see 7.4.3. and 7.4.4. above). This question of non-discriminatory measures is considered at 10.2.1.3. below.

The Court concluded that the measures in issue in *Du Pont de Nemours* were caught by **Article 30.** They precluded a certain quantity of supplies from being procured from outside Italy, and thus they were discriminatory and hindered the normal course of intra-Community trade (para. 11 of the judgment). As indicated, the fact that a measure which affects trade in any way is discriminatory is generally sufficient to show a breach of **Article 30**.

An argument advanced by Italy was that some of the products adversely affected by the measure were Italian. In other words, the legislation in issue favoured only part of national production, discriminating against the other part as well as against foreign products. This was the first measure with such a characteristic to be considered by the European Court in the context of **Article 30**. The court clearly ruled that the measure was not saved by this characteristic (paras. 12-13 of the judgment). The court emphasised the fact that all the products benefiting from the policy were domestic products (para. 13), even though not all such products were benefited.

10.2.1.2. Is there a de minimis rule?
Advocate General Lenz pointed out in his opinion that the impact on trade of the legislation in question was greater in economic terms than a number of other measures which previously had been held to be within **Article 30**. It was noted earlier in considering the *Dundalk* case that it is generally not necessary to show a measure has any significant impact on trade for it to fall within **Article 30**: there is generally no *de minimis* rule applicable in such a case (see 7.4.3. above). Certainly this is generally accepted to be the case whenever a measure is discriminatory, as it was in *Du Pont de Nemours*. It thus should not have mattered how insignificant the impact of the measures on the market - a stipulation relating to a single small contract would, it is submitted, have infringed the Treaty.

10.2.1.3. Is discrimination necessary?
As has been explained, where measures which have the potential for restricting imports operate in a discriminatory manner, they are generally caught by **Article 30**. The measures in *Du Pont de Nemours* were held to be discriminatory and thus *prima facie* within **Article 30**.

It may also be noted, however, that **Article 30** may also apply to measures which are not discriminatory. Certainly it applies to non-discriminatory measures concerned to regulate the characteristics of products sold in a market. Such measures are generally prohibited, unless they can be justified to the European Court in terms of mandatory requirements or under **Article 36**. Effectively this means that with measures of this kind a degree of discretion in policy-making is taken away from the member states, through its being subject to the scrutiny of the European Court.

There is considerable controversy over the extent to which **Article 30** covers non-discriminatory measures concerned with matters other than the characteristics of products themselves. There has recently been consideration of this issue by the European Court and by writers in relation to restrictions concerned with the marketing of goods - in particular, restrictions on the sale of goods on a Sunday. Unfortunately, it is not at all clear from the rulings given by the court what is the position, and there is considerable disagreement amongst writers. One view is that non-discriminatory measures with the potential to restrict trade are generally within **Article 30,** regardless of the nature of the restriction (see Gormley (1990) 27 CML Rev 825 at 826-833). Another is that measures not concerned with the characteristics of goods are generally, though with possible exceptions, outside **Article 30** if not discriminatory (White, (1989) 26 CML Rev 235; Mortelmans, (1991) 28 CML Rev 115). A further view, put forward by Advocate General Van Gerven in the *Torfaen* case (*Torfaen BC v B & Q plc,* case 145/88 [1989] ECR 3851, [1990] 1 CMLR 337) is that non-discriminatory rules on market circumstances are within **Article 30** only if their effect is such as to partition off the national market. This seems effectively to suggest the introduction of a fairly stringent *de minimis* requirement for the application of **Article 30** to rules of this kind.

It is not possible to go further into the details of the controversy here: the issues, as well as the case law of the court, are discussed in the works mentioned above. However, it is mentioned in order to raise the possibility that some secondary procurement policies providing for the reservation of contracts for limited groups might possibly be caught by **Article 30** even though they are not discriminatory; their effect is to close off the government market for certain imported products. To the extent that such policies are caught, they will only be permissible if justified by **Article 36** or mandatory requirements.

10.2.2. Justification under Article 36 and mandatory requirements

The court concluded that the measures in *Du Pont de Nemours* were not within the exceptions to **Article 30** which are laid out in **Article 36** (as to which see 7.4.4. above): they were not concerned with any of the objectives listed in that article (para. 15 of the judgment). Nor could they be justified by reference to mandatory requirements (as to which see also 7.4.4.), since these cannot be invoked in relation to measures which are discriminatory in effect (para. 14).

As the Advocate General pointed out, another reason which might have been given for concluding that the measures were not saved either by **Article 36** or mandatory requirements was that these cannot be relied on in relation to measures which have economic aims, as was the case in *Du Pont de Nemours.* He also considered that the Italian legislation constituted a measure of regional support which was an objective justified by **Article 92 (3)** and **Article 130A of the Treaty of Rome.** He considered that measures to promote such an objective could only be taken on the basis of these provisions.

10.2.3. Relevance of Commission Directive 70/50/EEC

It had been contended in the written procedure that the preference policy constituted an infringement of **Directive 70/50** ([1970] OJ L13/29). This Directive provided specifically for the abolition of measures having an equivalent effect to a quantitive restriction on imports not covered by other Community measures, prior to the time when **Article 30** itself became directly effective. **Article 2 (2)** provides that amongst measures considered to hinder imports are measures which favour domestic producers or grant them a preference, and **Article 2 (3) (k)** cites as an example measures which *inter alia* require or give preference to the purchase of domestic products only.

It is generally considered that from the time that **Article 30** became directly effective, this Directive has merely served as a guide to interpretation of **Article 30**, and can not have the effect of imposing any *autonomous* prohibition on certain measures. To the extent that it may be used as an interpretive guide, it is considered that it is intended to provide only a list of illustrations of the **Article 30** principle, and not an exhaustive list. This general view of the significance of the Directive was stated by the Advocate General, who discussed the Directive in his opinion. He also considered that in any case the Directive was not of a kind capable of having direct effect in the national courts. He did, however, consider the scope of the Directive, as a guide to the interpretation of **Article 30**, and concluded that the preference system fell within it, since it both required and gave preference to, the purchase of domestic products.

The Directive was not mentioned at all by the court.

10.2.4. Public procurement and state aids

10.2.4.1. Relationship between Article 30 and state aids provisions
The Treaty provisions on state aids, **Articles 92** and **93 of the Treaty of Rome,** make special provision for "aid" provided by government to domestic enterprise, such as grants made to industry for the purchase of equipment, or more indirect benefits such as preferential pricing of the raw materials which an industry needs. Such aid may be undesirable in that it may distort free competition. However, it is also accepted that some aid may be desirable even in a free market economy, both to achieve maximum efficiency (for example, by promoting technological development which firms cannot afford to finance themselves), and also to achieve other, including social, objectives. The problem of determining, in the light of

these concerns, which aid is allowable and which is not, is dealt with in the **Treaty of Rome** by providing for all proposed aids to be notified to the Commission. The Commission then assesses whether the aid should be permitted in accordance with certain principles which are set out in **Articles 92-93.**

A difficult question for the European Court has been the relationship between **Articles 92** and **93,** on the one hand, and **Article 30** on the other. The effect of some aids is to assist home industry in the production of goods. To this extent aid will put imports at a disadvantage in the market and thus potentially restrict imports, so satisfying the usual conditions for the application of **Article 30.** Does the aid in this case fall within **Article 30,** in which case it must effectively be treated as null and void by the national courts and the state aids provisions will have no application? Or is it instead left to be assessed by the Commission in accordance with the state aid provisions? If the latter is the case, and an aid of this type is not caught by **Article 30,** it is possible that the aid might be upheld by the Commission as justified in the light of the objectives listed in the state aids provisions. (In addition, it may be noted that unlike **Article 30, Articles 92** and **93** do not have direct effect, and thus may not be generally invoked before the national courts). If all aids affecting the free movement of goods are within **Article 30,** then it seems that the aids provisions will be almost entirely redundant in this sphere.

The position before *Du Pont de Nemours:* Unfortunately the case law in the area is unsatisfactory and the relevant principles uncertain.

One view might be that **Article 30** generally has no application to state aids. This has has much to recommend it. It seems that the intention of the Treaty was to allow the Commission to authorise aids even though they may interfere with free trade under present conditions, in order to promote other objectives; and that it was intended that the balance between possible competing objectives was to be made by the Commission itself. However, this approach has not been followed by the court.

An approach which comes quite close to this was, however, put forward in the leading case of *Ianelli & Volpi SpA v Ditta Paola Meroni* (case 74/76 [1977] ECR 557, [1977] 2 CMLR 688). Here the court seemed to suggest that the general principle is that **Article 30** does not apply to aids, but, however, that it may apply to measures and conditions relating to the aid which are not necessary to achieve the aid's objectives, and can be severed from it. These ancillary matters can then be assessed under **Article 30** though the aid itself must then be evaluated under the aid provisions.

Some later cases have contained statements that aids relating to goods are to be assessed under **Article 30,** without making reference at all to *Ianelli.* (see case 18/84, *Commission v France* [1985] ECR 1339, [1986] 1 CMLR 605; case 103/84, *Commission v Italy* [1986] ECR 1759, [1987] 2

CMLR 825; case 244/81, *Commission v Ireland* [1982] ECR 4005, [1983] 2 CMLR 104). The pronouncements in these cases seemed to indicate that the court was rejecting the "general principle" stated in *Ianelli*, that state aids are normally to be assessed under **Article 92** and *not* under **Article 30**, in favour of a much wider role for the strict Article 30 provision (see Oliver, (1986) 23 CML Rev 325).

However, a number of writers suggested that the *Ianelli* test still stood after these cases, and that later cases in which **Article 30** has been applied to aids could be reconciled with it: it was argued that these later cases concerned aids which were not notified to the Commission as required by the Treaty, and that where theis has not been done they cannot be "saved" from **Article 30** by their alleged character as aids (see, for example, Flynn, (1987) 12 EL Rev 131 at pp. 131-137; Wyatt and Dashwood, p.474; White, (1989) 26 CML Rev 235 at p.272 *et seq.*). These writers clearly preferred this restrictive interpretation of the three cases mentioned above, for the policy reasons noted - that is, that the desirability of all aids, including those affecting the free movement of goods, is a matter intended normally to be left to the discretion of the Commission (and see also the views of Fernandez Martin and Stehmann, (1991) 16 EL Rev 216, writing after the *Du Pont de Nemours* decision).

The preference scheme in issue in *Du Pont de Nemours* had in fact been notified by the Italian government to the Commission on the basis that it was a state aid. One of the questions raised by the Italian court in the *Du Pont de Nemours* case, therefore, was whether the assistance given to firms in southern Italy through the public procurement preference rules constituted a state aid, and, if so, whether this meant that **Article 30** was inapplicable. The *Du Pont de Nemours* case thus provided an important opportunity for the court to develop and to clarify its case law on the question of the relationship between **Article 30** and the aid provisions.

The approach in *Du Pont de Nemours:* The court concluded in *Du Pont de Nemours* that even if the measures did constitute an aid under **Articles 92** and **93**, the application of **Article 30** was not thereby ousted. This case cannot be explained like previous cases since *Ianelli* on the basis of absence of notification of the aid, since, as indicated, the aid had been notified. Nor, it seems, can it be explained on the basis that it concerned a measure "severable" to the aid and unnecessary to it, since the whole aid scheme was considered by the court as caught by **Article 30**. The case thus seems to indicate that the *Ianelli* principle is now rejected.

Unfortunately, the court did not explain expressly the principle on which its conclusion was based. It did state, however, that "the fact that a national measure might be regarded as an aid within the meaning of **Article 92** is not therefore a sufficient reason to exempt it from the prohibition contained in **Article 30**" (para. 20 of the judgment). This is a broad statement which does seem to negate any general principle favouring the exclusivity of **Article 92** in matters of state aids. The Advocate General also makes reference to a statement made by the court in *Commission v France*, above, that the provisions on state aids cannot be used to frustrate the operation of those on the free movement of goods. Thus the case arguably means that the general rule is that **Article 30** applies even to measures covered by **Articles 92** and **93**, and that those Articles are thus substantially redundant in the field of the free movement of goods. Such an interpretation would mean that aids restricting the free movement of goods would never be permissible unless falling within the **Article 36** derogations or the scope of mandatory requirements. This would be most unsatisfactory: it would substantially reduce the ability of member states to give state aids.

A narrower interpretation is also possible, however. This is that **Article 30** only applies where a measure goes further than necessary to achieve its objective as an aid. This finds support in the opinion of the Advocate General, who emphasises that regional development could have been achieved here by measures which would be less restrictive of the free movement of goods than a procurement preference policy. Such an approach can be seen as an extension of *Ianelli* which allowed the court to assess under **Article 30** particular measures which were not necessary to the aid package, and could be severed from it; now it can be argued that the court can assess the package as a whole on this basis. This is similar to the judicial balancing of the open market policy of the Community against other objectives which occurs in the application of the **Article 36** derogations and of mandatory requirements. However, the mandatory requirements approach cannot be adopted to deal with state aids, since these aids should be permissible though they may operate in a discriminatory manner and/or have economic objectives, and mandatory requirements cannot be invoked in such circumstances (see 10.2.2. above).

If the correct test for the application of **Article 30** to aids provisions is indeed whether the measures are justifiable with regard to their aims, it leaves open the possibility that measures which do potentially restrict the free movement of goods may still be upheld as justifiable aids: if the court thinks they go no further than necessary to achieve their objective, **Article 30** is held inapplicable, and the measure is then left to be assessed by the Commission under **Articles 92** and **93**. This is certainly preferable to an interpretation by which *all* aids which restrict free movement of goods are prohibited under **Article 30**. However, it is still open to objection on the basis that under this approach it is for the court to assess and balance the objectives of any aid policy against the Community's open competition policy. This involves the formulation of Community policy on a sensitive issue, and also the analysis of complex economic matters (see further

10.2.4.2.). It was surely intended that these should be matters for the Commission under **Article 92**, and this is certainly the best way of dealing with such issues. The approach here leaves very little discretion for the Commission regarding state aids policy affecting the free movement of goods.

10.2.4.2. Justification of the preference policy as an aid
Whatever the general implications of the decision in *Du Pont de Nemours* regarding the relationship between **Article 30** and the aid provisions, the case does clearly indicate that a procurement preference policy is generally to be assessed under **Article 30**; that under that Article it is a measure of equivalent effect to a restriction on imports; and that therefore it is not a permissible method of promoting regional development under Community law.

If the correct view is that the application of **Article 30** to aids is determined by asking whether they go further than necessary, there might be room for argument that in some circumstances - different from those in *Du Pont de Nemours* - such a policy is justifiable in the light of the particular circumstances. However, it seems unlikely that the court would distinguish between different procurement preference policies: every policy is likely to be considered as going further than necessary to achieve regional objectives, and hence as within **Article 30** and unlawful, even if such a policy can be considered an aid (a matter considered at 10.2.4.3. below).

The conclusion that the preference policy in Italy which was in issue in *Du Pont de Nemours* is not justifiable in the light of its objective of regional aid has been questioned by Fernandez Martin and Stehmann ((1991) 16 EL Rev 216, at pp. 231-239). They point out that there are good reasons why, in the short term, regional development may best be pursued by a procurement preference regime rather than by other methods which might be used, notably direct subsidies. For example, a procurement preference policy does not involve as many state resources as a direct subsidy, since part of the benefit is achieved by diverting funds which would have been expended elsewhere (the only direct cost being any additional price payable beyond that payable on an open market). Further, it circumvents the bureaucracy inherent in other types of aid scheme, a particular advantage in Italy where the bureaucracy is said to be corrupt and inefficient; and it means that benefits are channelled directly into enterprises rather than being hived off by organised crime. Whatever the significance of these types of arguments, their assessment, and their evaluation against competing concerns in individual cases, certainly seem to be matters more appropriate for the Commission than for the European Court. Neither the Advocate General nor the court in *Du Pont de Nemours* in fact attempted any serious assessment of the social and economic factors in issue in the case.

10.2.4.3. Is a procurement preference policy an aid?
It was argued that the measures in this case constituted an aid for the purposes of **Articles 92** and **93** on the basis that higher prices would be paid by the state for goods from southern Italy than would be paid in a free market. Having decided that even if the measures amounted to aid **Article 30** applied, the court did not proceed to consider whether they did in fact fall within the definition of "aid". This issue was however addressed by the Advocate General. His view appeared to be that they did not; he noted a number of considerations which "militate against the proposition that the contested system is in the nature of an aid".

First, he thought that in this particular case any aid did not come from resources of the *state*, since the health authorities were not dependent on "the state" for funding. Thus a narrow view is taken of the meaning of "the state" for the purpose of state aid provisions, which is perhaps questionable. He also noted that a part of any increase would be borne by the market, not other sources of funding.

The second reason for suggesting that these measures might not amount to aids, was that the amount of an aid had to be capable of being objectively determined, and here it could not be calculated what extra costs were incurred because of the preference policy, if indeed any in some cases (since some firms in the region might, of course, have won contracts even on an open market). However, there seems no justification for adopting such a criterion to define an aid. In the light of the objective of the aids provisions, the test should be simply whether there is provision of a recognisable benefit. This seems to be so in the present case - enterprises in the assisted region benefit from higher prices; a larger market; and increased stability in the demand for their products (see Fernandez Martin and Stehmann, (1991) 16 EL Rev 216 at pp. 239-241).

The Advocate General also noted that paying a price supplement was not the sole object of the policy, which was also concerned to maintain plant in the area, and might also have the effect of setting up new industries which in fact are competitive. This is irrelevant since these are the objectives of many aids given in other ways, and indeed the promotion of such objectives is one of the main reasons why aids should sometimes be permitted even though their short term effect is to distort free competition.

10.2.4.4. Conclusion
The court's conclusion that the state aids provisions did not apply to the preference policy in *Du Pont de Nemours* is open to serious criticism. The court should have taken the view that the preference scheme was an aid, and as such should not have been assessed under **Article 30** of the Treaty. However, the court's view that the preference scheme was unlawful under **Article 30** has now been reiterated in its later decision in *Laboratori*

Bruneau, which is considered at 15. below. It thus seems to be well established that procurement preference schemes are not a permissible method of pursuing regional development. This view of the law seems to be accepted by the Commission: see 10.3. below.

10.3. THE REGIONAL POLICY PROVISIONS IN THE SUPPLIES DIRECTIVE

Having concluded that the measures in *Du Pont de Nemours* appeared to be within **Article 30,** the court then went on to consider an argument made by the Italian government that these measures were nevertheless lawful by virtue of a specific provision in the **Supplies Directive** dealing with the question of regional policy. The provision in force at the relevant time was the original **Article 26 of the 1977 Supplies Directive** which stated: "The Directive shall not prevent the implementation of provisions contained in Italian Act 835 of 6 October 1950 and in modifications thereto in force on the date on which this Directive is adopted; this is without prejudice to the compatibility of these provisions with the Treaty". The Italian Act mentioned in the provision was the Act which had made mandatory the quota system which was in issue in the *Du Pont de Nemours* case.

The court concluded that the provision did not save the regional preference measures (see para. 17 of the judgment). It pointed out that **Article 26** specifically stated that its provisions were without prejudice to the Treaty. Since the measures infringed the Treaty they were thus not within the scope of the provision. Second, the court stated that in any case a Directive cannot be interpreted as authorising conduct which is contrary to the Treaty, implying that the provision of **Article 26** would thus have to be interpreted as qualified by the Treaty even if this had not been stated expressly. The court might also have noted that in any case a Directive *cannot* lawfully authorise something which is contrary to the Treaty, and to the extent that it purports to do so its provisions will be void. Finally, the court noted that the Italian legislation relied on in this case was in some measure more extensive than that in force when the derogation was introduced, implying that modifications amounting to extensions of the policy were not covered.

Article 26 of the Supplies Directive has subsequently been replaced by an amended **Article 26,** under the **1988 Supplies Directive.** It still deals with the question of regional policy but in more general terms than the original provision which referred only to specific Italian legislation. This Article now provides: "This Directive shall not prevent, until 31 December 1992, the application of existing national

provisions on the award of public supply contracts which have as their
objective the reduction of regional disparities and promotion of job creation
in the most disadvantaged regions and in declining industrial regions, on
condition that the provisions concerned are compatible with the Treaty and
with the Community's international obligations".

This provision had been adopted at the time of the court's judgment in
Du Pont de Nemours but was not in force at the time of the conduct which
was in issue in that case, and was not discussed by the court. Clearly,
though, the court's reasoning indicates that the same conclusion would
apply to conduct occurring after this more general provision came into force:
if contrary to the Treaty, it would not be saved.

As was indicated at 10.2.4. above, the effect of the court's ruling in *Du
Pont de Nemours* seems to be that regional policy designed to promote
home industry will always be incompatible with **Article 30**. Thus it
might appear that **Article 26 of the Supplies Directive** can have no
application in practice, at least in so far as provisions to aid domestic
industry are concerned. This is the view which appears to be taken by the
Commission. In its original proposal for a Directive on services contracts
the Commission included a provision comparable to that found in **Article
26 of the Supplies Directive** (see COM (90) 372, 1991 OJ C23,
proposed Article 35). This was omitted from the amended proposal (COM
(91) 322 Final, Aug. 30 1991) on which a Common Position was adopted
by the Council on 25th February 1992, one reason being the
"Commission's view regarding the compatibility of preference systems with
Article 30" and the decision of the court in *Du Pont de Nemours* (see para.
27 of the Commission's comments on the above proposal). Another reason
for deleting this provision was that the implementation date for the proposed
Directive on services seemed in any event unlikely to be before 31st
December 1992, when the provision would cease to operate.

11. Case 103/88, Fratelli Costanzo SpA v Commune di Milano ("Costanzo")

22nd June 1989; [1989] ECR 1839; [1990] 3 CMLR 239

SUMMARY

This case concerned a request for a preliminary ruling from the European Court under Article 177 of the Treaty of Rome.

The court ruled that Article 29 (5) of the Works Directive as it stood prior to amendment in 1989 precluded authorities from rejecting bids as abnormally low simply through the application of an objective mathematical formula, and was required to be transposed without material departure from its stipulations. It also ruled that this provision applied to tenders considered merely abnormally low, and not just those obviously abnormally low.

The court also ruled that Article 29 (5) was capable of having direct effect.

11.1. INTRODUCTION AND FACTS

This case concerned a request for a preliminary ruling from the European Court, made by an Italian authority, the *Tribunale amministrativo regionale par la Lombardia* (hereafter "the tribunal"). The preliminary ruling procedure is explained at 1.3.3. above.

The proceedings before the tribunal concerned certain decisions made by the Milan Municipal Executive Board and the Milan Municipal Council in relation to a contract for construction work on a football stadium. The sole criterion for the award had, effectively, been stated to be "lowest price". Costanzo had submitted the lowest tender for the work, but the Executive Board had decided to disqualify it from the competition on the basis that the tender which it had submitted was abnormally low, and the contract had been awarded to another bidder. The Council subsequently ratified the award decision. Costanzo alleged before the tribunal that these various decisions were vitiated by a breach of **Article 29 (5) of the Works Directive**, as it stood before an amendment in 1989, which regulated the exclusion of abnormally low bids.

The tribunal referred to the European Court several questions relating to the application and effect of **Article 29 (5)**.

11.2. PROCEDURE FOR REJECTING ABNORMALLY LOW BIDS

The Executive Board had characterised Costanzo's tender as abnormally low and excluded it from the competition in accordance with an Italian law which regulated the procedure for excluding abnormally low bids. The law provided, essentially, that the price of each bid should be compared with the average price of all the bids, and that if this bid were lower than the average by a certain amount, as determined by the application of an objective mathematical formula, it should automatically be rejected as abnormally low.

Article 29 (5) of the Works Directive stated, however, in the form which applied at the relevant time, that where a tender was "obviously abnormally low" the authority was required to examine the details of the tender and to take this examination into account, and that for the purpose of this examination it was required to seek explanations from the bidder. (For the full text of the relevant provision see 3.3. above). The automatic disqualification procedure clearly contemplated that the authorities would not follow the precise steps set out in the above provision - the Italian procedure did not require examination of the details of the individual tender nor require that explanations be sought from bidders. Costanzo thus contended that the procedure set out in the Italian legislation, and which had been applied in relation to its own bid, was not in compliance with the Directive.

In connection with this ground of challenge, one of the questions put by the tribunal to the European Court asked whether the Italian Republic was obliged to "transpose [the Directive] without any amendment of substance" or whether it was possible to provide for a procedure involving automatic elimination without the need to examine the tender or seek explanations. Another question asked directly whether the Italian law was compatible with **Article 29 (5)** in so far as it omitted to provide for the procedural steps stipulated in that article. As the Advocate General pointed out, these two questions sought essentially to establish the same thing - that is, the legality of the automatic exclusion procedure.

The argument advanced by Italy was that the aim of **Article 29 (5)** was to provide protection for bidders against wrongful exclusion, and that if this could be achieved equally well through methods other than those stipulated in the Directive, then states should be able to implement the

Directive through these other methods. It was argued that the identification of abnormally low bids through application of a mathematical formula was not only as good a method of protection as that stipulated, but better, since it provided for objectivity in making the decision to exclude. Italy also pointed to other alleged advantages of this method of exclusion: it speeds up the award process, and it also obviates the need for an authority to make subjective judgements on matters which it may not be qualified to decide.

The court rejected this argument, considering that the procedural steps laid out in **Article 29 (5)** were required to be followed. It stated emphatically that "Article 29 (5) of Council Directive 71/305 prohibits member states from introducing provisions which require the automatic exclusion from procedures for the award of public works contracts of certain tenders according to a mathematical criterion, instead of obliging the awarding authority to apply the examination procedure laid down in the Directive, giving the tenderer an opportunity to furnish explanations" (para. 19 of the judgment). The reason given was that the automatic exclusion procedure deprives a bidder whose low bid is genuine of the opportunity of demonstrating this which, as the court noted, can be anti-competitive, eliminating the most competitive bidders (para. 18 of the judgment). The court also went on to state further that this aim of the provision, of allowing low bidders to prove their bids to be genuine, would be jeopardised if states were allowed to depart to a material extent from the precise and detailed procedure stipulated, and that this was thus impermissible (paras. 20-21) . This indicates that not only the use of a formula, but also any other departure from the procedure, will not be permitted. This is in line with the court's previous ruling in *Transporoute,* in which the court refused to admit an exception to **Article 29 (5)** for the case of a tender appearing so low that it bore no relation to reality (see 3.3. above).

It may be noted that one of the questions to the court on this issue had asked directly whether the Italian legislation which had been relied on was compatible with the Directive. However, as was explained at 1.3.3. above, the court may not in answering a request for a ruling pronounce on the validity of national legislation: this is a matter for the national courts to decide in the light of the general guidance given by the European Court. Hence the court merely pronounced generally on the permissibility of automatic exclusion procedures, leaving the question of the consequences for the Italian legislation to be determined by the Italian courts.

The court's rulings on the points discussed above were confirmed in the later case of *Donà Alfonso,* discussed at 13. below. In that case almost identical questions were put to the European Court concerning the same Italian legislation, and they received the same answers.

Article 29 (5) of the Works Directive in the form which was applicable at the time of the *Costanzo* decision has now been replaced, under

Article 1 (20) of the 1989 Works Directive by a new **Article 29 (5)**. The new text is set out in full at 3.3.3. above. There seems to be nothing in the new wording, however, which would affect the court's conclusions on the issues discussed above.

11 3.　THE DIRECT EFFECT OF THE PROVISIONS ON LOW BIDS

A further question put to the court was whether, if the Italian legislation on low tenders were incompatible with the Directive, the awarding authority was permitted, or obliged, to disregard the legislation and follow the Directive. This required the court to consider whether **Article 29 (5) of the Works Directive** had direct effect. (On direct effect see 1.3.2. above). In the earlier case of *Beentjes* the court had stated that **Article 29**, as well as certain other Articles of the **Works Directive**, could have direct effect, but this had been stated not in the context of a dispute over **Article 29 (5)**, but in relation to other aspects of **Article 29** (see 8. above). In *Transporoute*, considered at 3. above, it seems to have been assumed that **Article 29 (5)** had direct effect, but the point was not argued and was not expressly considered by the court. In *Costanzo* the court stated clearly, however, that **Article 29 (5)** could have direct effect (see para. 32 of the judgment).

There is nothing in the nature of the changes made to the low bid provision by the **1989 Works Directive**, which were noted at 11.2. above, to suggest that the amended provisions would not also have direct effect.

11.4.　CONDITIONS FOR APPLYING ARTICLE　29 (5)

The low bid procedure in **Article 29**, before its amendment in 1989, was stated to be applicable to a tender which is "obviously abnormally low". The Italian law which had originally been passed to implement the Directive had provided for the procedural steps set out in **Article 29** to be followed where a tender was "abnormally low" (Article 24 of Law No 584 of 8 August 1977). It stated that where tenders were abnormally low, the authority had to request explanations and examine the details of the tenders, and could disallow them if took the view that they were "not valid". (This law had subsequently been amended by the provisions on the automatic exclusion of low bids which were considered at 11.2. above). One further question referred by the tribunal to the European Court asked whether this provision was compatible with **Article 29 (5)**, in referring to tenders which were "abnormally low", rather than "obviously abnormally low" as in the Directive.

The court took the view that the provision of the Directive was in this respect not required to be transposed *verbatim*. It considered that the objective of the procedural provisions on low bids is to ensure bidders whose elimination is contemplated on the basis that their bids are not genuine are not disqualified without an opportunity to furnish explanations to prove that indeed their bids *are* genuine (para. 26 of the judgment). In this light it was in order for states to require examination when bids are merely abnormally low: this meets the objective of protecting all those who might be eliminated. The court concluded that the Directive allowed states "to require that tenders be examined when those tenders appear to be abnormally low, and not only when they are obviously abnormally low" (para. 27 of the judgment). The court again did not pronounce on the validity of the particular legislation, though this was the question put by the court; as indicated above, the consequence of a ruling of the court for specific national measures is for the national court to determine.

It is rather curious that there could be thought to be any room for argument over whether states are *permitted* to require procedural protection for bidders whose bids appear only "abnormally low", rather than "obviously abnormally low", which the terms of the court's ruling might suggest was the matter of dispute. Clearly it would be odd, assuming a power to eliminate all such bids, to allow bids merely abnormally low to be eliminated *without* seeking explanations, whilst such explanations *must* be sought for those *obviously* abnormally low - that is, those appearing the least likely to be genuine bids!

In fact, it seems that any argument that the Italian legislation was incompatible with **Article 29 (5)** could have been based only on the view that low bids can only be excluded *at all* in some circumstances to the extent that exclusion is authorised by **Article 29 (5)**, and that the Article did not authorise national authorities to exclude merely "abnormally low" bids, but only those "obviously abnormally low". This does seem to be one effect of **Article 29 (5)**: without this Article authorities choosing the "lowest price" criterion for awards would arguably be unable to reject low bids, whilst those choosing "most advantageous bid" would arguably be unable to do so unless this was stated as a selection factor in the tender documents. Only on this basis is it sensible to suggest that states cannot require explanations of merely "abnormally low" bids - they cannot require such explanations, since bids falling into this category cannot be excluded from the award process *at all*. If this were the case, then it seems the Italian legislation would have been incompatible with the Directive since, as indicated above, this legislation expressly gave to awarding authorities the power to exclude abnormally low bids from the award process.

On the assumption that the effect of **Article 29 (5)** is positively to authorise the exclusion of low bids, as well as providing procedural protection for those whose bids might be excluded under the provision, the court's ruling can be seen to make it clear that the decision as to when to invoke the scrutiny procedure for bids which might be within the "low bid" category is for national authorities.

The court's ruling on this point, as well as on the matters discussed at 11.2., was confirmed in the later case of *Donà Alfonso*, discussed at 13. below, in which a question in identical terms and concerning the same Italian legislation was put to the court.

Finally, it should be pointed out that the new **Article 29 (5)**, which was introduced by **Article 1 (20) of the 1989 Works Directive**, now refers specifically to "abnormally low bids" rather than bids which are "obviously abnormally low".

12. Case 194/88R, Commission of the European Communities v Italy

i) 20th July 1988; [1988] ECR 4547 (Order on *ex parte* application for interim relief)

ii) 27th September 1988; [1988] ECR 5647; [1990] 1 CMLR 813 (Order on hearing of application for interim relief)

SUMMARY

This case concerned an application by the Commission for interim measures in connection with proceedings brought under Article 169 of the Treaty of Rome.

The President of the court first ordered measures to suspend the award of the contract in dispute on an ex parte application; and then at the hearing of the application for interim measures ordered further suspension of the award until the date of delivery of judgment in the Article 169 proceedings.

12.1. INTRODUCTION AND FACTS

This case concerned an application for interim measures by the Commission, sought in connection with proceedings brought by the Commission against Italy under the procedure laid down in **Article 169 of the Treaty of Rome**. The **Article 169** procedure is explained at 1.2. above.

The proceedings under Article 169 arose in connection with a proposed contract for the renovation of a solid waste incinerator which was operated by a consortium of Italian public authorities. This contract was not advertised in accordance with the requirements of the **1971 Works Directive**. It was contended by the Commission that the Directive applied and that the contract should be advertised.

The Commission first sought relief on an *ex parte* application, to prevent any award being made pending a hearing on the question of interim measures. The relief requested was granted by the President, and the order made is reported at [1988] ECR 4547.

The Commission then sought measures to have any award suspended until judgment had been given in the main (**Article 169**) proceedings. This relief was also granted, and the order made is reported at [1988] ECR 5647 and [1990] 1 CMLR 813.

These two stages will be considered in turn.

12.2. THE *EX PARTE* APPLICATION

Article 84 (2) of the Rules of Procedure of the European Court provide for suspensory measures to be granted in certain cases after an *ex parte* hearing (see 1.2.1.3. above). As indicated, in the present case the Commission applied for measures to be granted *ex parte*.

At this *ex parte* stage the President of the court simply noted briefly, in paragraphs 2 and 3 of his order, that interim measures were necessary to allow the court to give the matter fuller consideration (which would be done at the hearing of the application for interim measures, after Italy had had a chance to make observations); and suspension was ordered. It was suggested at 7.2.2. above in considering the *Dundalk* case that there should be a strong presumption in favour of ordering suspension at the *ex parte* stage since the delay caused will be minimal - normally a matter only of several weeks. This case seems to confirm that this is the correct approach: the assumption of the President seems to be that such measures should be granted as a matter of course, since he does not inquire into the particular circumstances of the matter.

In this particular order, which was made on 20th July 1988, Italy was ordered to take measures to suspend the award of the contract until 15th September 1988 (or such other date as subsequently fixed by the court). It was also required to lodge its observations on the Commission's application for interim measures by 5th September 1988. The order was later extended to apply until such time as the hearing on interim relief should take place since this would not occur until after 15 September (see [1988] ECR 4559). (In the event the order requiring suspensory measures until the date of judgment in the main action was made on 27th September).

12.3. INTERIM MEASURES PENDING JUDGMENT

At the hearing on the application for interim measures which took place in September the Commission argued that measures should be granted to require Italy to take steps to suspend the award until the date of judgment in the **Article 169** proceedings. The principles which apply in determining whether interim relief should be granted were outlined at 7.2. above in considering the *Dundalk* cases.

Legal and factual grounds for relief: For such relief to be given it is first necessary, under **Article 83 (2) of the Rules of Procedure**, that there should be legal and factual grounds for relief - that is, a *prima facie* case. This condition the President of the court found to be satisfied in this case.

It was not disputed that the contract had not been advertised in accordance with the advertisement provisions in the **Works Directive**, but the Italian government argued that advertisement was not required for two reasons.

First, the call for tenders was merely an "exploratory" call for tenders, for which a special procedure was laid down in Italian law. This was stated by the President to be irrelevant. As he rightly pointed out, the scope of the Directive cannot depend on national rules: if the contract in question falls within the Directive, its procedures must be followed, regardless of what is stated in national legislation (para. 10 of the order).

Second, Italy argued that even if this situation generally fell within the Directive, there was no need to follow the advertising requirements in the particular circumstances because the case fell under **Article 9 (d)**, which at the relevant time provided for a derogation from the procedures of the Directive for reasons of "extreme urgency" unforeseen by the awarding authorities. (The "urgency" derogation, with slightly different wording but identical in substance, is now found in **Works Directive Article 5 (3) (c)**: see **1989 Works Directive Articles 1 (8) and (9)**). The argument was based on the circumstances that the contract was for renovation of a solid waste incinerator, which the Italian government had ordered to be closed down until renovations were carried out, since it did not comply with technical specifications laid down in a Presidential decree of 1982. It was contended that delay to the renovations would result in insufficient capacity for safe and hygienic waste disposal in the area with consequent risks to public health and the environment. The President, however, considered that the urgency derogation could not apply here even if this were so. This was because the events giving rise to urgency were not unforeseeable by the awarding authorities since the need for renovation had been know since 1982, though steps had not been taken in the matter until 1986 (see para. 14 of the order). Thus it was concluded that there were sufficient factual and legal elements to assume that *prima facie* the Directive applied.

Circumstances of urgency: It was then necessary to consider whether there were circumstances of "urgency" which would justify the grant of interim measures - that is, whether the applicant would suffer serious and irreparable damage if relief were not given. It was explained at 7.2.3. above in discussing the interim order made in *Dundalk* that the President there considered that there would be damage to the Community's open procurement policy if breaches could not be corrected, and that the potential for this type of damage would suffice as "serious and irreparable" damage for the purposes of interim relief without any need for the Commission to show precisely the nature and extent of damage which would occur. This view seems to be confirmed by the fact that the President was prepared to grant such relief in the present case. It was obviously also assumed here that such damage could occur if interim measures were not adopted - that the award procedure might go ahead and work begin, and the court thus presented with a *fait accompli* so that there could be no rectification of the breach. No doubt the court will always assume that interim measures are necessary to prevent such damage in a procurement case.

Balance of interests: Having satisfied itself on the above two points, the court in an application for interim relief must then proceed to a weighing exercise to decide if interim measures should be awarded on the facts - that is, it must consider the balance of interests.

On the one hand, the court must consider the prejudice which would result if interim relief were refused and the allegation of a breach of Community law turned out to be well founded. Obviously, the court must consider the prejudice which will result to the open procurement policy, both from the disincentive to compliance if adequate remedies are not provided, and also from the failure to correct the particular breach (though the latter is likely to be fairly small). It was also contended in the *Dundalk* case that the court should take account of the interests of other contractors affected by a breach of the Community rules. Whether this may be done was not considered by the President in *Dundalk*. In the present case, however, the President did seem to indicate that this would be a relevant factor: he specifically noted, in considering the arguments in favour of relief, that a declaration of illegality under **Article 169** "cannot make good the damage suffered by undertakings established in other member states which were excluded from the tendering procedure" (para. 16). The arguments for and against taking this factor into consideration, and the options open to the court, were examined in discussing *Dundalk* at 7.2.3. above. It was suggested that even if these interests can be taken into account they are unlikely anyway to tip the balance (see further 7.2.3.).

On the other side, the court must take account of the interests which will be adversely affected if a delay to a procurement results in a delay to the project to which it relates. In this case it was argued that a delay to the procurement would have adverse consequences for public health and for the environment, as has already been explained above, and this argument was accepted by the President (see para. 16 of the order). It was contended by Italy that even if the urgency derogation did not apply these consequences of

delay meant that the balance of interests in this case was against granting interim measures. It has been explained that in the *Dundalk* case the President had concluded that interim measures should not be given, on the basis that public health and safety would be adversely affected if the project in that case were delayed (see 7.2.3.).

In the present case, however, the President concluded that interim measures should be given despite the possible adverse effects on health and safety. Two particular factors were mentioned relating to the adverse consequences of delay.

The first was that the delay was the fault of the contracting authorities (para.16), suggesting that this fact might lead the court to grant interim measures when otherwise they might be refused. It has been noted above that under the **Works Directive** the derogation from the advertising requirements based on urgency can be used only where urgency is not the fault of the contracting authority. It is consistent with this approach, which puts the need to prevent evasion of the open procurement rules above specific considerations of public interest in the member states, that the fault of the authority should also be taken into account at the interim relief stage.

Second, the President noted that the delay from complying with the Directive -which would be 40 days, or as little as 25 if the matter could be considered urgent -would be minimal compared with the delay which would occur before the incinerator would come into operation, and, in particular, that Italian legislation on the issue of urgent waste disposal allowed around 22 months for the completion of this type of work once necessary loans had been granted (para. 17). Of course, delay caused by the grant of interim measures would be much longer than 40 days, since the procurement would be delayed until the main action which could take very many months; but this could be avoided if the authorities complied with the procedure in the Directive. This reasoning perhaps indicates that the strength of the Commission's case is a relevant factor, since if it is clear there is non-compliance the offending authority can reasonably be expected to take action straightaway, whilst this cannot be expected if the application of Community rules are not clear.

It may be suggested then, that in a case of manifest breach, the court will be very willing to grant interim measures even in the face of serious prejudice to the public interest, in order to deter and correct deliberate breaches of the procurement rules. Further, when urgency is due to the fault of the contracting authorities, the court likewise will not be prepared to accept public interest arguments as a reason for refusing relief. On the other hand, it can be argued that where these factors are not present, and to grant interim measures might cause serious prejudice to the public interest, such measures may be refused, as happened in *Dundalk*. The court's robust attitude towards enforcing the procurement rules in the present case does suggest, however, that it might be reluctant to accept "public interest" arguments, and that immediate and serious prejudice to important interests, such as health and safety, would have to be shown. This view finds confirmation in the *Italian lottery* case discussed at 16. below, which does seem to indicate that there is a strong presumption in favour of interim relief.

13. Case 295/89, Impresa Donà Alfonso di Donà Alfonso & Figli s.n.c. v Consorzio per lo sviluppo industriale del Commune di Monafalcone ("Donà Alfonso")

18th June 1991; not yet reported

SUMMARY

This case concerned a request for a preliminary ruling under Article 177 of the Treaty of Rome.

The court ruled that Article 29 (5) of the Works Directive as it stood prior to amendment in 1989 precluded authorities from rejecting bids as abnormally low simply through the application of an objective mathematical formula, and was required to be transposed without material departure from its stipulations. It also ruled that it was permissible to invoke this provision for tenders considered merely abnormally low, and not just those obviously abnormally low. In these respects the court confirmed its previous rulings in Costanzo.

FACTS AND RULING

This case concerned a request for preliminary ruling made by an Italian tribunal, the *tribunale amministrativo regionale del Friuli-Venezia Giulia* ("the tribunal"). The case before the tribunal involved an action by Donà Alfonso to annul a decision by an Italian authority to disqualify the firm's tender from a competition for a public works contract, the tender being alleged to be abnormally low. This decision had been taken in accordance with Italian legislation which required certain tenders be disqualified as abnormally low. Abnormally low tenders were to be identified on the basis of an objective mathematical formula, which related the price quoted in each tender to an average price quoted by bidders on the contract.

The tribunal referred to the European Court a number of questions regarding the operation of **Article 29 (5) of the Works Directive**, as it stood prior to amendment in 1989, which deals with the rejection of abnormally low bids. These questions were almost identical in their terms to the questions on abnormally low bids which were put to the court in the

Costanzo case, and they concerned the same legislation which was at issue in *Costanzo*. This case was discussed at 11. above.

The court took the view that the questions put should be answered in the same way as in *Costanzo*, and reiterated the following points which it had stated in the *Costanzo* case:

i) Exclusion of bids as abnormally low on the basis of objective mathematical formula was not permissible, and in implementing **Article 29 (5)** (as it stood prior to amendment) it was not permissible to depart to any material extent from its stipulations. (On the discussion on this point in *Costanzo* (see 11.2. above).

ii) The text of the provision before amendment did not preclude the examination of tenders which were merely abnormally low, as opposed to *obviously* abnormally low. (On the discussion in *Costanzo* see 11.4. above).

One argument put to the European Court was that the amended version of **Article 29** now permits an objective mathematical formula to be used, but the court did not consider the argument since the old version applied here. The amended version does provide for an exception to the usual procedure when the number of apparently low tenders is so great that exceptional costs would be involved in following the procedure, an exception which may be invoked until the end of 1992. If this exception does not apply, however, it seems most improbable that the court's rulings would have differed had the amended version applied: there is nothing in this version (set out at 3.3.3. above) to suggest that changes were intended to be introduced in respect of either of these points.

14. Case C-247/89, Commission of the European Communities v Portugal ("the Lisbon airport case")

11th July 1991; not yet reported

SUMMARY

This case concerned an action brought by the Commission under Article 169 of the Treaty of Rome.

The court ruled that the exclusion from the scope of the Supplies Directive for contracts "awarded by bodies which administer transport services", which applied under Article 2 (2) (a) of the Directive before amendment in 1988, applied not only to transport carriers but also to bodies providing infrastructure for the transport sector.

14.1. INTRODUCTION AND FACTS

This case concerned proceedings by the Commission against Portugal brought in the European Court under the procedure laid down in **Article 169 of the Treaty of Rome.** This procedure is described at 1.2. above.

The Commission's complaint related to the actions of a Portuguese authority, the Aeroportas e Navegaçao Aerea (ANA-EP). This body had various responsibilities connected with the support of civil aviation in Portugal, including the provision of airport infrastructure. The case concerned a call for tenders by the authority for a contract for the supply and installation of a telephone exchange at Lisbon airport. The contract had been advertised in a Portuguese newspaper, but not in the Official Journal. If the contract had been subject to the **Supplies Directive** the authority's conduct would clearly have constituted a breach of the Directive, which requires advertisement of major contracts in the Official Journal, and which also forbids any prior advertisement in national publications. The Commission considered that the **Supplies Directive** did apply, and brought an action under **Article 169** alleging breach of the Directive's provisions.

Portugal argued that the Directive did not apply because ANA-EP was a body administering transport services, and, as such, Portugal contended, outside the scope of the Directive. Portugal also argued *inter alia* that, in any case, 169 proceedings could not be brought against Portugal in relation to this matter since ANA-EP was not the kind of authority for which the Portuguese government could be held responsible.

14.2. APPLICATION OF THE SUPPLIES DIRECTIVE

At the time of the call for tenders the **Supplies Directive** stated, in **Article 2 (2) (a)**, that its provisions were not to apply to contracts "awarded by bodies which administer transport services". Portugal argued that the contract in this case was covered by this exclusion. The Commission, on the other hand, contended that the administration of transport services referred only to the actual provision of transport (whether of goods or persons) and did not include the provision of back-up services. Since ANA-EP was concerned only with the provision of related services and not directly with the provision of transport, it was thus argued by the Commission that contracts awarded by the authority were not covered by the exclusion, and thus were required to be advertised in accordance with the Directive's requirements.

The court rejected the Commission's argument, and found that ANA-EP's contracts were in fact excluded from the Directive. A very wide meaning was given to the concept of transport services for the purposes of the exclusion, which the court considered to embrace the whole transport sector, including, it seems, not only the provision of transport infrastructure, but also the administration of all services connected with that infrastructure (see paras. 35, 36 and 37 of the judgment). The court therefore rejected the Commission's application for a declaration that Portugal was in breach of its obligations under the Treaty.

The exclusion from the **Supplies Directive** which applied at the time of the relevant call for tenders has subsequently been amended by **Directive 88/295/EEC**. This Directive has repealed the former **Article 2 of the Supplies Directive**, including the exclusion on transport services. With respect to the latter, **Directive 88/295** inserted into the **Supplies Directive** a new **Article 3 (4) (a)**, which excludes from the scope of the **Supplies Directive** "contracts awarded by carriers by land, air, sea, and inland waterway". This amendment is now in force. The exclusion provided for by the amendment is clearly much narrower than that which applied formerly and was in issue in the *Lisbon airport* case, and it seems not to apply to authorities concerned with the provision of transport infrastructure. Under this new, narrower, exclusion, it thus appears that a contract of the type in issue in the *Lisbon airport* case is at present within the **Supplies Directive**, and must be advertised in accordance with the requirements of that Directive, whenever it is awarded by a body which is generally within the scope of the Directive (as is ANA-EP). In support of its argument regarding the scope of the old exclusion, so that the contract in issue in the *Lisbon airport* case would have been within the **Supplies Directive**, the Commission had argued that the scope of the former exclusion was intended to be the same as the amended version - that the amendment had been introduced simply for clarification purposes. However, as explained, the Commission's narrow view of the old exception was rejected favour of a much wider one.

The width of the transport exemption under the **Supplies Directive** will not have significance for long, since procedures for the award of contracts in the transport sector are now covered by the **Utilities Directive**. Most member states are required to adopt implementing measures by 1st July 1992, though these need not be brought into effect until 1st January 1993. (For Spain the date of implementation is 1st January 1996; for Greece and Portugal 1st January 1998). Once this Directive is implemented contracts relating to transport infrastructure, as well as those concerned with the provision of transport directly, will fall under this Directive - both those currently within the **Supplies Directive** (such as contracts relating to infrastructure contracts made by public bodies), and those outside it altogether (see **Article 2 (2)**).

The obligations imposed by the **Utilities Directive** are slightly different to those under the **Supplies Directive** - in particular, contracting procedures are more flexible, and under the **Utilities Compliance Directive** the remedies system is slightly different. It was considered that contracts in the transport sector awarded by public bodies which are currently within the **Supplies Directive** should be moved instead to this special Directive on utilities, so that obligations relating in this sector are the same whether the body is a public one of the type covered by the **Supplies Directive,** or one more towards the private end of the public-private spectrum. This is particularly important in light of the fact that transport services - and the other activities which are covered by the **Utilities Directive** - are carried on by different types of bodies in different member states, and it is important to secure equality of treatment as between states.

14.3. RESPONSIBILITY OF STATES FOR PUBLIC UNDERTAKINGS

An action under **Article 169** cannot be brought against a member state in respect of a breach of Community law by any person in that state, but only in respect of a breach by those persons for which the national government is regarded as properly accountable, which broadly means those in some way connected with the public sector. This issue was considered in general terms at 1.2.1.4. above. In the *Lisbon airport* case the Portuguese government argued that it could not be brought to account in the European Court for the actions of ANA-EP, because of the nature of that authority as an independent undertaking. The court having found that there was no breach of Community law in this case declined to consider whether or not Portugal could indeed be held responsible for the activities of this body.

It may be noted, however, that Advocate General Lenz, took the view that the fact that an authority was covered by the **Supplies Directive** did not necessarily entail that the relevant state would be held responsible for its non-compliance with Community law. If this is true then it seems probable that a number of bodies covered by the **Utilities Directive** will certainly not be bodies for which states will be held responsible under **Article 169**, since the link between central governments and many of the bodies covered by this latter Directive is fairly remote.

15. Case C-351/88, Laboratori Bruneau Srl v Unità Sanitaria Locale RM/24 de Monterondo ("Laboratori Bruneau")

11th July 1991; not yet reported

SUMMARY

This case concerned a request for a preliminary ruling under Article 177 of the Treaty of Rome.

The court confirmed its ruling in Du Pont de Nemours that a policy of reserving a certain percentage of public supplies contracts for firms in a particular region of the state of the awarding authority is a measure equivalent to a restriction on imports under Article 30 of the Treaty of Rome, and that even if such a policy constitutes a state aid under Article 92 this does not exempt it from the scope of Article 30.

FACTS AND RULING

This case concerned a request for a preliminary ruling from the European Court made by an Italian authority, the *Tribunale Amministrativo Regionale del Lazio* ("the tribunal"). The preliminary ruling procedure is explained at 1.3.3. above.

The proceedings before the tribunal concerned certain decisions made by the *Unità Sanitaria*, the local health authority, in connection with a restricted tender procedure for the purchase of suture equipment. These decisions had been taken in accordance with Italian legislation which required the health authority, along with other public bodies, to reserve a percentage of its supplies contracts to firms with certain connections with southern Italy. This was the same legislation as was in issue in the case of *Du Pont de Nemours*, discussed at 10. above. The tribunal put before the court certain questions concerning the application of **Article 30 of the Treaty of Rome** to the procurement preference policy, and the relationship between this Article and **Article 92**. These questions were, according to the court in the present case, essentially identical to the questions put in the *Du Pont de Nemours* case (see para. 7 of the court's judgment).

In answering the questions put the court confirmed the views which it stated in *Du Pont de Nemours*. Having made reference to its rulings in that case that a preference scheme of the type in issue here was contrary to **Article 30**, and that even if the relevant measures were an aid under **Article 92** this would not save them from being caught by the **Article 30** provisions, the court stated that there was nothing about this case to require a different response (see paras. 7 and 8 of the judgment).

The legal and policy issues involved in the court's rulings are discussed in examining the *Du Pont de Nemours* decision, at 10.2.3. above, and need not be considered further here.

16. Case C-272/91R, Commission of the European Communities v Italy ("the Italian lottery case")

31st January 1992; not yet reported

SUMMARY

This case concerned an application by the Commission for interim measures in connection with proceedings brought under Article 169 of the Treaty of Rome.

The President of the court granted interim measures to suspend the legal effects of a contract award decision and also to suspend the effects of any contract actually concluded.

16.1. INTRODUCTION AND FACTS

This case concerned an application for interim measures by the Commission, sought in connection with proceedings brought by the Commission against Italy under the procedure laid down under **Article 169 of the Treaty of Rome**. The **Article 169** procedure is explained at 1.2. above.

The **Article 169** proceedings arose in connection with the award by the Italian central authorities of a concession contract for the establishment and operation of a computerised lottery system. Participation in the competition to obtain the concession had been limited to firms, or groups of firms, of which the majority of the shares were in Italian public ownership. The Commission contended that this limitation contravened **Articles 52 and 59 of the Treaty of Rome**, which are concerned with the freedom of establishment and freedom to provide services (as to which see 9.2.1. above), and also **Article 30**, concerned with the free movement of goods (see 7.4. above). It also alleged that there had been certain breaches of the **Supplies Directive**. In a reasoned opinion the Commission alleged that Italy was in breach of these provisions of Community law and demanded compliance. In its opinion it pointed to the European Court's decision in *Re Data Processing,* discussed at 9. above, in which the court had ruled that a requirement for contracts for certain data processing firms to be awarded only to firms in Italian public ownership infringed **Articles 52 and 59** of the Treaty. Italy contended, however, that these Articles did not apply to the lottery contract, arguing that that contract fell within the derogation which applies for activities connected with the exercise of official authority (**Articles 55 and 66**). The Commission disagreed with this view and instituted proceedings under **Article 169.**

The decision to award the lottery contract had already been made. The Commission therefore sought interim measures from the court first, to suspend the legal effects of the Ministerial decree awarding the contract and, second, to suspend the legal effects of any contract which had actually been concluded with the successful contractor.

The interim measures requested were granted by the President of the court.

16.2. PRINCIPLES GOVERNING INTERIM RELIEF

When proceedings have been instituted under **Article 169 of the Treaty of Rome** there is provision, under **Article 186** of the Treaty, for the court to order interim measures. The procedure for this has been noted briefly above at 1.2.1.3., and the principles which apply to the grant of relief were outlined at 7.2. above in considering the *Dundalk* cases.

For such relief to be granted it is first necessary, under **Article 83 (2) of the Rules of Procedure**, that there should exist legal and factual grounds for relief - that is, a *prima facie* case. This the President found existed in the *Italian lottery* case. In particular, the President noted that he did not think that Italy could show that **Articles 52 and 59** of the Treaty did not apply because the contract required participation in the exercise of official authority (see further 16.4. below). Thus there seemed to be a *prima facie* case that these Articles of the Treaty had been breached.

According to **Article 83 (2) of the Rules of Procedure**, to obtain interim relief it is also necessary to show circumstances of urgency. This has been interpreted to mean that the applicant must show that he would suffer serious and irreparable damage if interim measures were not given. It has already been explained that in *Dundalk* the President of the court stated that there would be damage to the Community's open procurement policy if breaches could not be corrected, and that the potential of this type of damage would suffice as "serious and irreparable damage" to justify interim relief, without any need to show precisely the nature and extent of damage which would occur (see 7.2.3. above). This view was implicitly accepted in case 194/88R (see 12.3. above) and was also clearly accepted in the present case (see para. 25 of the order). The President also took the view that such damage would indeed occur if interim measures were not granted: in the present case the lottery system would be well in place by the date of trial if measures were not granted to prevent it's going ahead, and the court would then be presented with a *fait accompli* and no means of redressing the situation (see para. 25 of the order).

Once a *prima facie* case and "serious and irreparable damage" have been shown the court must proceed to a weighing exercise to decide whether interim relief should be granted on the facts of the individual case - that is, to consider the "balance of convenience". On the one hand, the court must consider the prejudice which would result if interim relief were refused and the allegation of breach of Community law turned out to be well founded. This will include prejudice to the open procurement policy, both from the disincentive to compliance if adequate remedies are not provided, and also from the failure to correct the particular breach (though the latter is likely to be small). It has also been suggested by the President in considering interim measures in case 194/88R that the interests of individual contractors prejudiced by the government's conduct may also be taken into account at this balancing stage (see 12.3. above). On the other side the court must consider the adverse consequences which would flow from a grant of interim relief. Usually this will arise from the delay to the provision of public services which might be caused by holding up the project to which the procurement relates whilst the dispute is settled.

In the *Italian lottery* case the Italian government argued that the delay which would be caused to the implementation of the lottery scheme as a result of the grant of interim measures would cause two types of prejudice. First, it would cause the Italian government to lose revenue of around 500 000 million lira a year. Second, it would delay the cessation of illicit gambling schemes which it was hoped would be killed off by the more efficient official lottery.

The President of the court, however, stated that the Community interests at stake should prevail over the interests of the member state (para. 28 of the order). Thus he granted the interim measures sought by the Commission.

It was suggested in considering the *Dundalk* and case 194/88R, the two previous cases on interim relief, that such relief will generally be granted once a *prima facie* case and serious and irreparable damage are shown, and that it is likely to be refused only in exceptional cases, where delay might cause prejudice to health and safety (as the court found to be the case in *Dundalk*). The order made in the *Italian lottery* case clearly provides support for this view. It shows that the court is determined to take a robust approach towards the implementation of Community procurement policy, and will be unwilling to give much weight to arguments of domestic convenience in the face of apparent breaches of the procurement rules.

It may finally be noted that in weighing the competing arguments at the balancing stage, the President specifically noted as relevant the existence of the court's prior decision in *Re Data Processing*. This might suggest that he was particularly minded to grant interim relief because he believed that there had been a *deliberate* breach of Community law. Alternatively, this might be taken to indicate that the strength of the Commission's case is a factor to take into account: relief is more likely to be granted where the case is a strong one, even though this does not necessarily imply that the breach itself was intentional.

16.3. IMPLICATION FOR THE SETTING ASIDE OF CONCLUDED CONTRACTS

When in **Article 169** proceedings a state is declared to be in breach of its obligations under Community law, it is required under **Article 171 of the Treaty of Rome** to take necessary measures to comply with the judgment of the court. It was considered at 5.2.2. above, in discussing case 199/85, whether this requirement might include an obligation to take steps to set aside any contract which has been concluded in breach of the procurement rules. The issue was not addressed by the court in that case, but it was touched on by the Advocate General, who seemed to think that this might sometimes be required.

In the *Italian lottery* case the court, as noted earlier, ordered the suspension of the legal effects of a concluded contract, until such time as the main proceedings should be resolved. The fact that the court was willing to order suspension of a concluded contract at the interim relief stage indicates that it might be willing to find that a state must set aside a concluded contract if it is declared in **Article 169** proceedings to be in breach of the procurement rules.

Of course, this does not *necessarily* follow from the fact that interim relief to suspend an award is granted. One view could be that if the state is ultimately declared to be in breach it is up to that state to decide whether to reopen the award procedure or to continue with the contract which has already been awarded. The purpose of interim relief to suspend the award would then be to prevent work from continuing as far as possible, so that it will be easier for the member state to reopen the procedure should it choose to do so. Whether, and how, the contract may be set aside in such a situation will, of course, depend on the applicable rules of national law.

It may be suggested, however, that if the European Court is willing to hold the successful contractor in suspense until the resolution of **Article 169** proceedings, it is likely also to be willing to require the setting aside of his contract once the proceedings have been resolved. It might be thought unlikely that the court would be willing to give such interim measures, and then to allow the member state ultimately to proceed with the contract at its discretion even though it is finally shown that it was awarded in breach of

Community law: if states are to have this discretion it seems logical that they should have it at the interim stage also. The *Italian lottery* case thus seems to provide support for the argument that the effect of **Article 171** may be that a concluded contract is required to be set aside when made in breach of Community law. However, the Article does not seem to have direct effect and a failure on the part of the state concerned to take steps to set aside the contract could not be invoked in the national courts. What steps will be required by the state or public authorities to achieve any necessary set aside will, of course, depend on the applicable rules of national law.

16.4. DEROGATIONS RELATING TO THE EXERCISE OF OFFICIAL AUTHORITY

Article 52 and Article 59 of the Treaty of Rome do not apply to activities which are "connected, even occasionally, with the exercise of official authority" (see **Article 55 and 66**). Italy argued that this derogation covered the lottery concession contract which was in issue in the present case. This argument was considered by the President in deciding whether the Commission had a *prima facie* case, one of the necessary conditions for the grant of interim relief (see 16.2 above).

This derogation was also considered by the court in *Re Data Processing* (see 9.2.3. above). It was explained that official authority generally covers only those activities which involve some special power or prerogative of the state. This condition was satisfied in the present case since, as was pointed out by Italy, the power to run a lottery system was in Italy reserved by legislation to the Italian state.

However, as explained in the discussion of *Re Data Processing*, the derogation does not apply to the award of a contract simply because that contract involves the supply of goods or services to be used in connection with the exercise of official authority: for the derogation to apply it is necessary that the contractor is "directly and specifically" involved in the exercise of that authority. The derogation was held inapplicable in *Re Data Processing* on the basis that there was no direct and specific involvement in the relevant official functions by a contractor who supplies and operates data processing systems connected with those functions.

Here it was argued that there had been an actual "transfer" of official authority in connection with the lottery system to the contractor: the contract could not be equated with an ordinary contract for the provision of goods or services in connection with the activity. However, the court rejected the view that this alone sufficed to render the contractor a "direct" participant in the exercise of any official function in running the lottery (see paras. 22 and 23 of the judgment). The court noted that the responsibility for controlling the issue of tickets and prizes, including the power to annul and correct errors, the mere operation of the computerised system remained with the administration. It considered that the functions exercised under the contract in this case were comparable to those exercised under the contracts which were at issue in the *Re Data Processing* case. It was specifically noted that this conclusion was not affected by the fact the present contract was a contract of concession under which payment was made in the form of a percentage of receipts from the lottery; nor by the fact that property in the automated system had not passed to the state.

Assuming that the operation of the lottery itself involves the exercise of official authority, the question of the extent of contractor responsibility required for the contractor to be regarded as participating directly in this function is one of degree. In view of the fact that derogations must be strictly construed, it seems likely that a very substantial degree of autonomy by the contractor in running the system would be required before the derogation would be considered to apply.

Appendix

Judgments of the Court of Justice

Case 10/76, Commission of the European Communities v Italy

22nd September 1976

(for discussion see 1. above)

JUDGMENT

[The account of the facts and issues which is contained in the complete text of the judgment is not reproduced.]

1   By an application which was received at the Registry on 5 February 1976 the Commission has brought before the Court under Article 169 of the EEC Treaty an action seeking a declaration that the Italian Republic has failed to fulfil its obligations under Directive No 71/305/EEC of the Council of 26 July (OJ, English Special Edition, 1971 (II), p. 682.

2   In conjunction with Directive No 71/304/EEC of the same date concerning the abolition of restrictions on freedom to provide services in respect of public works contracts, Directive No 71/305/EEC seeks to coordinate the national procedures for the award of these contracts. Under Article 32 Member States were to adopt the measures necessary to comply with the directive within twelve months of its notification to them, which period expired on 29 July 1972.

3   Subsequent to this directive the Italian Republic adopted the Law of 2 February 1973 relating to the procedures for the award of public contracts by restricted invitation to tender (licitazione privata) the text of which was conveyed to the Commission on 16 August 1973.

In application of Article 169 of the Treaty of the Commission, however, informed the Italian Republic by letter of 10 June 1974 that it considered that the obligations arising from the abovementioned directive had not been satisfied by the adoption of the Law.

4   In the first place it was claimed that the defendant had excluded from the scope of the Law procedures for the award of public works contracts other than by restricted invitation to tender.

5   Secondly, it was alleged that the defendant had not complied with Article 29 of the directive whereby the Italian 'anonymous envelope' procedure had to be abolished by 29 July 1975 or 29 July 1979 according to the estimated value of the contract as the Italian Law of 2 February 1973 made no provision in this respect.

6   In addition, under Article 12 of the directive, authorities awarding contracts who wish to award a public works contract by open of restricted procedure must make their intention known by means of a notice published in the Official Journal of the Communities whereas the Italian Law limits itself to providing for the publication of a notice in the Official Journal of the Italian republic.

7   The Italian Law does not contain the provisions referred to in Article 14, 15, 16 and 17 of the directive concerning the time-limit for the receipt of requests to participate, the form required for tenders and the compulsory indication of the time-limit for the completion of the works put out to tender.

8   Finally, Articles 20, 24, 25 and 26 of the directive lay down the criteria for qualitative selection which allow certain undertakings to be excluded from participation in the contracts, while the Italian Law contains no provision to this effect and retains the wide discretion conferred on authorities awarding contracts by Article 89 of the Royal Decree of 23 May 1924.

9   The defendant did not contest the alleged failures and on 6 July 1974, conveyed to the Commission a preliminary draft of a bill containing the Community rules in full.

1 0   The draft, which according to the Commission satisfies the essential requirements of the directive, was conveyed to the Italian Parliament on 13 August 1974 but has still not been adopted with the result that the measures intended to ensure the implementation of the directive are not yet in force at the date of this judgment.

1 1   Article 189 of the Treaty provides that a directive shall be binding, as to the result to be achieved, upon each Member State to which it is addressed but leaves to the national authorities the choice of form and methods.

1 2   The mandatory nature of directives entails the obligation for all Member States to comply with the time-limits contained therein in order that the implementation shall be achieved uniformly within the whole Community.

1 3   It follows that as the Italian Republic has failed to adopt, within the prescribed period, the measures necessary to comply with Directive No 71/305/EEC of the Council concerning the coordination of procedures for the award of public works contracts, it has failed to fulfil an obligation under the Treaty.

Costs

1 4   Under Article 69 (2) of the Rules of Procedure of the Court of Justice, the unsuccessful party shall be ordered to pay the costs.

The defendant has failed in its submissions.

It must therefore be ordered to pay the costs.

On those grounds,

THE COURT

hereby rules:

1.   As the Italian Republic has failed to adopt, within the prescribed period, the measures necessary to comply with Directive No 71/305/EEC of the Council concerning the coordination of procedures for the award of public works contracts, it has failed to fulfil an obligation under the Treaty.

2.   The defendant shall pay the costs.

Lecourt	Kutscher	O'Keefe	Donner
Mertens de Wilman	Pescatore	Sørensen	Mackenzie Stuart

Capotorti

Delivered in open court in Luxembourg on 22 September 1976.

A. Van Houtte   R. Lecourt
Registrar   President

Case 76/81, S.A. Transporoute v Minister of Public Works

10th February 1982

(for discussion see 3. above)

JUDGMENT

[The account of the facts and issues which is contained in the complete text of the judgment is not reproduced.]

Decision

1 By judgment of 11 March 1981 which was received at the Court on 7 April 1981 the Comite du Contentieux d'État (Judical Committee of the State Council) of the Grand Duchy of Luxembourg referred to the Court for a preliminary ruling under Article 177 of the EEC Treaty two questions concerning the interpretation of the Council Directives 71/304 and 71/305 of 26 July 1971 concerning, respectively, the abolition of restrictions on freedom to provide services in respect of public works contracts and on the award of public works contracts to contractors acting through agencies or branches (Official Journal, English Special Edition 1971 (II), p. 678), and the coordination of procedures for the award of public works contracts (idem, p. 682).

2 The questions arose in the course of a dispute the origin of which lay in a notice of invitation to tender issued by the Administration des Ponts et Chaussées (Bridges and Highways Authority) of the Grand Duchy of Luxembourg, in response to which SA Transporoute et Travaux (hereinafter referred to as "Transporoute"), a company incorporated under Belgian law, had submitted the lowest tender.

3 The tender was rejected by the Minister of Public Works because Transporoute was not in possession of the Government establishment permit required by Article 1 of the Réglement Grand-Ducal (Grand-Ducal Regulation) of 6 November 1974 (Mémorial [Gazette] A, 1974, p. 1663 et seq.) and because the prices in Transporoute's tender were considered by the Minister of Public Works to be abnormally low within the meaning of the fifth and sixth paragraphs of Article 32 of that regulation. As a result, the

Minister of Public Works of the Grand Duchy of Luxembourg awarded the
contract to a consortium of Luxembourg contractors whose tender was
considered to be economically the most advantageous.

4   Transporoute brought an action before the Conseil d'État for the
annulment of the decision. In support of its application it contended inter
alia that the reasons given for rejecting its tender amounted to an
infringement of Council Directive 71/305, in particular Articles 24 and 29
(5) thereof.

5   Considering that the dispute thus raised questions concerning the
interpretation of Community law, the Conseil d'État referred to the Court
for a preliminary ruling two questions concerning the interpretation of
Council Directives 71/304 and 71/305.

First question

6   The first question asks whether it is contrary to the provisions of
Council Directives 71/304 and 71/305, in particular those of Article 24 of
Directive 71/305, for the authority awarding the contract to require as a
condition for the award of a public works contract to a tenderer established in
another Member State that in addition to being properly enroled in the
professional or trade register of the country in which he is established the
tenderer must be in possession of an establishment permit issued by the
Government of the Member State in which the contract is awarded.

7   Directives 71/304 and 71/305 are designed to ensure freedom to provide
services in the field of public works contracts. Thus the first of those
directives imposes a general duty on Member States to abolish restrictions
on access to, participation in and the performance of public works contracts
and the second directive provides for coordination of the procedures for the
award of public works contracts.

8   In regard to such coordination Chapter 1 of Title IV of Directive 71/305
is not limited to stating the criteria for selection on the basis of which
contractors may be excluded from participation by the authority amending
the contract. It also prescribes the manner in which contractors may furnish
proof that they satisfy those criteria.

9   Thus Article 27 states that the authority awarding contracts may invite
the contractor to supplement the certificates and documents submitted only
within the limits of Article 23 to 26 of the directive, according to which
Member States may request references other than those expressly mentioned
in the directive only for the purpose of assessing the financial and economic
standing of the contractors as provided for in Article 25 of the directive.

1 0 Since the establishment permit in question is intended, as the
Luxembourg Government has acknowledged in its written observations, to
establish not the financial and economic standing of undertakings but the

qualifications and good standing of those in charge of them, and since the exception provided for in Article 25 of Directive 71/305 does not apply, the permit constitutes a means of proof which does not come within the closed category of those authorized by the directive.

11 The Luxembourg Government submits, however, that the grant of an establishment permit is equivalent to registration of the contractor in question in a list of recognized contractors within the meaning of Article 28 of Directive 71/305 and therefore complies with the terms of that provision.

12 It should be pointed out, in reply to that argument, that even if the establishment permit may be equated with registration in an official list of recognized contractors within the meaning of Article 28 of Directive 71/305, there is nothing in that provision to justify the inference that registration in such a list in the State awarding the contract may be required of contractors established in other Member States.

13 On the contrary, Article 28 (3) entitles contractors registered in an official list in any Member State whatever to use such registration, within the limits laid down in that provision, as an alternative means of proving before the authority of another Member State awarding contracts that they satisfy the qualitative criteria listed in Articles 23 to 26 of Directive 71/305.

14 It should be noted that the result of that interpretation of Directive 71/305 is in conformity with the scheme of the Treaty provisions concerning the provision of services. To make the provision of services in one Member State by a contractor established in another Member State conditional upon the possession of an establishment permit in the first State would be to deprive Article 59 of the Treaty of all effectiveness, the purpose of that article being precisely to abolish restrictions on the freedom to provide services by persons who are not established in the State in which the service is to be provided.

15 Accordingly, the reply to the first question must be that Council Directive 71/305 must be interpreted as precluding a Member State from requiring a tenderer established in another Member State to furnish proof by any means, for example by an establishment permit, other than those prescribed in Articles 23 to 26 of that directive, that he satisfies the criteria laid down in those provisions and relating to his good standing and qualifications.

Second question

16 The second question asks whether the provisions of Article 29 (5) of Directive 71/305 require the authority awarding the contract to request a tenderer whose tenders, in the authority's opinion, are obviously abnormally low in relation to the transaction, to furnish explanations for those prices before investigating their composition and deciding to whom it will award

the contract, or whether in such circumstances they allow the authority awarding the contract to decide whether it is necessary to request such explanations.

1 7   Article 29 (5) of Directive 71/305 provides that if a tender is obviously abnormally low the authority awarding the contract is to examine the details of the tender and, for that purpose, request the tenderer to furnish the necessary explanations. Contrary to the view expressed by the Luxembourg Government, the fact that the provision expressly empowers the awarding authority to establish whether the explanations are acceptable does not under any circumstances authorize it to decide in advance, by rejecting the tender without even seeking an explanation from the tenderer, that no acceptable explanation could be given. The aim of the provision, which is to protect tenderers against arbitrariness on the part of the authority awarding contracts, could not be achieved if it were left to that authority to judge whether or not it was appropriate to seek explanations.

1 8   The reply to the second question must therefore be that when in the opinion of the authority awarding a public works contract a tenderer's offer is obviously abnormally low in relation to the transaction Article 29 (5) of Directive 71/305 requires the authority to seek from the tenderer before coming to a decision as to the award of the contract, an explanation of his prices or to inform the tenderer which of his tenders appear to be abnormal, and to allow him a reasonable time within which to submit further details.

Costs

1 9   The costs incurred by the Government of the Kingdom of Belgium, the Government of the Italian Republic and the commission of the European Communities, which have submitted observations to the court, are not recoverable. As the proceedings are, in so far as the parties to the main action are concerned, in the nature of a step in the action before the national court, the decision as to costs is a matter for the court.

On those grounds,

THE COURT

in answer to the questions referred to it by the Comité du Contentieux of the Conseil d'État of the Grand Duchy of Luxembourg by judgment of 11 March 1981, hereby rules:

Council Directive 71/305 must be interpreted as precluding a Member State from requiring a tenderer in another Member State to furnish proof by any means, for

example by an establishment permit, other than those prescribed in Articles 23 to 26 of that directive that he satisfies the criteria laid down in those provisions and relating to his good standing and qualifications.

When in the opinion of the authority awarding a public works contract a tenderer's offer is obviously abnormally low in relation to the transaction Article 29 (5) of Directive 71/305 requires the authority to seek from the tenderer, before coming to a decision as to the award of the contract, an explanation of his prices or to inform the tenderer which of his tenders appear to be abnormal, and to allow him a reasonable time within which to submit further details.

Bosco	Touffait	Pescatore	Mackenzie Stuart
Koopmans	Everling	Chloros	Grévisse

Delivered in open court in Luxembourg on 10 February 1982

P. Heim
Registrar

G. Bosco
President of the First Chamber
Acting as President

Case 274/83, Commission of the European Communities v Italy

28th March 1985

(for discussion see 4. above)

JUDGMENT

[The account of the facts and issues which is contained in the complete text of the judgment is not reproduced.]

1   By application lodged at the Court Registry on 16 December 1983, the Commission of the European Communities brought an action pursuant to Article 169 of the EEC Treaty for a declaration that, by adopting certain provisions concerning the award of public works contracts and by failing to notify the Commission of the main provisions of national law which is adopted in the field covered by Council Directive 71/305/EEC of 26 July 1971 concerning the coordination of procedures for the award of public works contracts (Official Journal, English Special Edition 1971 (II), p. 682), the Italian Republic had failed to fulfil its obligations under the EEC Treaty.

2   On 26 July 1971, the Council of the European Communities adopted two directives for attaining freedom of establishment and freedom to provide services in relation to public works contracts.   The first, Directive 71/304/EEC (Official Journal, English Special Edition 1971 (II), p. 678) implements, with regard to public works contracts, the principle of the prohibition of discrimination based on nationality in the matter of freedom t provide services.   The second, Directive 71/305/EEC (Official Journal, English Special Edition 1971 (II), p. 682), provides for the coordination of national procedures for the award of public works contracts and lays down in particular:

Common advertising rules (Article 12 et seq.);

Common rules on participation (Title IV) comprising the introduction of objective criteria both for qualitative selection of undertakings (Article 23 et seq.) and for the award of contracts (Article 29).

3   In its judgment of 22 September 1976 (Case 10/76 Commission v Italy [1976] ECR 1359) the Court held that by failing to adopt, within the prescribed period, the measures necessary to comply with Council Directive 71/305, the Italian Republic had failed to fulfil an obligation under the Treaty. On 8 August 1977 the Italian Republic adopted, in response to that judgment, Law No 584 (Gazzetta Ufficiale [Official Gazette] No 232 of 26 August 1977, p. 6272), which in the Commission's opinion duly implemented the directive.

4   On 10 December 1981, the Italian legislature adopted Law No 741 concerning supplementary rules to speed up procedures for the performance of public works (Gazzetta Ufficiale No 344 of 16 December 1981, p. 8271). Since the Commission considered that several of the provisions of that Law, especially Articles 9, 10, 11, 13 and 15, infringed in particular the provisions of Directive 71/305 concerning the publication of contract notices in the Official journal of the European Communities, proof of the financial, economic and technical capacity of the contractor and the criteria for the award of contracts and that, moreover, by failing to notify it of the text of that Law, Italy had failed to fulfil its obligations under Article 33 of the directive, it requested the Italian Government, by a letter dated 17 December 1982, pursuant to Article 169 of the EEC Treaty, to submit its observations with regard to the eight allegations therein contained within two months of receipt of the letter.

5   By a letter dated 24 February 1983 from its Permanent Representation, the Italian Government admitted that the complaints with regard to the third, fourth and fifth paragraphs of Article 10 and Article 13 of Law No 741 were justified but contested the allegations with regard to Article 9, the first paragraph of Article 10 and Article 11 and the first sentence of the second paragraph of Article 15 of the Law. The Italian Government sent to the Commission, in an annex to that letter, the text of a preliminary draft law drawn up by the Minister of Public Works in response to the requests made by the Commission.

6   Since the Commission took the view that it was unable to take the preliminary draft law into account in so far as it amounted merely to 'a vague and incomplete intention on the part of the competent authorities to comply with provisions of the directive', it delivered a reasoned opinion dated 2 August 1983 which repeated all the complaints which had already appeared in its initial letter. In that opinion, the Italian Republic was invited to adopt the necessary measures within one month.

7   By a telex message dated 27 September 1983, the Italian Government, in response to the reasoned opinion, informed the Commission of the intention of the Minister of Public Works to lay the aforementioned draft before the Italian Parliament once again since it had at the end of the

previous legislative period. Since no further steps were taken the Commission decide to bring an action before the Court.

8 Law No 687 amending Law 741 and the provisions relating to provisional security and advertising was not adopted until 8 October 1984.

9 In this action the Commission alleges in the first place that on 10 December 1981, Italy adopted Law No 741 concerning supplementary rules to speed up procedures for the performance of public works (Gazzetta Ufficale No 344 of 16 December 1981, p. 8271) Articles 9, 10, 11, 13 and 15 of which infringe certain provisions of Directive 71/305 and in the second place that contrary to Article 33 of that directive Italy did not notify the text of the Law to the Commission.

I - The Adoption of certain provisions in Law No 741

(a) *Admissibility of increased tenders*

1 0 The Commission contends that Article 29 (1) of the directive provides for only two criteria for the award of contracts, that is to say the lowest price or the most economically advantageous tender, whilst Article 9 of the Italian Law permits the acceptance of an increased tender not corresponding to either of those two criteria in the case of a restricted invitation to tender.

1 1 The Italian Government replies to that allegation that the possibility of submitting tenders increased with regard to the basic price for tenders fixed by the administration conforms to the criterion of 'the lowest price' provided for in Article 29 (1) of the directive. Article 9 of the Italian Law provides that the contract is to be awarded to the tenderer who submits the offer which exceeds the price fixed by the smallest margin so that the contract is always awarded to the person who tenders 'the lowest price'.

1 2 In the light of the submissions made by the Italian Government, the commission has withdrawn its complaint with regard to that matter.

(b) *Procedure for making increased tenders*

1 3 According to the Commission, Article 9 of Italian Law No 741 of 10 December 1981, in conjunction with the third paragraph of Article 1 of Law No 504 of July 1970 (Gazetta Ufficiale No 179 of July 1970), provides that the calculation of prices in the context of tendering procedures is to include the possibility of making higher tenders according to the 'anonymous envelope' procedure whereas Article 29 (3) of the directive prohibits the calculation of prices in accordance with that procedure after the expiry of the time-limits referred to therein.

1 4 The Italian Government replies to the allegation that recourse to the anonymous envelope procedure does not follow from Article 9 of the Law of

1981 and that in practice that procedure is neither provided for nor used in connection with the award of contracts under Article 9. It is only in order to clarify the position and to eliminate the Commission's doubts that Article 1 of the draft law, approved on 22 December 1983, prohibits the use of the anonymous envelope procedure provided for in Article 1 of the Law No 504/70 with regard to contracts falling within the scope of the directive.

1 5   Since the draft law was adopted on 8 October 1984 the Commission has withdrawn its complaint in the course of the oral procedure.

(c)   *Secret tender equal to or closest to the average tender*

1 6   According to the Commission the criterion for the award of a contract, for which in Italy the first paragraph of Article 10 Law No 741 refers to Article 4 of Law No 14 of 2 February 1973 and therefore to Article 1 (d) of that Law which provides that the contract is to be awarded to the tenderer whose tender equals the average tender of failing that is the nearest tender below that average, does not correspond to either of the two criteria provided for in Article 29 (1) of the directive, that is to say the lowest price of the most economically advantageous tender according to various criteria depending on the contract.

1 7   Italian Government on the contrary, considers that the criterion of the average price enables the most economically advantageous tender to be determined by virtue of the specific rules relating to the application of that criterion as defined in Article 4 of Law No 14/73. Moreover, in the course of the oral procedure the .Italian Government has raised an objection of inadmissibility on the ground that in the Commission's initial letter the first paragraph of Article 10 of Law No 741 was alleged to be incompatible only with Article 29 (3) of the directive, whereas in its reasoned opinion the Commission maintained that the criterion for the award of a contract in question did not correspond to either of the criteria provided for in Article 29 (1) of the directive.

1 8   It should be recalled that under Article 169 of the treaty the Commission may bring before the court an action for a declaration that a State has failed to fulfil its obligations only if that State does not comply with the reasoned opinion within the period laid down therein by the Commission. The Commission does not deliver its reasoned opinion until the Member State has been given an opportunity to submit its observations.

1 9   It follows from the purpose assigned to the preliminary stage of the procedure under Article 169 that the initial letter is intended to define the subject-matter of the dispute and to indicate to the Member state which is invited to submit its observations the factors enabling it to prepare its defence.

2 0 As the court held in its judgment of 11 July 1984 (Case 51/83 Commission v Italy [1984] ECR 2793) the opportunity for the Member State concerning to submit its observations constitutes an essential guarantee required by the Treaty and, even if the Member State does not consider it necessary to avail itself thereof, observance of that guarantee is an essential formal requirement of the procedure under Article 169.

2 1 Although it follows that the reasoned opinion provided for in Article 169 of the EEC Treaty must contain a coherent and detailed statement of the reasons which led the Commission to conclude the the State in question has failed to fulfil one of its obligations under the treaty, the court cannot impose such strict requirements as regards the initial letter, which of necessity will contain only an initial brief summary of the complaints. As the Court stated in its judgment of 31 January 1984 (Case 74/82 Commission v Ireland [1984] ECR 317) there is nothing therefore to prevent the Commission from setting out in detail in the reasoned opinion the complaints which it has already made more generally in its initial letter.

2 2 In that respect it is clear from the documents on the file that in its initial letter dated 17 December 1982 the Commission alleged the the first paragraph of Article 10 of Law No 741 infringed Article 29 (3) of Directive 71/305 which prohibits the anonymous envelope procedure. But it also stated, after citing the text of the Law, that the provision infringed the directive 'in a manner analagous to that indicated in the preceding paragraph'. In that paragraph it complained that Article 9 of Law No 741 inter alia for a criterion for the award of contracts which was not compatible with either of the two criteria provided for in Article 29 (1) of the directive.

2 3 Consequently, although its wording is not very explicit, the initial letter did give notice to the Italian Government of the complaint against it. The Commission's complaint is therefore admissible.

2 4 With regard to the substance of the complaint it appears the the first paragraph of Article 10 of Law No 741 contains, in addition to the criteria for the award of contracts of the lowest price and the most economically advantageous tender, which are provided for in the directive, the criterion of the average price calculated on the basis of the tenders in the lower half of the scale between the lowest and highest tenders.

2 5 The Italian Government's contention that the criterion for the award of the contract to the person who submits 'the tender which equals the average tender or is the closest to it' serves to determine 'the most economically advantageous tender' within the meaning of Article 29 of the directive is incorrect. In order to determine the most economically advantageous tender, the authority making the decision must be able to exercise its discretion in taking a decision on the basis of qualitative criteria that vary according to the contract in question and cannot therefore rely solely on the quantitative criterion of the average price.

26 It is therefore necessary to declare that the first paragraph of Article 10 (1) of Law No 741 is not compatible with Directive 71/305 in so far as it contains a criterion for the award of contracts which is not provided for in Article 29 (1) of the directive.

(d) *Publication of contract notices*

27 The Commission also maintains that the paragraph of Article 10 of Law No 741, in so far as it suspends until 31 December 1983 the operation of Article 7 of Law No 14 of 2 February 1973 and the provisions of Law 584 of August 1977 with regard to the publication of contract notices, is incompatible with Article 12 of the directive which lays down an obligation to publish contract notices falling within the scope of the directive in the Official Journal of the European Communities.   According to the Commission the fourth paragraph of Article 10 concerning the publication of awards is also incompatible with Article 12 of the directive which provides that contract notices are not to be published in the daily press before they have been dispatched to the Official Journal.

28 The Italian Government does not dispute that these complaints are well-founded. It is therefore necessary to declare that it has failed to fulfil its obligations in the manner alleged.

(e) *The contractor's financial and economic standing and technical knowledge and ability*

29 The fifth paragraph of Article 10 of Law No 741, to the extent to which it suspends until 31 December 1983 Articles 17 and 18 of Law No 584 of 8 August 1977, which implement Articles 25 and 26 of the directive, is in the commission's opinion incompatible not only with the provisions listing the references which the authority awarding the contract may require in order to assess the contractor's financial and economic standing and technical knowledge and ability, but also with Articles 17 (d), 20, 22 and 27 of the directive, according to which the suitability of contractors is to be checked in accordance with the criteria of economic and financial standing and technical knowledge and ability referred to in Article 25, 26 and 27 of the directive.

30 The Italian Government does not dispute that these complaints are well-founded. It is therefore necessary to declare that it has failed to fulfil its obligations.

(f) *Additional or modified works*

3 1 The Commission contends that Article 11 of Law No 741, by authorizing the administration to proceed with 'the award of additional or modified works, once a favourable 'opinion has been delivered by the competent consultative body or deliberative body with regard to approval of the relevant expertise' is incompatible with Article 9 (f) of the directive in so far as it fails to take account of any of the conditions provided for by that provision with regard to the award of additional works to the contractor who successfully tendered for the main works.

3 2 The Italian Government states, on the contrary, that Article 11 relates solely to 'the award of additional or modified works' and does not relate to the conditions on which additional works are to be awarded to the contractor who was awarded the main contract provided for in Article 9 (f) of the directive. Those conditions continue to be governed by Article 5 (f) of Law No 584/77 which conforms to the aforementioned Article 9 (f) of the directive. Where the conditions in Article 5 (f) are satisfied, Article 11 permits, at the most, the award of works to the successful tenderer before the contract for additional works has been approved in order to speed up procedures for the performance of public works. The hypothesis on which the Commission's complaint is based, namely that Article 11 introduces a derogation from the provisions of Article 9 (f) of the directive, therefore lacks any foundation.

3 3 In the light of the submissions made by the Italian Government, the commission has stated that it is not proceeding with this complaint.

(g) *Urgency*

3 4 The Commission maintains that Article 13 of Law No 741, in so far as it permits, by reference to Article 41 (5) of the Regolamento [Regulation] approved by Regio Decreto [Royal Decree] No 827 of 23 May 1924, the award of private contracts 'when the urgency of the works, purchases, transport and materials is such that there must be no delay', is incompatible with Article 9 (d) of the directive to the extent to which it permits urgency to be relied upon in circumstances which do not correspond to the conditions provided for expressly in Article 9 (d).

3 5 The Italian Government has not contested that allegation. It is therefore necessary to declare that it has failed to fulfil its obligations in the manner alleged.

(h) *Security*

3 6 Finally the Commission considers that the first sentence of the second paragraph of Article 15 of Law No 741, according to which 'if it is provided that the undertaking invited to tender can be awarded only one contract that undertaking shall provide only one provisional deposit, calculated on the basis of the amount of the most valuable contract', is incompatible with Articles 25 and 26 of the directive to the extent to which the provision of security is not mentioned in the exhaustive list of references in Articles 25 and 26 that may be required at the tendering stage as proof of the contractor's financial and economic standing and technical knowledge and ability. Since as a deposit serves as a guarantee to the authority awarding in the contract that the works will be performed properly, it can be required only of the contractor to whom the contract is awarded.

3 7 According to the Italian Government, this complaint is inadmissible on the ground that the Commission has no interest in the matter in so far as the complaint is based solely on the first sentence of the second paragraph of Article 15 of Law No 741 since it is not that provision which requires contractors to provide a provisional deposit in order to take part in the tendering procedure, but other provisions which are not impunged. The first sentence of the second paragraph of Article 15 merely provides a power to permit a contractor who is taking part in several tender procedures to lodge only one provisional deposit.

3 8 In additon, the Italian Government contends that Article 16 (i) of the directive refers in general terms to 'deposits and any other guarantees, whatever their form, which may be required by the authorities awarding contracts' and therefore refers not only to the definitive deposits to be paid by the tenderer to whom the contract is awarded, but also to a provisional deposit whose specific purpose is to guarantee that the tender is serious and to compensated the administration in advance for any injury. The provisional deposit merely reinforces the obligation laid down in Article 16 (m) of the directive that the tenderer must keep his tender open for a certain period of time.

3 9 Since Italian Law 687 amending Law No 741 and in particular the provisions relating to provisional securities was adopted on 8 October 1984, the Commission has withdrawn its complaint in the course of the oral procedure.

II - Failure to notify the text of Law 741

4 0 The Commission claims that, by failing to notify it of the text of Law No 741 of 10 December 1981, Italy has failed to fulfil its obligations under Article 33 of Directive 71/305.

41 The Italian Government for its part considers that this complaint has ceased to be material in so far as the Commission was well aware of the text of the Law when it delivered its reasoned opinion.

42 In that respect it is necessary to declare that even if the Commission was aware of Law No 741 when it delivered its reasoned opinion, the fact remains that the Italian Government has not notified it officially of the text of the law as it is obliged to do under Article 33. It should be emphasized in that respect that the Member States are obliged, by virtue of Article 5 of the EEC Treaty to facilitate the achievement of the Commission's tasks which, under Article 155 of the EEC Treaty, consists in particular of ensuring that the provisions of the Treaty and the measures adopted by the institutions pursuant thereto are applied. It is for those reasons that Article 33 of the directive in question, like other directives, imposes upon the Member States, an obligation to provide information. In the absence of such information, the Commission is not in a position to ascertain whether the Member State has effectively and completely implemented the directive.

43 It is therefore necessary to declare that the Italian Republic, by failing to notify the Commission officially of the text of Law 741, has failed to fulfil its obligations under Article 33 of Directive 71/305.

III - Costs

44 Under Article 69 (2) of the Rules of Procedure, the unsuccessful party is to be ordered to pay the costs. As the defendant has failed in the majority of its submissions, it must be ordered to pay the costs.

On those grounds,

THE COURT

hereby:

1) **Declares that the Italian Republic, by adopting Article the first, third and fifth paragraphs of 10 and Article 13 of Law 741, has failed to fulfil its obligations under Directive 71/305/EEC.**

2) **Declares that the Italian Republic, by failing to notify the Commission officially of the text of Law No 741, has also failed to fulfil its obligations under Article 33 of Directive 71/305.**

3) **Orders the defendant to pay the costs.**

Mackenzie Stuart   Bosco   Due

Pescatore   Koopmans   Bahlmann

Joliet

Delivered in open court in Luxembourg on 28 March 1985.
P. Heim   A.J. Mackenzie Stuart
Registrar   President

Case 199/85, Commission of the European Communities v Italy

10th March 1987

(for discussion see 5. above)

JUDGMENT

1   By an application lodged at the Court Registry on 28 June 1985 the Commission of the European Communities brought an action under Article 169 of the EEC Treaty for a declaration that the Italian republic, more particularly the Municipality of Milan, as a local public authority, by deciding to award by private contract a contract for the construction of a plant for the recycling of solid urban waste and thus failing to publish a notice thereof in the Official journal of the European Communities, has failed to fulfil its obligations under Council Directive 71/305 of 26 July 1971 concerning the co-ordination of procedures for the award of public works contracts (Official Journal, English Special Edition 1971 (II), p. 682.

2   Reference is made to the Report for the Hearing for the facts and the submissions and arguments of the parties, which are mentioned or discussed hereinafter only in so far as is necessary for the reasoning of the Court.

I - Admissibility

3   The Italian republic has raised an objection of inadmissibility. It maintains that it fully complied with the reasoned opinion delivered by the Commission and that, consequently, an action before the Court of Justice under Article 169 of the EEC Treaty is no longer admissible.

4   In its reasoned opinion delivered in the pre-litigation procedure the Commission requested the Italian Republic "to adopt the measures necessary to comply with this reasoned opinion within 30 days of notification hereof" in the final paragraph thereof stated that "by necessary measures is meant above all a written undertaking by the Municipality of Milan that will comply with all the provisions of Directive 71/305/EEC in future".

5   In response to the reasoned opinion, the Italian authorities sent to the Commission a copy of a letter in which the Minister of the Interior

instructed the Prefect of Milan to enjoin the Municipality of Milan strictly to ensure that the directive was complied with in full in future together with the following written declaration by the Mayor of Milan dated 19 April 1984:

"....although convinced that the Municipal Administration acted, as on every other occasion, in a lawful manner in authorizing the award by private contract of a contract for the construction of the said plant for the recycling of solid urban waste,

I HEREBY DECLARE,

as requested in the aforementioned opinion, that the Municipality of Milan will ensure that, in the future, too its administrative action is in conformity with the provisions of primary and secondary legislation, including all the provisions of Directive 71/305/EEC, by according them full respect, in both form and substance".

6   It is clear from the documents before the Court that subsequently there were considerable delays in the construction of the proposed plant,the award of the contract for which was objected to by the Commission in its reasoned opinion, and that considerable changes had to be made to the project. However, no steps were taken with a view to proceeding to a fresh invitation to tender under conditions complying with the terms of the reasoned opinion.

7   It must be pointed out that the purpose of the procedure provided for in Article 169 of the EEC Treaty is, inter alia, to avoid a situation in which a Member State's conduct is put in issue before the Court when, following the Commencement by the Commission of the infringement procedure, the State admits the breach of obligations with which it is charged and remedies that breach within the period fixed by the Commission.

8   In this case, however, the declaration issued by the Mayor of Milan disputes the view expressed by the Commission in its reasoned opinion as to the existence of an infringement and no practical measure entailing acceptance of that point of view has been adopted by the Italian authorities.

9   In those circumstances, the Italian Republic cannot be considered to have complied with the reasoned opinion delivered by the Commission and therefore the action brought by the Commission under Article 169 of the EEC Treaty cannot be considered inadmissible. Consequently, the action must be declared admissible.

II - Substance

1 0 By reference to the observations submitted to the Commission by the Municipality of Milan during the pre-litigation procedure, the defendant

justified the award by private contract of the contract in question by relying upon Article 9 (b) and (d) of Directive 71/305.

1 1 According to the defendant, the construction of the type of plant envisaged involved the use of exclusive rights by the undertakings to which the contract was awarded and secondly, as the result of certain events, in particular the accident at Seveso, the construction of the plant was a matter of extreme urgency.

1 2 It should be observed that Directive 71/305 is intended to facilitate the effective attainment within the Community of freedom of establishment and freedom to provide services in respect of public works contracts. To that end it lays down common rules, in particular regarding advertisements and participation, so that public works contracts in the Member States are open to all undertakings in the Community.

1 3 Article 9 of the directive permits awarding authorities to award their works contracts without applying the common rules, except those contained in Article 10, in a number of situations, including (b) and (d), described under the following:

"when, for technical or artistic reasons or for reasons connected with the protection of exclusive rights, the works may only be carried out by a particular contractor," (b).

"in so far as is strictly necessary when, for reasons of extreme urgency brought by events unforeseen by the authorities awarding contracts, the time-limit laid down in other procedures cannot be kept," (d).

1 4 Those provisions, which authorize derogations from rules intended to ensure the effectiveness of the rights conferred by the Treaty in the field of public works contracts, must be interpreted strictly and the burden of proving the actual existence of exceptional circumstances justifying a derogation lies on the person seeking to rely on those circumstances.

1 5 In the present case, no facts of such a nature as to show that the conditions justifying the derogations provided for in the aforementioned provisions were satisfied have been put forward. Consequently, the Commission's application must be granted without any need to examine the facts at issue more closely.

1 6 It must therefore be declared that since the Municipality of Milan decided to award by private contract for the construction of a plant for the recycling of solid urban waste and thus did not publish a contract notice in the Official Journal of the European Communities, the Italian Republic has failed to fulfil its obligations under Council Directive 71/305 of 26 July 1971 concerning the co-ordination of procedures for the award of public works contracts.

Costs

1 7   According to Article 69 (2) of the Rules of Procedure, the unsuccessful party is to be ordered to pay costs. Since the defendant has failed in its submissions, it must be ordered to pay the costs.

on those grounds,

THE COURT

hereby:

1) Declares that since the Municipality of Milan decided to award by private contract a contract for the construction of a plant for the recycling of solid urban waste and thus did not publish a contract notice in the Official Journal of the European Communities, the Italian Republic has failed to fulfil its obligations under Council Directive 71/305/EEC of 26 July 1971 concerning the co-ordination of procedures for the award of public works contracts.

2)   Orders the Italian Republic to pay the costs.

Mackenzie Stuart   O'Higgins   Schockweiler   Koopmans

Bahlmann   Joliet   Rodriguez Iglesias

Delivered in open court in Luxembourg on 10 March 1987.

P. Heim   A.J. Mackenzie Stuart
Registrar   President

Joined cases 27, 28 and 29/86, Construction et Entreprises Industrielles (CEI) and others v Societé Co-operative "Association Intercommunales pour les Autroutes des Ardennes" and others

9th July 1987

(for discussion see 6. above)

JUDGMENT

1   By three judgments of 15 January 1986, which were received at the Court on 3 February 1986, the Conseil d'État of Belgium referred to the Court for a preliminary ruling under Article 177 of the EEC Treaty several questions on the interpretation of Council Directive 71/305/EEC of 26 July 1971 concerning the co-ordination of procedures for the award of public works contracts (Official Journal, English Special Edition 1971 (II(, p. 682).

2   Those questions arose in the context of proceedings for the annulment of decisions awarding various public works contracts.

3   The plaintiff in the main proceedings in Case 27/86 (CEI) was excluded in favour of an undertaking which had submitted a higher tender on the ground that the total value of the works, both public and private, which CEI had in hand at the time of the award of the contract exceeding the limit laid down by the applicable Belgian rules.

4   The tenders submitted by the plaintiff in the proceedings in Cases 28 and 29/86 (Bellini) were also excluded in favour of undertakings which had submitted higher tenders on the ground that Bellini did not satisfy the criteria laid down by the Belgian legislation for recognition in the classes required by the contract documents notwithstanding the fact that it had submitted a certificate of recognition issued in Italy in a class which entitled it to bid in Italy for contracts of a value corresponding to that of the Belgian contracts in question.

5   In three main proceedings, the plaintiffs allege in support of their application for annulment of the decisions awarding the contracts, inter alia, that those decisions were contrary to the provisions of Directive 71/305.
6   Since it considered that an interpretation of certain provisions of that directive was necessary, the Conseil d'État stayed proceedings and referred the following questions to the Court of Justice for a preliminary ruling:

a)   In Case 27/86

"1. Are the references enabling a contractor's financial and economic standing to be determined exhaustively enumerated in Article 25 of Directive 71/305/EC?

2.   If not, can the value of the works which may be carried out at one time be regarded as a reference enabling a contractor's financial and economic standing to be determined within the meaning of Article 25 of the directive?"

b)   In Cases 28 and 29/86

"Does Directive 71/305/EEC of July 1971 concerning the co-ordination of procedures for the award of public works contracts, and in particular Article 25 and Article 26 (d) thereof, permit a Belgian awarding authority to reject a tender submitted by an Italian contractor on the grounds that the undertaking has not shown that it possesses the minimum amount of own funds required by Belgian legislation and that it does not have in its employ on average the minimum number of workers and managerial staff required by that legislation, when the contractor is recognized in Italy in a class equivalent to that required in Belgium by virtue of the value of the contract to be awarded?"
7   Reference is made to the Report for the Hearing for a fuller account of the background to the main proceedings, the Community and national legislation at issue, the written observations submitted to the Court and the conduct of the procedure, which are mentioned or discussed hereinafter only in so far as is necessary for the reasoning of the Court.

The question concerning the exhaustive nature of the list references in Article 25 of the directive.

8   The first paragraph of Article 25 of the directive provides that proof of the contractor's economic and financial standing may, as a general rule, be furnished by one or more of the references mentioned therein. Under the second paragraph, the authorities awarding contracts are required to specify in the notice or in the invitation to tender which references they have chosen

from among those mentioned in the previous paragraph "and what references other than those mentioned under (a), (b) or (c) are to be produced".

9   It can be seen from the very wording of that article and in particular, the second paragraph thereof, that the list of references mentioned therein is not exhaustive.

1 0   The reply to the national court must therefore be that the references enabling a contractor's financial and economic standing to be determined are not exhaustively enumerated in Article 25 of Directive 71/305/EEC.

The question concerning the value of the works which may be carried out at one time.

1 1   With regard to the national court's second question in Case 27/86, it should be noted that the total value of the works awarded to a contractor at a particular moment may be a useful factor in determining, in a specific instance, the financial and economic standing of a contractor in relation to his obligations. Since the references are not exhaustively enumerated in Article 25 of the directive, there is therefore no reason why such information should not be required of tenderers by way of a reference within the meaning of that article.

1 2   However, in the light of the grounds of the order for reference, the content of the Belgian legislation mentioned therein and the arguments before this Court, the national court's question must be understood as also seeking to ascertain whether a national rule fixing the maximum value of works which may be carried out at one time is compatible with the directive.

1 3   In that regard, it should be noted that the fixing of such a limit is neither authorized nor prohibited by Article 25 of the directive, because the purpose of that provision is not to delimit the power of the Member States to fix the level of financial and economic standing required in order to take part in procedures for the award of public works contracts but to determine the references or evidence which may be furnished in order to establish the contractor's financial and economic standing.

1 4   In order to rule on the compatibility of such a limit with the directive as a whole, the purpose and object of the directive must be borne in mind. The purpose of Directive 71/305 is to ensure that the realization within the Community of freedom of establishment and freedom to provide services in regard to public works contracts involves, in addition to the elimination of restrictions, the co-ordination of national procedures for the award of public works contracts. Such co-ordination "should take into account as far as possible the procedures and administrative practices in force in each Member State" (second recital in the preamble to the directive). Article 2 expressly

provides that the authorities awarding contracts are to apply their national procedure adapted to the provisions of the directive.

1 5 The directive therefore does not lay down a uniform and exhaustive body of Community rules. Within the framework of the common rules which it contains, the Member States remain free to maintain or adopt substantive and procedural rules in regard to public works contracts on condition that they comply with all the relevant provisions of Community law and in particular, the prohibitions flowing from the principles laid down in the Treaty in regard to the right of establishment and the freedom to provide services.

1 6 The fixing in a Member State of a maximum value for works which may be carried out at one time is not contrary to the said principles and there is nothing to suggest that it has the effect of restricting access by contractors in the Community to public works contracts.

1 7 In those circumstances, it must be held that as Community law now stands, there is no reason why the Member States, in the context of their powers in regard to public works contracts, should not fix a maximum value for works which may be carried out at one time.

1 8 The reply to the national court should therefore be that a statement of the total value of the works awarded to a contractor may be required from tenderers as a reference within the meaning of Article 25 of Directive 71/305 and that neither that article nor any other provision of the directive precludes a Member State from fixing the value of the works which may be carried out at one time.

The question concerning the effect of being included in an official list of recognized contractors in one Member State vis-à-vis the authorities awarding contracts in other Member States.

1 9 In order to reply to this question, it is necessary to make clear the function of a contractor's inclusion in an official list of recognized contractors on a Member State in the overall scheme of the directive.

2 0 Under Article 28 (1), Member States which have official lists of recognized contractors must adapt them to the provisions of Article 23 (a) to (d) and (g) and Articles 24 to 26.

2 1 The said provisions of Article 23 define the circumstances relating to the insolvency or dishonesty of a contractor justifying his exclusion from participation in a contract. The provisions of Articles 25 and 26 concern the references which may be furnished as proof of the contractor's financial and economic standing, on the one hand, and technical knowledge of ability on the other.

2 2   The harmonization of official lists of recognized contractors provided for in Article 28 (1) therefore of limited scope. It concerns in particular references attesting to the financial and economic standing of contractors and their technical knowledge and ability. On the other hand, the criteria for their classification are not harmonized.

2 3   Article 28 (2) provides that contractors registered in such lists may, for each contract, submit to the authority awarding contracts a certificate of registration issued by the competent authority. That certificate is to state the references which enabled them to be registered in the list and the classification given in that list.

2 4   Article 28 (3) entitles contractors registered in an official list in any Member state whatever to use such registration, within the limits laid down in that provision, as an alternative means of providing before the authority of another Member State awarding contracts that they satisfy the qualitative criteria listed in Article 23 to 26 of the directive (judgment of 10 February 1982 in Case 76/81, Transporoute v Minister of Public Works [1982] ECR 417).

2 5   In regard, in particular, to evidence of contractor's economic and financial standing and technical knowledge or ability, registration in an official list of recognized contractors may therefore replace the references referred to in Article 25 and 26 in so far as such registration is based upon equivalent information.

2 6   Information deduced from registration in an official list may not be questioned by the authorities awarding contracts. None the less, those authorities may determine the level of financial and economic standing and technical knowledge and ability required in order to participate in a given contract.

2 7   Consequently, the authorities awarding contracts are required to accept that a contractor's economic and financial standing and technical knowledge and ability are sufficient for works corresponding to his classification only in so far as that classification is based on equivalent criteria in regard to the capacities required. If that is not the case, however, they entitled to reject a tender submitted by a contractor who does not fulfil the required conditions.

2 8   The reply to the national court should therefore be that Article 25, Article 26 (d) and Article 28 of the directive must be interpreted as not precluding an awarding authority from requiring a contractor recognized in another Member State to furnish proof that his undertaking has the minimum own funds, manpower and managerial staff required by national law even when the contractor is recognized on the Member States in which he is established in a class equivalent to that required by the national law by virtue of the value of the contract to be awarded.

Costs

29 The costs incurred by the Commission of the European Communities, the Kingdom of Spain and the Italian Republic, which have submitted observations to the Court, are not recoverable. Since these proceedings are, in so far as the parties to the main proceedings are concerned, in the nature of a step in the action pending before the national court, the decision on costs is a matter for that court.

on those grounds,

THE COURT (Sixth Chamber)

in answer to the question referred to it by the Conseil d'État of Belgium by judgments of 15 January 1986, hereby rules:

1. The references enabling a contractor's financial and economic standing to be determined are not exhaustively enumerated in Article 25 of Council Directive 71/305 of 26 July 1971 concerning the co-ordination of procedures for the award of public works contracts.

2. A statement of the total value of the works awarded to a contractor may be required from tenderers as a reference within the meaning of Article 25 of Directive 71/305 and neither that article nor any other provision of the directive precludes a Member State from fixing the value of the works which may be carried out at one time.

Article 25, Article 26 (d) and Article 28 of Directive 71/305 must be interpreted as not precluding an awarding authority from requiring a contractor recognized in another Member State to furnish proof that his undertaking has the minimum own funds, manpower and managerial staff required by national law even when the contractor is recognized in the Member State in which he is established in a class equivalent to that required by the national law by virtue of the value of the contract to be awarded.

Kakouris,   O'Higgins,   Koopmans,   Bahlmann,

Rodriguez Iglesias

Delivered in open court in Luxembourg on 9 July 1987.
P. Heim   C.N. Kakouris
Registrar   President of the Sixth Chamber

Case 45/87R, Commission of the European Communities v Ireland

16th February 1987 and 13th March 1987

(for discussion see 7. above)

ORDER (16th February 1987)

1   Dundalk Urban District Council is the promoter of a project known as the Dundalk Water Supply Augmentation Scheme. Contract No 4 of this Scheme concerns the construction of a water main to transport water from the River Fane source to a treatment plant at Cavan Hill and thence into the existing town supply system. The invitation to tender for this Contract by open procedure was published in Supplement 50/13 of the Official Journal of the European Communities dated 13 March 1986. At point 13 of the published notice it was stated that:

"The contract will be awarded, subject to the Dundalk Urban District Council being satisfied as to the ability of the contractor to carry out the work, to the contractor who submits a tender, in accordance with the tender documents, which is adjudged to be the most economically advantageous to the Council in respect of price, period of completion, technical merit and running costs.

The lowest or any tender need not necessarily be accepted."

2   The Commission received complaints that one of the tenders submitted was being unfairly excluded from consideration.. One of the complaints is an Irish contractor tendering for the contracts, P.J. Walls (Civil) Ltd. ("Walls") and the other is the Spanish company offering to supply asbestos cement pipes for the contract, Uralita S.A. ("Uralita").

3   Walls submitted three offers in response to the tender invitation, one of which based on the use of pipes supplied by "Uralita" of Spain, was the lowest tender offered. The consulting engineers to the project have, however, stated that this tender is not in accordance with Clause 4.29 of the Specification to the Contract which provides that:

"Asbestos Cement Pressure pipes shall be certified as complying with Irish Standard Specification 188 - 1975 in accordance with the Irish Standard Mark Licensing Scheme of the Institute for Industrial Research and Standards. All asbestos Cement Water-mains are to have a bituminous coating internally and externally. Such coatings shall be applied at the factory by dipping".

Only pipes made by Tegral Pipes Ltd. of Drogheda, Ireland, are currently certified to this standard.

4 Following various discussions, the Commission instituted proceedings under Article 169 of the EEC Treaty on 20 October 1986, setting out its view that this clause of the Specification constituted a breach of Article 30-36 of the EEC Treaty and of Article 10 of Council Directive of 71/305/EEC of 26 July 1971 co-ordinating procedures for the award of public works contracts (OJ L 185 of 25 August 1971, p. 5 (English Special Edition p. 682)). The Irish Government replied on 14 November 1986. The Commission was not satisfied with this reply and addressed a reasoned opinion to the Irish Government on 13 January 1987. The Irish Government replied on 3 February 1987. The Irish Government agreed to undertake not to award the contract until 20 February 1987.

5 By an application lodged at the Court Registry on 13 February 1987, the Commission applied for a declaration that by the inclusion of Clause 4.29 in the Contract and by the refusal to accept the use of asbestos cement pipes manufactured to an equivalent standard, Ireland has failed to fulfil its obligations under Article 30 of the EEC Treaty and Article 10 of Council Directive 71/305/EEC.

6 By an application lodged at the Court Registry on 13 February 1987, the applicant requested the Court, pursuant to Article 186 of the EEC Treaty and Article 83 of the Rules of Procedure, to order Ireland to take such measures as may be necessary to prevent, until such time as the Court has given final judgment in this case or a settlement has been reached between the Commission and Ireland, the award of a contract for the works to which this case relates, or if such a contract should already have been awarded, to order Ireland to take such measures as may be necessary to cancel such a Contract.

7 According to Article 84 (2) of the Rules of Procedure, the President may grant an application for interim measures even before the observations of the opposite party have been submitted. That decision may be varied or cancelled even without any application being made by any party.

8 It appears necessary to make use of this power in the present case so as to ensure that the application for interim measures is not prejudiced by the existence of a fait accompli. If the contract in question were awarded before the application for interim measures is decided, difficult questions might arise as to the possibility of subsequently cancelling it. Moreover, the Commission state that other phases of the scheme (for example the pumping station) are still at the design stage and that a delay in the award is thereof unlikely to delay the ultimate objective of increasing water supply in the Dundalk area. The interests of justice and of the parties involved can therefore best be maintained by an order maintaining the status quo until there has been the possibility of hearing the parties and deciding the application for interim measures with all due deliberation.

On those grounds,

THE PRESIDENT

by way of interim decision,

hereby

ORDERS

as follows:

1) Ireland shall take such measures as may be necessary to prevent, until such time as the application by the Commission for interim measures has been disposed of or until further order, the award by Dundalk Urban District Council of Contract No 4 of the Dundalk Water Supply Augmentation Scheme.

2) The costs are reserved.

Done at Luxembourg on 16 February 1987.

P. Heim   A.J. Mackenzie Stuart
Registrar   President

ORDER (13th March 1987)

1   By an application lodged at the Court Registry on 13 February 1987, the Commission of the European Communities brought an action under Article 169 of the EEC Treaty for a declaration that by adopting the tendering procedure relating to the Dundalk Water Supply Augmentation Scheme: Contract No 4, Ireland had failed to comply with its obligations

under Article 30 of the EEC Treaty and Council Directive 71/305/EEC of 26 July 1971 concerning the coordination of procedures for the award of public works contracts (Official Journal, English Special Edition 1971 (II), p. 682), and in particular Article 10 (2) thereof.

2   By an application lodged at the Court Registry on the same day, the applicant requested the Court under Article 186 of the EEC Treaty and Article 83 of the Rules Procedure, primarily to make an interim order that Ireland should take such measures as may be necessary to prevent, until such time as the Court has given final judgement in this case or a settlement has been reached between the Commission and Ireland, the award of a contract for the work relating to the Dundalk Water Supply Augmentation Scheme: Contract No 4. Also in that application, in the event that such a contract should already have been awarded, the Commission requested the Court to order the defendant to take such measures as may by necessary to cancel that contract.

3   It appears from the documents in the case, in particular a letter dated 3 February 1987, that Ireland gave an undertaking to the Commission not to award the contract before 20 February 1987. Ireland stated, moreover, that it would not be able to delay the award any further unless the Court of Justice so ordered.

4   By order of 16 February 1987 pursuant to Article 84 (2) of the Rules of Procedure, the President of the Court of Justice therefore decided in the interests of justice and in order to maintain the status quo to order the defendant to take such measures as might be necessary to prevent the award of the contract in question by Dundalk Urban District Council before the final order was delivered in the proceedings for interim measures in Case 45/87 R.

5   Ireland presented its written observations on 2 March 1987. The parties presented oral argument on 9 March 1987.

6   Before considering the merits of this application for interim measures it may be useful to give a brief description of the background to this case and in particular of the various facts that promoted the Commission to bring the main proceedings.

7   Dundalk Water Supply Augmentation Scheme. Contract No 4 of that scheme concerns the construction of a water main to transport water from the River fane source to a treatment plant at Craven Hill and thence into the existing town supply system. The invitation to tender for this contract by open procedure was published on page 13 of Supplement No S 50 of the Official Journal of the European Communities.

'The contract will be awarded, subject to the Dundalk Urban District Council being satisfied as to the ability of the contractor to carry out the work, to the contractor who submits a tender, in accordance with the tender documents, which is adjudged to be the most economically advantageous to the council in respect of price, period of completion, technical merit and running costs. The lowest or any tender need not necessarily be accepted.'

8   In response to that invitation to tender, an Irish contractor, P. J. Walls (Civil) Ltd (herein after referred to as 'Walls'), submitted 3 tenders. One was based on the use of asbestos cement pipes supplied by a Spanish company, Uralita SA. Walls considered that that tender, which was the lowest it had submitted, offered it the best possibility of obtaining the contract. However, the engineers consulted by the Dundalk authorities concerning the project considered that the tender did not comply with Clause 4.29 of the specification for the contract. That clause provides that:

'Asbestos cement pressure pipes shall be certified as complying with Irish Standard Specification 188-1975 in accordance with the Irish Standard Mark Licensing Scheme of the Institute for Industrial Research and Standards. All asbestos cement water mains are to have a bituminous coating internally and externally. Such coatings shall be applied at the factory by dipping'.

The consulting engineers therefore informed Walls that that tender could not be considered. Walls and Uralita then complained to the Commission that their tender had not been duly considered.

9   In fact only one manufacturer has obtained approval from the Institute for Industrial Research and Standards as regards Irish Standard (IS) 188 and is authorized to affix the Irish Standard Mark to pipes of the type required for the work in question. That company is Tegral Pipes Ltd, of Drogheda, Ireland.

1 0 The Commission took the view that Clause 4.29 infringed Article 30 to 36 of the EEC Treaty and Article 10 of Council Directive 71/305/EEC and therefore initiated the pre-litigation procedure under Article 169 of the EEC Treaty by a telex dated 11 August 1986. That telex drew Ireland's attention to the alleged infringements and invited it to submit its observations. Bt latter dated 9 September 1986 the defendant stated that it did not accept the validity of the complaint since the complaints had not submitted any evidence that their products met the requirements of IS 188 or any equivalent recognized international standard.

1 1 By letter dated 20 October 1986 the Commission formally reiterated its views to the defendant and invited it to submit its observations within two weeks of receiving the letter. Ireland's reply did not satisfy the Commission which, by letter of 13 January 1987, delivered a reasoned opinion stating that Clause 4.29 infringed Articles 30 to 36 of the EEC Treaty and Article 10 of the Council Directive 71/305/EEC; the Commission requested Ireland to take all necessary measures to comply with the reasoned opinion within 15 days following notification. By letter dated 3 February 1987 Ireland stated that it stood by the views expressed in its letter of 9 September 1986. It did, however, also undertake not to award the contract before 20 February

1987. Since Ireland had not complied with the reasoned opinion, the Commission applied to the Court on 13 February 1987 pursuant to Article 169 of the Treaty for a declaration that Ireland had failed to fulfil its obligations under the Treaty.

12 Pursuant to Article 186 of the Treaty, the court of Justice may in cases before it prescribe any necessary interim measures.

13 As a condition for the grant of a measure such as that requested, Article 83 (2) of the Rules of Procedure provides that an application for interim measures must state the circumstances giving rise to urgency and the factual and legal grounds establishing a prima facie for the interim measures applied for.

14 In order to establish a prima facie case for the interim measures it seeks the applicant refers to the two submissions on which it bases its main application. Its first submission is that, having regard to its detailed technical requirements, Clause 4.29 of the specifications for the contract is incompatible with Article 10 of Council Directive 71/305/EEC.

15 Article 10 (1) of Directive 71/305 states that the 'technical specifications may be defined by reference to national standards'. However, Article 10 (2) lays down certain conditions with which such technical specifications must comply. It proves: 'Unless such specifications are justified by the subject of the contract Member States shall prohibit the production into the contractual clauses relating to a given contract of technical specifications which mention products of a specific make or source or of a particular process and which therefore favour or eliminate certain undertakings. In particular, the indication of trade marks, patents, types or of a specific origin or production, shall be prohibited. However, if such indication is accompanied by the words "or equivalent", it shall be authorized in cases when the authorities awarding contracts are unable to give a description of the subject of the contract using specifications which are sufficiently precise and intelligible to all parties concerned.'

16 The Commission's second submission is that Clause 4.29 inserted in the specifications by Dundalk Urban District Council, a body subject to the authority of the Irish Department of the Environment, creates a barrier to trade which is contrary to Article 30 of the EEC Treaty since it has the affect of excluding the use of pipes manufactured in other Member States which would provide guarantees of the safety performance and reliability equivalent to those offered by pipes manufactured by the Irish company, Tegral Pipes Ltd, which is the only undertaking certified to ISS 188 as required by that clause. Ireland has, moreover, not put forward any ground based on Article 36 of the EEC Treaty or on the 'mandatory requirements' within the meaning of the Court's case-law to justify that infringement of Article 30 of the EEC Treaty. The existence of such an infringement is also clearly borne out by the fact that contractors which might have considered

submitting a tender base on the use of imported pipes were deterred from doing so and a contractor who did in fact submit such a tender was hampered by the fact that he was unaware of the additional conditions which might be imposed if other pipes were to be used.

1 7   In the written observations submitted by it in these proceedings for interim measures, the defendant argues that Article 30 of the EEC Treaty is not applicable since there is no barrier to trade or, in any event, no barrier to trade as a result of a commercial provision or other measure adopted by Ireland. It refers to the judgement of the Court of 22 March 1977 (Case 74/76, Iannelli & Volpi SpA v Meroni [1977] ECR 577) in paragraph 9 of which the Court stated that the field of application of Article 30 of the EEC Treaty 'does not include obstacles to trade covered by other provisions of the Treaty'. It points out that , in any event, any barrier to trade in this field would be covered by other provisions of Community law, namely Council Directive 71/305/EEC adopted pursuant to Article 57 (2) and Article 66 and 100 of the EEC Treaty, and is thus excluded from the scope of Article 30 of the Treaty. The proper course fort he Commission to take in order to put an end to the barriers to trade resulting from disparity between national standards is to propose measures of harmonization under Article 100 of the EEC Treaty rather than to apply Article 30.

1 8   It does not appear that the first submission relied on by the Commission can establish a prima facie case for the interim measures applied for. It is clear from the sixth recital in the preamble to Directive 71/305/EEC read in conjunction with Article 5 (3), which provides that:

'The provisions of this Directive shall not apply to public works contracts awarded by the production, distribution, transmission or transportation services for water and energy', that the public works Contract No 4 of the Dundalk Water Supply Augmentation Scheme does not fall within the scope of that directive and is not subject to the requirements laid down therein.

1 9   As regards the Commission's second submission, it should be pointed out that once it is found that prima facie Directive 71/305/EEC did not apply to the public works contract in question, Ireland's arguments against the applicability of Article 30 of the EEC Treaty which it bases on the judgement in Iannelli & Volpi SpA v Meroni become wholly irrelevant. Furthermore, as the Commission has rightly pointed out, secondary Community legislation such as a directive cannot derogate from directly applicable provision of the EEC Treaty such as Article 30.

2 0   The next step is to examine whether Clause 4.29 of the specifications may amount to a barrier to trade and whether such a barrier is imputable to a measure adopted by Ireland.

2 1   Although it would seem normal that in a public works contract such as that issue the materials to be used may be required to comply with a certain

technical standard, even a national standard, in order to ensure that they are appropriate and safe, such a technical standard cannot, without creating prima facie a barrier trade which is contrary to Article 30 of the EEC Treaty, have the effect excluding, without so much as an examination, any tender based on another technical standard recognized in another Member State as providing equivalent guarantees of safety, performance and reliability.

2 2 In this case it should be observed that the automatic effect of Clause 4.29 of specifications, by itself and without any justification, is to exclude any term based on the use of any types of pipes other than those certified to comply with 188, that is to say those manufactured by the only undertaking certified to standard, Tegral Pipes Ltd, Ireland, although there are a number of features in documents before the Court that suggest that the possibility cannot necessary ruled out that equivalent technical standards exist in other Member States.

2 3 Since that clause was inserted in the specifications by Dundalk Urban District Council, a body subject to the authority of the Minister for the Environment for whose acts Ireland is responsible, the barrier to intra-Community trade which it prima facie gives rise is imputable to Ireland.

2 4 In the light of the foregoing it must be considered that the Commission has indeed raised a material argument which establishes a prima facie case for the interim measure applied for.

2 5 Although it may be considered that in this case the Commission has indicated factual and legal grounds establishing a prima facie case for the interim measure applied for, the Court still has to assess the circumstances giving rise to urgency.

2 6 The Court has consistently held that the urgency required by Article 83 (2) of the Rules of Procedure in regard to an application for interim measures must be assessed on the basis of the need to adopt such measures in order to avoid serious and irreparable damage to the party seeking those measures.

2 7 The Commission submits that if contract in question were awarded in a manner contrary to Community law, irreparable harm would be caused not only to the interests of the Community but also to those of contractors whose tenders were not considered as a result of Clause 4.29 and their suppliers. The award of the contract will create a situation whereby the infringement becomes progressively irreversible as commitments are entered into by the contractor, orders are placed and physical work commences on the execution of the contract. The urgency for the interim measures applied for is sufficiently highlighted by the mere fact that Ireland's undertaking not to award the contract in question expired on 20 February 1987.

2 8 The Commission also states that a delay in the award of the contract will not involve serious inconvenience for the Irish authorities since other phases of the Dundalk Water Supply Augmentation Scheme are still at the

design stage. A delay in the award of the contract in question will therefore scarcely delay the achievement of the ultimate objective of increasing the water supply in the Dundalk area.

2 9 Ireland contends that the Commission has not raised any serious arguments showing that the damage to which the situation would allegedly give rise would be serious and irreparable. The Commission has merely inferred as much from the trite observation that the pipeline can only be constructed once and reference to all the consequences that entails. It has not stated who will suffer damage and how or the nature and extent of the damage. Besides, tenderers wrongly excluded from consideration for the contract can always claim damages.

3 0 Ireland emphasizes that contrary to what the Commission asserts, the interim measure applied for would have the effect of delaying completion of the scheme itself which would have very serious implications for the people of Dundalk and the surrounding region.

3 1 Ireland cites the following examples of the repercussions for the people of Dundalk if the interim measure applied for is granted:

The overall project, whose objective is to provide water to the town of Dundalk by 1990, has been subdivided into eight contracts. The completion of three of those contracts is dependent on the commencement of work on the contract at issue, Contract no 4. The work under Contract No 4 must be started by June at the latest if the project is to be completed by 1990.

From a public enquiry held in 1982 it emerged that the 30,000 inhabitants of Dundalk have for many years been faced by acute water shortages which have frequently necessitated water rationing. Evidence was also given at the inquiry that the water shortage constitutes a serious fire hazard and even a health hazard. It is also a serious disincentive to attracting industry to the region.

3 2 Although at first sight the problem seems to be a matter of some urgency, particularly since the damage to the Commission, as guardian of the interests of the Community, will arise as soon as the contract at issue is awarded, it may be necessary in proceedings for interim measures under Article 185 and 186 of the EEC Treaty to weigh against each other all the interests at stake.

3 3 In this case the objective of the public works contract in question, namely to secure water supplies for the inhabitants of the Dundalk are by 1990 at the latest, and the aggravation of the existing health and safety hazards for them if the award of the contract as issue is delayed tilt the balance of interests in favour of the defendant. It should be stressed that a quite different assessment might be arrived at in the case of other public works contracts serving different purposes where a delay in the award of the contract would not expose a population to such health and safety hazards.

On the grounds,

THE PRESIDENT,

by way of interim decision,

hereby orders as follows:

(1) The application is dismissed.

(2) This order cancels and replaces the order of 16 February 1987.

(3) Costs are reserved.

Luxembourg, 13 March 1987.

P. Heim   A. J. Mackenzie Stuart
Registrar   President

Case 45/87, Commission of the European Communities v Ireland

22nd September 1988

(for discussion see 7. above)

JUDGMENT

1 By application at the Court Registry on 13 February 1987, the Commission of the European Communities brought an action under Article 169 of the EEC Treaty for a declaration that by allowing the inclusion in the contract specification for the Dundalk Water Supply Augmentation Scheme - Contract No. 4 of a clause providing that the asbestos cement pressure pipes should be certified as complying with Irish Standard 188:1975 in accordance with the Irish Standard Mark Licensing Scheme of the Institute for Industrial Research and Standards (IIRS) and consequently refusing to consider (or reject without adequate justification) a tender providing for the use of asbestos cement pipes manufactured to an alternative standard providing equivalent guarantees of safety, performance and reliability, Ireland has failed to fulfil its obligations under Article 30 of the EEC Treaty and Article 10 of the Council Directive 71/305/EEC of 26 July 1971 concerning the co-ordination of procedures for the award of public works contracts (Official Journal, English Special Edition 1971 (II), p. 682).

2 Dundalk Urban District Council is the promoter of a scheme for the augmentation of Dundalk's drinking water supply. Contract No. 4 of that scheme is for the construction of a water main to transport water from the river Fane source to a treatment plant at Cavan Hill and thence into existing town supply system. The invitation to tender for that contract by open procedure was published in the Official Journal of the European Communities on 13 March 1986 (Official Journal No. S 50, p. 13).

3 Clause 4.29 of the specification relating to Contract No.4, which formed part of the contract specification, including the following paragraph:

"Asbestos cement pressure pipes shall certified as complying with Irish Standard Specification 188:1975 in accordance with the Irish Standard Mark Licensing Scheme of the Institute for Industrial Research and Standards. All asbestos cement water-mains are to have a bituminous coating internally and externally. Such coatings shall be applied at the factory by dipping."

4   The dispute stems from complaints made to the Commission by an Irish undertaking and a Spanish undertaking. In response to the invitation to tender for Contract No. 4, the Irish undertaking had submitted three tenders, one of which provided for the use of pipes manufactured by the Spanish undertaking. In the Irish undertaking's view, that tender, which was the lowest of the three submitted by it, gave it the best chance of obtaining the contract. The consulting engineers to the project wrote a letter to the Irish undertaking concerning that contract stating that there would be no point in its coming to the pre-adjudication interview if proof could not be provided that the firm supplying the pipes was approved by the IIRS as a supplier of products complying with Irish Standard 188:1975 ("I.S.188"). It is common ground that the Spanish undertaking in question had not been certified by the IIRS but that its pipes complied with international standards, and in particular with ISO 160-1980 of the International Organization for Standardization.

5   Reference is made to the Report for the Hearing for a fuller account of the relevant provisions, the background to the case and the submissions and arguments of the parties and of the intervener, which are mentioned or discussed hereinafter only in so far as is necessary for the reasoning of the Court.

6   In the Commission's view, this action raises inter alia the question of the compatibility with Community law, in particular Article 30 of the EEC Treaty and Article 10 of the Directive 71/305, of the inclusion in a contract specification of clauses like the disputed Clause 4.29. It further argues that the Irish authorities' rejection, without any examination, of a tender providing for the use of Spanish-made pipes not complying with Irish standards also infringed those provisions of Community law. It is appropriate to examine first the issues raised by Clause 4.29.

Directive 71/305

7   Article 10 of Directive 71/305, to which the Commission refers, provides that Member States are to prohibit the introduction into the contractual clauses relating to a given contract of technical specifications which mention products of a specific make or source or of a particular process and which therefore favour or eliminate certain undertakings. In particular, the indication of types or of a specific origin or production is to be prohibited. However, such indication is permissible if it is accompanied by the words "or equivalent" where the authorities awarding contracts are unable to give a description of the subject of the contract using specifications which are sufficiently precise and intelligible to all parties concerned. The words "or equivalent" do not appear in Clause 4.29 of the contract notice at issue in this case.

8 The Irish Government argues that the provisions of Directive 71/305 do not apply to the contract in question. It points out that Article 3 (5) of the provides that the directive is not to apply to "public works contracts awarded by the production, distribution, transmission or transportation services for water and energy". There is no doubt that the contract in this case was a public works contract to be awarded by a public distribution services for water.

9 The Commission does not deny that but points out that Ireland requested the publication of the relevant notice in the Official Journal by reference to the obligatory publication of contract notices laid down by the directive. The Commission, in common with the Spanish Government, which intervened in support of its conclusions, considers that, having voluntarily brought itself within the scope of the directive, Ireland was obliged to comply with its provisions.

1 0 With regard to this point, the Irish Government's argument must be accepted. The actual wording of Article 3(5) is wholly unambiguous, in so far as it excludes public works contracts of the type at issue from the scope of the directive. According to the preamble to the directive, that exception to the general application of the directive was laid down in order to avoid the subjection of distribution services for water to different systems for their works contracts, depending on whether they come under the State and authorities governed by public law or whether they have separate legal personality. There is no reason to consider that the exception in question no longer applies, and the reasons underlying it are no longer valid, where a Member State has a contract notice published in the Official Journal of the European Communities, whether through an error or because it initially intended to seek a contribution from the Community towards the financing of the work.

1 1 The application must therefore be dismissed in so far as it is based on the infringement of Directive 71/305.

Article 30 of the Treaty

1 2 It must be observed at the outset that the Commission maintains that Dundalk Urban District Council is a public body for whose acts the Irish Government is responsible. Moreover, before accepting a tender Dundalk has to obtain the authorization of the Irish Department of the Environment. Those facts have not been challenged by the Irish Governement.

1 3 It must also be noted that according to the Irish Government the requirement of compliance with Irish standards is the usual practice followed in relation to public works contracts in Ireland.

1 4 The Irish government points out that the contract at issue relates not to the sale of goods but to the performance of work, and the clauses relating to the materials to be used are completely subsidiary. Contracts concerned with the performance of work fall under the Treaty provisions relating to the free supply of services, without prejudice to any harmonization measures which might be taken under Article 100. Consequently, Article 30 cannot apply to a contract for works.

1 5 In that connection, the Irish Government cites the case-law of the Court and, in particular, the judgment of 22 March 1977 in case 74/76 (Iannelli & Volpi v Meroni, [1977] ECR 557), according to which the field of application of Article 30 does not include obstacles to trade covered by other specific provisions of the Treaty.

1 6 That argument cannot be accepted. Article 30 envisages the elimination of all measures of the Member States which impede imports in intra-Community trade, whether the measures bear directly on the movement of imported goods or have the effect of indirectly impeding the marketing of goods from other Member States. The fact that some of those barriers must be considered in the light of specific provisions of the Treaty, such as the provisions of Article 95 relating to fiscal discrimination, in no way detracts from the general character of the prohibitions laid down by Article 30.

1 7 The provisions on the freedom to supply services invoked by the Irish Government, on the other hand, are not concerned with the movement of goods but the freedom to perform activities and have them carried out; they do not lay down any specific rule relating to particular barriers to the free movement of goods. Consequently, the fact that a public works contract relates to the provision of services cannot remove a clause in an invitation to tender restricting the materials that may be used from the scope of the prohibitions set out in Article 30.

1 8 Consequently, it must be considered whether the inclusion of Clause 4.29 in the invitation to tender and in the tender specifications was liable to impede imports of pipes into Ireland.

1 9 In that connexion, it must first be pointed out that the inclusion of such a clause in an invitation to tender may cause economic operators who produce or utilize pipes equivalent to pipes certified as complying with Irish standards to refrain from tendering.

2 0 It further appears from the documents in the case that only one undertaking has been certified by the IIRS to I.S. 188 to apply the Irish Standard Mark to pipes of the type required for the purpose of the public works contract at issue. That undertaking is located in Ireland. Consequently, the inclusion of Clause 4.29 had the effect of restricting the supply of the pipes needed for the Dundalk scheme to Irish manufacturers alone.

2 1 The Irish Government maintains that it is necessary to specify the standards to which materials must be manufactured, particularly in a case such as this where the pipes utilized must suit the existing network. Compliance with another standard, even an international standard such as 160-1980, would not suffice to eliminate certain technical difficulties.

2 2 That technical argument cannot be accepted. The Commission's complaint does not relate to compliance with technical requirements but to the refusal of the Irish authorities to verify whether those requirements are satisfied where the manufacturer of the materials has not been certified by the IIRS to I.S.188. By incorporating in the notice in question the words "or equivalent" after the reference to the Irish standard, as provided for by Directive 71/305 where it is applicable, the Irish authorities could have verified compliance with the technical conditions without from the outset restricting the contract only to tenderers proposing to utilize Irish materials.

2 3 The Irish Government further objects that in any event the pipes manufactured by the Spanish undertakings in question whose use was provided for in the rejected tender did not meet the technical requirements, but that argument, too, is irrelevant as regards the compatibility with the Treaty of the inclusion of a clause like Clause 4.29 in an invitation to tender.

2 4 The Irish Government further maintains that protection of public health justifies the requirement of compliance with the Irish standard in so far as that standard guarantees that there is no contact between the water and the asbestos fibres in the cement pipes, which would adversely affect the quality of the drinking water.

2 5 That argument must be rejected. As the Commission has rightly pointed out, the coating of the pipes, both internally, was the subject of a separate requirement in the invitation to tender. The Irish Government has not shown why compliance with that requirement would not be as to ensure that there is no contract between the water and the asbestos fibres, which it considers to be essential for reasons of public health.

2 6 The Irish Government has not put forward any other argument to refute the conclusions of the Commission and the Spanish Government and those conclusions must consequently be upheld.

2 7 It must therefore be held that by allowing the inclusion in the contract specification for tender for a public works contract of a clause stipulating that the asbestos cement pressure pipes must be certified as complying with Irish Standard 188:1975 in accordance with the Irish Standard Mark Licensing Scheme of the Institute for Industrial Research and Standards, Ireland had failed to fulfil its obligations under Article 30 of the EEC Treaty.

The rejection of the tender providing for the use of the Spanish-made pipes.

2 8 The second limb of the Commission's application is concerned with the Irish authorities' attitude to a given undertaking in the course of the procedure for the award of the contract at issue.

2 9 It became apparent during the hearing that the second limb of the application is in fact intended merely to secure the implementation of the measure which is the subject f the first limb. It must therefore be held that it is not a separate claim and there is no need to rule on it separately.

Costs

3 0 Under Article 69 (2) of the Rules of Procedure the unsuccessful party is to be ordered to pay the costs. Nevertheless, by virtue of the first subparagraph of Article 69 (3) the Court may order the parties to bear their own costs in whole or in part where each party succeeds on some and fails on other heads. As the Commission has failed in one of its submissions, the parties must be ordered to bear their own costs.

On those grounds,

THE COURT

hereby:

1. Declares that by allowing the inclusion in the contract specification for tender for a public works contract of a clause stipulating that the asbestos cement pressure pipes must be certified as complying with Irish Standard 188:1975 in accordance with the Irish Standard Mark Licensing Scheme of the Institute for Industrial Research and Standards, Ireland has failed to fulfil its obligations under Article 30 of the EEC Treaty;

2. Dismisses the remainder of the application

3. Orders the parties, including the intervener, to bear their own costs.

Mackenzie Stuart	Due	Moitinho de Almeida
Rodriguez Iglesias	Koopmans	Everling
Galmot	Kakouris	O'Higgins

Delivered in open court in Luxembourg on 22 September 1988.
J.G. Giraud   A.J. Mackenzie Stuart
Registrar   President

Case 31/87, Gebroeders Beentjes BV v The Netherlands

20th September 1988

(for discussion see 8. above)

JUDGMENT

1   By a judgment of 28 January 1987, which was received at the Court on February 1987, the Arrondissmentstrechtbank, The Hague, referred to the Court for a preliminary ruling under Article 177 of the EEC Treaty a number of questions on the interoperation of Council Directive 71/305/EEC of 26 July 1971 concerning the co-ordination of procedures for the award of public works contracts (Official Journal, English Special Edition 1971 (II) p. 682).

2   These questions arose in proceedings between Gebroeders Beentjes B.V. and the Netherlands Ministry of Agriculture and Fisheries in connection with a public works contract in connection with a land consolidation operation.

3   In the main proceedings. Beentjes, the plaintiff, claimed that the decision of the awarding authority rejecting its tender, although it was the lowest, in favour of the next-lowest bidder had been taken in breach of the provisions of the above-mentioned directive.

4   It was in these circumstances that the Arrondissmentsrechtbank stayed the proceedings and asked the Court for a preliminary ruling on the following questions:

"1. Is a body with the characteristics of a 'local committee' as provided for in the Ruilverkavelingswet 1954 and described in paragraph 5.3 of (the national court's) judgment t be regarded as 'the State' or a 'regional or local authority' for the purposes of Council Directive 71/305/EEC of 26 July 1971?

2.   Does Directive 71/305/EEC a low a tenderer to be excluded from a tendering procedure on the basis of considerations such as those mentioned in paragraph 6.2 of (the national court's) judgment if in the invitation itself no qualitative criteria are laid down in this regard (but reference is simply made to general conditions containing a general reservation such as that relied upon by the State in this case)?

3.   May parties such as Beentjes in a civil action such as this rely on the provisions of Directive 71/305/EEC indicating the cases in which and the conditions under which a tenderer may be excluded from the tendering procedure on qualitative grounds, even if in the incorporation of those provisions of the directive in national legislation the contracting authority is given wider powers to refuse to award a contract than are permitted under the directive?"

5   As regards the second question, it should be stated that the considerations referred to in the national court's judgment concern the reasons for which Beentjes' tender was rejected by the awarding authority, which considered that Beentjes lacked sufficient specific experience for the work in question, that its tender appeared to be less acceptable and that it did not seem to be in a position to employ long-term unemployed persons. It is apparent from the documents before the Court that the first two criteria cited above were provided for in Article 21 of the Uniform Rules on Invitations to Tender of 21 December 1971 (Uniform Aanbestedingsreglement, hereinafter referred to as "the Uniform Rules"), to which the contested invitation to tender referred, while the condition regarding the employment of long-term unemployed persons was expressly set out in the invitation to tender.

6   Reference is made to the Report for the Hearing for a more detailed account of the facts of the main proceedings, the relevant provisions of Community and national law, the written observations submitted to the Court and the course of the proceedings, which are mentioned or discussed hereinafter only in so far as is necessary for the reasoning of the Court.

The first question

7   By its first question, the national court seeks in substance to establish whether Directive 71/305/EEC applies to the award of public works contracts by a body such as the local land consolidation committee.

8   It appears from the documents before the Court that the local land consolidation committee is a body with no legal personality of its own whose functions and composition are governed by legislation and that its members are appointed by the Provincial Executive of the province concerned. It is bound to apply rules laid down by a central committee established by royal decree, whose members are appointed by the Crown. The State ensures observance of the obligations arising out of measures of the committee and finances the public works contracts awarded by the local committee in question.

9   The objective of Directive 71/305/EEC is to co-ordinate national procedures for the award of public works contracts concluded in Member

States on behalf of the State, regional or local authorities or other legal persons governed by public law.

1 0 Pursuant to Article 1 (b) of the Directive, the State, regional or local authorities and the legal persons governed by public law specified in Annex I are to be regarded as "authorities awarding contracts".

1 1 For the purposes of this provision, the term "the State" must be interpreted in functional terms. The aim of the directive, which is to ensure the effective attainment of freedom of establishment and freedom to provide services in respect of public works contracts, would be jeopardized if the provisions of the directive were to be held to be inapplicable solely because a public works contract is awarded by a body which, although it was set up to carry out tasks entrusted to it by legislation, is not formally a part of the State administration.

1 2 Consequently, a body such as that in question here, whose composition and functions are laid down by legislation and which depends on the authorities for the appointment of its members, the observance of the obligations arising out of its measures and the financing of the public works contracts which it is its task to award, must be regarded as falling within the notion of the State for the purpose of the above-mentioned provision, even though it is not part of the State administration in formal terms.

1 3 In reply to the first question put by the national court, it should therefore be stated that Directive 71/305/EEC applies to public works contracts awarded by a body such as the local land consolidation committee.

The second question

1 4 The second question put by the national court seeks, in the first place, to establish whether Directive 71/305/EEC precludes the rejection of a tender on the following grounds:

lack of specific experience relating to the work to be carried out;

the tender does not appear to be the most acceptable in the view of the awarding authority;

inability of the contractor to employ long-term unemployed persons.

Secondly, it seeks to determine what prior notice is required by the directive as regards the use of such criteria, should they be regarding as compatible with the directive.

1 5 According to the structure of the directive, in particular Title IV (Common rules on participation), the examination of the suitability of contractors to carry out the contracts to be awarded and the awarding of the

contract are two different operations in the procedure for the award of a works contract. Article 20 of the Directive provides that the contract is to be awarded after the contractor's suitability has been checked.

1 6 Even though the directive, which is intended to achieve the co-ordination of national procedures for the award of public works contracts while taking into account, as far as possible, the procedures and administrative practices in force in each Member Sate (second recital in the preamble), does not rule out the possibility that examination of the tenderer's suitability and the award of the contract may take place simultaneously, the two procedures are governed by different rules.

1 7 Article 20 provides that the suitability of contractors is to be checked by the authorities awarding contracts in accordance with the criteria of economic and financial standing and of technical knowledge or ability referred to in Articles 25 to 28. The purpose of these articles is not to delimit the power of the Member States to fix the level of financial and economic standing and technical knowledge required in order to take part in procedures for the award of public works contracts but to determine the references or evidence which may be furnished in order to establish the contractor's financial and economic standing and technical knowledge or ability (see judgment of 9 July 1987 in joined Cases 27 to 29/86, C.E.I. and Bellini [1987] ECR 3347). Nevertheless, it is clear from these provisions that the authorities awarding contracts can check the suitability of the contractors only on the basis of criteria relating to their economic and financial standing and their technical knowledge and ability.

1 8 As far as the criteria for the award of contracts is concerned, Article 29 (1) provides that the authorities awarding contracts must base their decision either on the lowest price only or, when the award is made to the most economically advantageous tender, on various criteria according to the contract: e.g. price, period for completion, running costs, profitability, technical merit.

1 9 Although the second alternative leaves it open to the authorities awarding contracts to choose the criteria on which they propose to base their award of the contract, their choice is limited to criteria aimed at identifying the offer which is economically the most advantageous. Indeed, it is only by way of exception that Article 29 (4) provides that an award may be based on criteria of a different nature "within the framework of rules whose aim is to give preference to certain tenderers by way of aid, on condition that the rules invoked are in conformity with the Treaty, in particular Articles 92 et seq."

2 0 Furhermore, the directive does not lay down a uniform and exhaustive body of Community rules; within the framework of the common rules which it contains, the Member States remain free to maintain or adopt substantive and procedural rules in regard to public works contracts on

condition that they comply with all the relevant provisions of Community law, in particular the prohibitions flowing from the principles laid down in the Treaty in regard to the right of establishment and the freedom to provide services (judgment of 9 July 1987, cited above).

2 1 Finally, in order to meet the directive's aim of ensuring development of effective competition in the award of public works contracts, the criteria and conditions which govern each contract must be given sufficient publicity by the authorities awarding contracts.

2 2 To this end, Title III of the Directive sets out rules for Community-wide advertising of contracts drawn up by awarding authorities in the Member States so as to give contractors in the Community adequate information on the work to be done and the conditions attached thereto, and thus enable them to determine whether the proposed contracts are of interest. At the time additional information concerning contracts must, as is customary in the Member States, be given in the contract documents for each contract or else in an equivalent document (cf. ninth and tenth recital in the preamble to the directive).

2 3 The different aspects of the question put by the national court must be examined in the light of the foregoing.

2 4 In this case specific experience relating to the work to be carried out was a criterion for determining the technical knowledge and ability of the tenderers. It is therefore a legitimate criterion for checking contractors' suitability under Articles 20 and 26 of the Directive.

2 5 The exclusion of a tenderer because its tender appears less acceptable to the authorities awarding the contract was provided for, as appears from the documents before the Court, in Article 21 of the Uniform Rules. Under Article 21 (3), 'the contract shall be awarded to the tenderer whose tender appears the most acceptable to the awarding authority".

2 6 The compatibility of such a provision with the directive depends on its interpretation under national law. It would be incompatible with Article 29 of the Directive it its effect was to confer on the authorities awarding contracts unrestricted freedom of choice as regards the awarding of the contract to a tenderer.

2 7 On the other hand, such a provision is not incompatible with the directive if it is to be interpreted as giving the authorities awarding contracts discretion to compare the different tenders and to accept the most advantageous on the basis of objective criteria such as those listed by way of example in Article 29 (2) of the Directive.

2 8 As regards the exclusion of a tenderer on the ground that it is not in a position to employ long-term unemployed persons, it should be noted in the first place that such a condition has no relation to the checking of contractors' suitability on the basis of their economic and financial standing

and their technical knowledge and ability or to the criteria for the award of contracts referred to in Article 29 of the Directive.

2 9 It follows from judgment of 9 July 1987, cited above, that in order to be compatible with the directive such a condition must comply with all the relevant provisions of Community law, in particular the prohibitions flowing from the principles laid down in the Treaty in regard to the right of establishment and the freedom to provide services.

3 0 The obligation to employ long-term unemployed persons could inter alia infringe the prohibition of discrimination on grounds of nationality laid down in the first paragraph of Article 7 of the Treaty if it became apparent that such a condition could be satisfied only by tenderers from the State concerned or indeed that tenderers from other Member States would have difficulty in complying with it. It is for the national court to determine, in the light of all the circumstances of the case, whether the imposition of such a condition is directly or indirectly discriminatory.

3 1 Even if the criteria considered above are not in themselves incompatible with the directive, they must be applied in conformity with all the procedural rules laid down in the directive, in particular the rules on advertising. It is therefore necessary to interpret those provisions in order to determine what requirements must be met by the various criteria referred to by the national court.

3 2 It appears from the documents before the Court that in this case the criterion of specific experience relating to the work to be carried out and that of the most acceptable tender were not mentioned in the contract documents or in the contract notice; these criteria are derived from Article 21 of the Uniform Rules, to which the notice made a general reference. On the other hand, the requirement regarding the employment of long-term unemployed persons was the subject of special provisions in the contract documents and was expressly mentioned in the notice published in the Official Journal of the European Communities.

3 3 As regards the criterion of specific experience relating to the work to be carried out, it should be stated that although the last sentence of Article 26 of the Directive requires the authorities awarding contracts to specify in the contract notice which of the references concerning the technical knowledge and ability of the contractor are to be produced, it does not require them to list in the notice the criteria on which they propose to base their assessment of the contractors' suitability.

3 4 Nevertheless, in order for the notice to fulfil its role of enabling contractors in the Community to determine whether a contract is of interest to them, it must contain at least some mention of the specific conditions which a contractor must meet in order to be considered suitable to tender for the contract in question. However, such a mention cannot be required

where, as in this case, the condition is not a specific condition of suitability but a criterion which is inseparable from the very notion of suitability.

3 5 As regards the criterion of "the most acceptable offer", it should be noted that even if such a criterion were compatible with the directive in the circumstances set out above, it is clear from the wording of Article 29 (1) and (2) of the Directive that where the authorities awarding the contract do not take the lowest price as the sole criterion for awarding the contract but have regard to various criteria with a view to awarding the contract to the most economically advantageous tender, they are required to state these criteria in the contract notice or the contract documents. Consequently, a general reference to a provision of national legislation cannot satisfy the publicity requirement.

3 6 A condition such as the employment of long-term unemployed persons is an additional sepecific condition and must therefore be mentioned in the notice, so that contractors may become aware of its existence.

3 7 In reply to the second question put by the national court it should therefore be stated that:

- the criterion of specific experience for the work to be carried out is a legitimate criterion of technical ability and knowledge for the purpose of ascertaining the suitability of contractors. Where such a criterion is laid down by a provision of national legislation to which the contract notice refers, it is not subject to the specific requirements laid down in the directive concerning publication in the contract notice or the contract document;

- the criterion of "the most acceptable tender", as laid down by a provision of national legislation, may be compatible with the directive if it reflects the discretion which the authorities awarding contracts have in order to determine the most economically advantageous tender on the basis of objective criteria and thus does not involve an element of arbitrary choice. It follows from Article 29 (1) and (2) of the Directive that where the authorities awarding contracts do not take the lowest price as the sole criterion for the award of a contract but have regard to various criteria with a view to awarding the contract to the most economically advantageous tender, they are required to state those criteria in the contract notice or the contract documents;

- the condition relating to the employment of long-term unemployed persons is compatible with the directive if it has no direct or indirect discriminatory effect on tenderers from other Member States of the Community. An additional specific condition of this kind must be mentioned in the contract notice.

The third question

3 8   The third question seeks in substance to establish whether Articles 20, 26 and 29 of Directive 71/305 may be relied upon by individuals before the national courts.

3 9   As the Court held in its judgment of 10 April 1984 in Case 14/83 (Von Colson and Kamann v Land Nordrhein-Westfalen [1984] ECR 1891),the Member States' obligation arising from a directive to achieve the result envisaged by the directive and their duty under Article 5 of the Treaty to take all appropriate measures, whether general or particular, to ensure fulfilment of that obligation are binding on all the authorities of the Member States, including, for matters within their jurisdiction, the courts. It follows that in applying national law, in particular the provisions of a national law specifically introduced in order to implement a directive, national courts are required to interpret their national law in the light of the wording and the purpose of the directive in order to achieve the result referred to in the third paragraph of Article 189 of the Treaty.

4 0   Furthermore, the court has consistently held (see most recently the judgment of 26 February 1986 in Case 152/84, Marshall v Southampton and South-West Hampshire Health Authority [1986] ECR 723) that where the provisions of a directive appear, as far as their subject-matter is concerned, to be unconditional and sufficiently precise, those provisions may be relied on by individuals against the State where that State fails to implement the directive in national law within the prescribed period or where it fails to implement the directive correctly.

4 1   It is therefore necessary to consider whether the provisions of Directive 71/305 in question are, as far as their subject-matter is concerned, unconditional and sufficiently precise to be related on by an individual against the State.

4 2   As the Court held in its judgment of 10 February 1982 in Case 76/81 (Transporoute v Minister of Public Works [1982] ECR 417), in relation to Article 29, the Directive's rules regarding participation and advertising are intended to protect tenderers against arbitrariness on the part of the authority awarding contracts.

4 3   To this end, as has been stated in relation to the reply to the second question, the rules in question provide inter alia that in checking the suitability of contractors the awarding authorities must apply criteria of economic and financial standing and technical knowledge and ability, and that contract is to be awarded either solely on the basis of the lowest price or on the basis of several criteria relating to the tender. They also set out the requirements regarding publication of the criteria adopted by the awarding authorities and the references to be produced.   Since no specific implementation measure is necessary for compliance with these

requirements, the resulting obligations for the Member States are therefore unconditional and sufficiently precise.

4 4 In reply to the third question it should therefore be stated that the provisions of Article 20, 26 and 29 of Directive 71/305 may be relied on by an individual before the national courts.

Costs

4 5 The costs incurred by the Commission of the European Communities and by the Italian Republic are not recoverable. As these proceedings are, in so far as the parties to the main proceedings are concerned, a step in the action before the national court, the decision on costs is a matter for that court.

On those grounds,

THE COURT (Fourth Chamber)

in answer to the questions referred to in it by the Arrondissementsrechtbank, The Hague, by a judgment of 28 January 1987, hereby rules:

1. Directive 71/305 applies to public works contracts awarded by a body as the local land consolidation committee.

2. The criterion of specific experience for the work to be carried out is a legitimate criterion of technical ability and knowledge for the purpose of ascertaining the suitability of contractors. Where such a criterion is laid down by a provision of national legislation to which the contract notice refers, it is not subject to the specific requirements laid down in the directive concerning publication in the contract notice or the contract documents.

The criterion of "the most acceptable tender", as laid down by a provision of national legislation, may be compatible with the directive if it reflects the discretion which the authorities awarding contracts have in order to determine the most economically advantageous tender on the basis of objective criteria and thus does not involve an element of arbitrary choice. It follows from Article 29 (1) and (2) of the directive that where the authorities awarding contracts do not take the lowest price as the sole criterion for the award of a contract but have regard to various criteria with a view to awarding the contract to the most

economically advantageous tender, they are required to state those criteria in the contract documents.

The condition relating to the employment of long-term unemployed persons is compatible with the directive of it has no direct or indirect discriminatory effect on tenderers from other Member States of the Community. An additional specific condition of this kind must be mentioned in the contract notice.

3. The provisions of Articles 20, 26 and 29 of Directive 71/305 may be relied on by an individual before the national courts.

Rodriguez Iglesias   Koopmans,   Kakouris

Delivered in open court in Luxembourg on 20 September 1988

J.G. Giraud   Rodriguez Iglesias
Registrar   President of the Fourth Chamber

Case C-3/88, Commission of the European Communities v Italy

(for discussion see 9. above)

JUDGMENT

1   By an application lodged at the Court registry on 6 January 1988 the Commission of the European Communities brought an action under Article 169 of the EEC Treaty seeking a declaration that, by adopting provisions under which only companies in which all or a majority of the shares are either directly or indirectly in public or State ownership may conclude agreements with the Italian state for the development of data-processing systems for the public authorities, the Italian Republic has failed to fulfil its obligations under Article 52 and 59 of the EEC Treaty and Council Directive 77/62 EEC of 12 December 1976 coordinating procedures for the award of public supply contracts (Official Journal 1977 No. L 13, p. 1, hereinafter referred to as "the directive").

2   It had come to the Commission's notice that the legislation in force in Italy authorized the State to conclude agreements, in a number of sectors of public activity (Taxation, health, agriculture and urban property), only with companies in which all or a majority of the shares were directly or indirectly in public or State ownership. The Commission considered that those rules were contrary to the above-mentioned provisions of Community law, and on 3 December 1985 it addressed a letter of formal notice to the Italian Government, thus setting in motion the procedure provided for in Article 169 of the Treaty.

3   On 1 July 1986, as no communication had been received from the Italian Government, the commission delivered the reasoned opinion provided for in the first paragraph of Article 169 of the Treaty.

4   At the request of the Italian Government, two meetings were held with officials of the Commission, one in Rome on 25 to 27 January 1987 and the other in Brussels on 10 March 1987, with a view to clarifying the situation. On 5 May 1987, the Italian Government statated its position on the reasoned opinion. The Commission considered that position unsatisfactory and decided to bring the present action.

5   Reference is made to the Report for the Hearing for a fuller account of the Italian legislation in issue, the course of the procedure and the

submissions and arguments of the parties, which are mentioned or discussed hereinafter only in so far as is necessary for the reasoning of the Court.

Failure to comply with Articles 52 and 59 of the EEC Treaty

6   In the Commission's view, by providing that only companies in which all or a majority of the shares are directly or indirectly in public or State ownership may conclude agreements for the development of data-processing systems for the public authorities, the laws and decree-laws in issue, although applicable without distinction to Italian undertakings and to those of other Member States, are discriminatory and constitute a barrier to the freedom of establishment and the freedom to provide services laid down in Article 52 and 59 of the Treaty.

7   The Italian Government claims first of all that the Laws and Decree-Laws in dispute make no distinction on the basis of the nationality of companies which may conclude the agreements in issue. Consequently, since the Italian State owns all or a majority of the share capital not only in certain Italian companies but also in certain companies of other Member States, both types of company may take part without any discrimination in the establishment of the data-processing systems in issue.

8   According to the Court's case-law the principle of equal treatment, of which Articles 52 and 59 of the Treaty embody specific instances, prohibits not only overt discrimination by reason of nationality but also all covert forms of discrimination which, by the application of other criteria of differentiation, lead in fact to the same result (see, in particular, the judgment of 29 October 1980 in Case 22/80, Boussac v Gerstenmeier [1980] ECR 3427).

9   Although the Laws and Decree-Laws in issue apply without discrimination to all companies, whether of Italian or foreign nationality, they essentially favour Italian companies. As the Commission has pointed out, without being contradicted by the Italian Government, there are at present no data-processing companies from other Member States all or the majority of whose shares are in Italian public ownership.

10   In justification of the public ownership requirement, the Italian Government claims that it is necessary for the public authorities to control the performance of the contracts in order to adapt the work to meet developments which were unforeseeable at the time when the contracts were signed. It also claims that for certain types of activity which the companies have to carry out, particularly in strategic sectors, which involve, as in the resent case, confidential data, the State must be able to employ an undertaking in which it can have complete confidence.

11   In that regard it must be stated that the Italian Government had sufficient legal powers at its disposal to be able to adapt the performance of

contracts to meet future and unforeseeable circumstances and to ensure compliance with the general interest, and that in order to protect the confidential nature of the data in question the Government could have adopted measures less restrictive of freedom of establishment and freedom to provide services than those in issue, in particular by imposing a duty of secrecy on the staff of the companies concerned, breach of which might give rise to criminal proceedings. There is nothing in the documents before the Court to suggest that the staff of companies none of whose share capital is in Italian public ownership could not comply just as effectively with such a duty.

1 2 The Italian Government also maintains that in view of their confidential nature the activities necessary for the operation of the data-processing systems in question are connected with the exercise of official authority within the meaning of Article 55.

1 3 As the Court has already held (see the judgment of 21 June 1974 in Case 2/74, Reyners v Belgium [197] ECR 631), the exception to freedom of establishment and freedom to provide services provided for by the first paragraph of Article 55 and by Article 66 of the EEC Treaty must be restricted to those of the activities referred to in Article 52 and 59 which in themselves involve a direct and specific connection with the exercise of official authority. That is not the case here, however, since the activities in question, which concern the design, programming and operation of data-processing systems, are of a technical nature and thus unrelated to the exercise of official authority.

1 4 Finally, the Italian Government claims that in view of the purpose of the data-processing systems in question and the confidential nature of the data processed, the activities necessary for their operation concern Italian public policy within the meaning of Article 56 (1) of the Treaty.

1 5 That argument must also be dismissed. It need merely be pointed out that the nature of the aims purposed by the data-processing systems in question is not sufficient to establish that there would be any threat to public policy if companies from other Member States were awarded the contracts for the establishment and operation of those systems. It must also be borne in mind that the confidential nature of the data processed by the systems could be protected, as stated above, by duty of secrecy, without there being any need to restrict freedom of establishment or freedom to provide services.

1 6 It follows from the foregoing considerations that the claim based on failure to comply with Articles 52 and 59 of the Treaty must be upheld.

Failure to comply with Directive 77/62/EEC

1 7   The Commission considers that the Laws and Decree-Laws in issue infringe the provisions of the directive as regards the purchase by the public authorities of the equipment necessary for the establishment of the data-processing systems in question. Since such equipment is to be regarded as "products" within the meaning of Article 1 (a) of the directive and since the value of the relevant public supply contracts exceeds the amount fixed in Article 5, the competent authorities should have followed the award procedures prescribed in the directive and complied with the obligations laid down in Article 9, which requires notices of such contracts to be published in the Official Journal of the European Communities.

1 8   The Italian Government objects, first, that in addition to the purchase of the hardware a data-processing system comprises the creation of software, the planning, installation, maintenance and technical commissioning of the system and sometimes its operation. The interdependence of those activities means that complete responsibility for the establishment of the data-processing systems provided for by the Laws and Decree-Laws in issue must be given to a single company. Therefore, and bearing in mind that the hardware is an ancillary element in the establishment of a data-processing system, the directive is inapplicable. The Italian Government adds that according to Article 1 (a) of the directive the concept of public supply contracts covers only contracts the principal object of which is the delivery of products.

1 9   That argument cannot be accepted. The purchase of the equipment required for the establishment of a data-processing system can be separated from the activities involved in its design operation. The Italian Government could have approached companies specializing in software development for the design of the data-processing systems in question and, in compliance with the directive, could have purchased hardware meeting the technical specifications laid down by such companies.

2 0   The Italian Government then claims that Council Decision 79/783/EEC of 11 September 1979 adopting a multiannual programme (1979 to 1983) in the field of data-processing (Official Journal 1979 No. L 231, p. 23), as amended by Decision 84/559/EEC of 22 November 1984 (Official Journal 1984 No. L 308, p. 49) should be interpreted as meaning that until such time as the programme is completed the temporary exemption referred to in Article 6 (1) (h) of the directive is to remain in force.

2 1   Under that provision, contracting authorities need not apply the procedures provided for in Article 4 (1) and (2) "for equipment supply contracts in the field of data-processing, and subject to any decisions of the Council taken on a proposal from the Commission and defining the categories of material to which the present exception does not apply. There

can no longer be recourse to the present exception after 1 January 1981 other than by a decision of the Council taken on a proposal from the Commission to modify this date".

2 2   The decisions mentioned by the Italian Government were adopted on the basis of Article 235 of the Treaty and not pursuant to Article 6 (1) (h) of the directive. They relate to the implementation of a programme in the field of data processing which does not concern, either directly or indirectly, the rules applicable to contracts for the supply of data-processing equipment.

2 3   In the Italian Government's submission, the supply contracts in issue also fall within the exceptions provided for in Article 6 (1) (g) of the directive, which authorizes contracting authorities not to follow the procedures referred to in Article 4 (1) and (2) "when supplies are declared secret or when their delivery must be accompanied by special security measures in accordance with the provisions laid down by law, regulation or administrative action in force in the Member State concerned, or when the protection of the basic interests of the State's security so requires". It refers, in that regard, to the secret nature of the data involved, which is essential in the fight against crime, particularly in the areas of taxation, public health and fraud in agricultural matters.

2 4   That objection concerns the confidential nature of the data entered in the data-processing systems in question. As has already been pointed out, however, observance of confidentiality by the concerned is not dependent on the public ownership of the contracting company.

2 5   The Italian Government also claims that the activities to be carried out by the specialized companies chosen for the development of the data-processing systems in question constitute a public service activity. Agreements concluded between the State and the companies chosen to carry out those activities are therefore excluded from the scope of the directive, Article 2 (3) of which provides:

"When the State, a regional or local authority or one of the legal persons governed by public law or corresponding bodies specified in Annex 1 grants to a body other than the contracting authority - regardless of its legal status - special or exclusive rights to engage in a public service activity, the instrument granting this right shall stipulate that the body in question must observe the principle of non-discrimination by nationality when awarding public supply contracts to third parties".

2 6   That argument cannot be accepted. The supply of the equipment required for the establishment of a data-processing system and the design and operation of the system enable the authorities to carry out their duties but do not in themselves constitute a public service.

2 7   Finally, the Italian Government claims that the derogation provided for in Article 6 (1) (e) of the directive should be applied in the case of the data-processing system at the Finance Ministry. Under that subparagraph,

contracting authorities need not apply the procedures referred to in Article 4 (1) and (2) "for additional deliveries by the original supplier which are intended either as part replacement of normal supplies or installations, or as the extension of existing supplies or installations where a change of supplier would compel the contracting authority to purchase equipment having different technical characteristics which would result in incompatibility or disproportionate technical difficulties of operation or maintenance".

2 8 In that regard it is sufficient to note that such cases of additional deliveries cannot justify a general rule that only companies in which all or a majority of the share capital is in Italian public ownership may be awarded supply contracts.

2 9 It follows from the foregoing that the claim based on failure to comply with Directive 77/62/EEC must also be upheld.

3 0 It must therefore be held that by providing that only companies in which all or a majority of the shares are either directly or indirectly in public or State ownership may conclude agreements for the development of data-processing systems for the public authorities, the Italian Republic has failed to fulfil its obligations under Articles 52 and 59 of the EEC Treaty and Council Directive 77/62/EEC of 21 December 1976.

Costs

Under Article 69 (2) of the Rules of Procedure, the unsuccessful party is to be ordered to pay the costs. Since the defendant has failed in its submissions, it must be ordered to pay the costs.

On those grounds,

THE COURT

hereby:

1. Declares that by providing that only companies in which all or a majority of the shares are either directly or indirectly in public or State ownership may conclude agreements for the development of data-processing systems for the public authorities, the Italian Republic has failed to fulfil its obligations under Articles 52 and 59 of the EEC Treaty and Council Directive 77/62/EEC of 21 December 1976;

2. Orders the Italian Republic to pay costs.

Due,   Slynn,   Schockweiler,   Mancini,

Joliet,   Moitinho de Almeida,   Rodriguez Iglesias

Delivered in open court in Luxembourg on 5 December 1989.

J.G. Giraud,   O. Due
Registrar   President

Case 21/88, Du Pont de Nemours Italiana Spa v Unità Sanitaria Locale No. 2 Di Carrara

20th March 1990

(for discussion see 10. above)

JUDGMENT

1   By order of 1 April 1987, which was received at the Court on 20 January 1988, the Tribunale Amministrativo Regionale della Toscana (Regional Administrative Tribunal for Tuscany) referred three questions to the Court pursuant to Article 177 of the EEC Treaty for a preliminary ruling on the interpretation of Articles 30, 92 and 93 of the EEC Treaty in order to determine the compatibility with those provisions of Italian rules reserving to undertakings established in the Mezzogiorno (Southern Italy) a proportion of public supply contracts.

2   Those questions were raised in a dispute between Du Pont de Nemours Italiana SpA, supported by Du Pont de Nemours Deutschland GmbH, and Unità Sanitaria Locale No. 2 di Carrara (Local Health Authority No. 2, Carrara, hereinafter referred to as "the local health authority"), supported by 3M Italia SpA, concerning the conditions governing the award of contracts for the supply of radiological films and liquids.

3   Under Article 17 (16) and (17) of Law No. 64 of 1 March 1986 (Disciplina Organica dell' Intervento Straordinario nel Mezzogiorno - system of rules governing special aid for Southern Italy), the Italian State extended to all public bodies and authorities, as well as to bodies and companies in which the State has a shareholding, and including local health authorities situated throughout Italy, the obligation to obtain at least 30% of their supplies from and agricultural undertakings and small businesses established in Southern Italy in which the products concerned undergo processing.

4   In accordance with the provisions of that national legislation, the local health authority laid down by decision of 3 June 1986 the conditions governing a restricted tendering procedure for the supply of radiological films and liquids. According to the special terms and conditions set out in the annex, it divided the contract into two lots, one, equal to 30% of the total amount, being reserved to undertakings established in Southern Italy. Du Pont de Nemours Italiana challenged that decision before the Tribunale

Amministrativo Regionale della Toscana, on the ground that it had been excluded from the tendering procedure for that lot because it did not have an establishment in Southern Italy. By decision of 15 July 1986 the local health authority proceeded to award the contract for the lot corresponding to 70% of the total amount in question. Du Pont de Nemours Italiana also challenged that decision before the same court.

5   In the course of its consideration of the two actions the national court decided to request the Court to give a preliminary ruling on the following questions:

1.   Must Article 30 of the EEC Treaty, in so far as it imposes a prohibition on quantitative restrictions on imports and all measures having equivalent effect, be interpreted as precluding the national legislation in question?

2.   Is the reserved quota which is provided for by Article 17 of Law No. 64 of 1 March 1986 in the nature of "aid" within the meaning of Article 92 inasmuch as it is intended "to promote the economic development" of a region "where the standard of living is abnormally low" by leading to the establishment of undertakings so as to contribute to the socio-economic development of such areas?

3   Does Article 93 of the EEC Treaty confer exclusively on the Commission the power to determine whether aid within the meaning of Article 92 of the EEC Treaty is permissible, or is that power also vested in the national court to be exercised in connection with the examination of any conflicts arising between national law and Community law?

6   Reference is made to the Report for the Hearing for a fuller account of the facts, the application legislation and the written observations submitted to the Court, which are mentioned or discussed hereinafter only in so far as is necessary for the reasoning of the Court.

A - First question

7   In its first question, the national court seeks to ascertain whether national rules reserving to undertakings established in certain regions of the national territory a proportion of public supply contracts are contrary to Article 30, which prohibits quantitative restrictions on imports and all measures having equivalent effect.

8   It must be stated in limine that, as the Court has consistently held since the judgment in Dassonville (judgment of 11 July 1974 in Case 8/74, Procureur du Roi v Dassonville [1974] ECR 837, paragraph 5), Article 30, by prohibiting as between Member States measures having an effect

equivalent to quantitative restrictions on imports, applies to all trading rules which are capable of hindering, directly or indirectly, actually or potentially, intra-Community trade.

9 It must be pointed out, moreover, that according to the first recital in the preamble to Council Directive 77/62/EEC of 21 December 1976 co-ordinating procedures for the award of public supply contracts (Official Journal 1977 No. L 13, p. 1), which was in force at the material time, "restrictions on the free movement of goods in respect of public supplies are prohibited by the terms of Article 30 et seq. of the Treaty"

1 0 Accordingly, it is necessary to determine the effect which a preferential system of the kind at issue in this case is likely to have on the free movement of goods.

1 1 It must be pointed out in that regard that such a system, which favours goods processed in a particular region of a Member State, prevents the authorities and public bodies concerned from procuring some of the supplies they need from undertakings situated in other Member States. Accordingly, it must held that products originating in other Member States suffer discrimination in comparison with products manufactured in the Member State in question, with the result that the normal course of intra-Community trade is hindered.

1 2 That conclusion is not affected by the fact that the restrictive effects of a preferential system of the kind at issue are borne in the same measure both by products manufactured by undertakings from the Member State in question which are not situated in the region covered by the preferential system and by products manufactured by undertakings established in other Member States.

1 3 It must be emphasized in the first place that, although not all the products of the Member State in question benefit by comparison with products from abroad, the fact remains that all the products benefiting by the preferential system are domestic products; secondly, the fact that the restrictive effect exercised by a State measure on imports does not benefit all domestic products but only some cannot exempt the measure in question from the prohibition set out in Article 30.

1 4 Furthermore, it must be observed that, on account of its discriminatory character, a system such as the one at issue cannot be justified in the light of the imperative requirements recognized by the Court in its case-law; such requirements may be taken into consideration only in relation to measures which are applicable to domestic products and to imported products without distinction (judgment of 17 June 1981 in Case 113/80, Commission v Ireland [1981] ECR 1625).

1 5 It must be added that neither does such a system fall within the scope of the exceptions exhaustively listed in Article 36 of the Treaty.

1 6   However, the italian Government has invoked Article 26 of Directive 77/62 (cited above), which provides that "this Directive shall not prevent the implimention of provisions contained in Italian Law No. 835 of October 1950 (Official Gazette No. 245 of 24 October 1950 of the Italian Republic) and in modifications thereto in force on the date on which this Directive is adopted; this is without prejudice to the compatibility of these provisions with the Treaty".

1 7   It should be pointed out in that regard, first, that the content of the national legislation to which the national court refers (Law No. 64/86) is in some respects different and more extensive than it was at the time of the adoption of the directive (Law No. 835/50) and, secondly, that Article 26 specifies that the directive is to apply "without prejudice to the compatibility of these provisions with the Treaty". In any event, the directive cannot be interpreted as authorizing the application of national legislation whose provisions are contrary to those of the Treaty and consequently, as impeding the application of Article 30 in a case such as this.

1 8   It must be therefore stated in answer to the national court's first question that Article 30 must be interpreted as precluding national rules which reserve to undertakings established in particular regions of the national territory a proportion of public supply contracts.

B - Second question

1 9   In its second question, the national court seeks to establish whether in the event that the rules in question might be regarded as aid within the meaning of Article 92 that might exempt them from the prohibition set out in Article 30.

2 0   In that regard, it is sufficient to recall that, as the Court has consistently held (see, in particular, the judgment of 5 June 1986 in Case 103/84, Commission v Italy [1986] ECR 1759), Article 92 may in no case be used to frustrate the rules of the Treaty on the free movement of goods. It is clear from the relevant case-law that those rules and the Treaty provisions relating to State aid have a common purpose, namely to ensure the free movement of goods between Member States under normal conditions of competition. As the Court made clear in the judgment cited above, the fact that a national measure might be regarded as aid within the meaning of Article 92 is therefore not a sufficient reason to exempt it from the prohibition contained in Article 30.

2 1   In the light of that case-law - there being no need to consider whether the rules in question are in the nature of aid - it must be stated in answer to the national court's second question that the fact that national rules might be

regarded as aid within the meaning of Article 92 cannot exempt them from the prohibition set out in Article 30.

C - Third question

2 2 It follows from the answers given to the preceding questions that, in a case such as this, the national court must ensure the full application of Article 30. Accordingly, the third question, which is concerned with the role of the national court in assessing the compatibility of aid with Article 92, has become otiose.

Costs

2 3 The costs incurred by the Italian Government, the French Government and the Commission of the European Communities, which have submitted observations to the Court, are not recoverable. As these proceedings are, in so far as the parties to the main proceedings are concerned, in the nature of a step in the proceedings before the national court, the decision on costs is a matter for that court.

On those grounds,

THE COURT,

in answer to the questions submitted to it by the Tribunale Amministrativo Regionale della Toscana, by order of 1 April 1987, hereby rules:

1. Article 30 of the EEC Treaty must be interpreted as precluding national rules which reserve to undertakings established in particular regions of the national territory a proportion of public supply contracts.
2. The fact that national rules might be regarded as aid within the meaning of Article 92 of the Treaty cannot exempt them from the prohibition set out in Article 30 of the Treaty.

Due,	Kakouris,	Schockweiler,	Zuleeg,
Koopmans,	Mancini,	Joliet,	Moitinho de Almeida,
Rodriguez Iglesias,		Grévisse,	Diez de Velasco

Delivered in open court in Luxembourg on 20 March 1990.

J.G. Giraud,   O. Due
Registrar   President

Case 103/88, Fratelli Costanzo Spa v Commune di Milano

(for discussion see 11. above)

JUDGMENT

1   By order of 16 December 1987, which was received at the Court registry on 30 March 1988, the Tribunale Amministrativo Regionale per la Lombardia referred to the Court for a preliminary ruling under Article 177 of the EEC Treaty a number of questions on the interpretation of Article 29 (5) of Council Directive 71/305/EEC of 26 July 1971 concerning the co-ordination of procedures for the award of public works contracts (Official journal, English Special Edition 1971 (II), p. 682 and the third paragraph of Article 189 of the EEC Treaty.

2   The questions were raised in proceedings brought by Fratelli Costanzo SpA. (hereinafter referred to as "Costanzo"), the plaintiff in the main proceedings, foar the annulment of a decision of the Giunta Municipale (Municipal Executive Board) of Milan eliminating the tender submitted by Costanzo from a tendering procedure for a public works contract and warding the contract in question to Ing. Lodigiani Spa. (hereinafter: "Lodigiani").

3   Article 29 (5) of Council Directive 71/305/EEC provides as follows:

"If, for a given contract, tenders are obviously abnormally low in relation to the transaction, the authority awarding contracts shall examine the details of the tenders before deciding to whom it will award the contract. The result of this examination shall be taken into account.

For this purpose it shall request the tenderer to furnish the necessary explanations and, where appropriate, it shall indicate which parts it finds unacceptable.

If the documents relating to the contract provide for its award at the lowest price tendered, the authority awarding conracts must justify to the Advisory Committee set up by the Council Decision of 26 July 1971 the rejection of tenders which it considers to be too low."

4   Article 29 (5) of Directive 71/305 was implemented in Italy by the third paragraph of Article 24 of Law No. 584 of 8 August 1977 amending the procedures for the award of public works contracts in accordance with the

directives of the European Economic Community (Gazzetta Ufficiale della Repubblica Italiana (Official journal of the Italian Republic) No. 232 of August 1977, p. 6272). That provision is worded as follows:

"If for a given contract, tenders are abnormally low in relation to the transaction, the authority awarding the contract shall, after requesting the tenderer to furnish the necessary explanations and after indicating, where appropriate, which part it considers unacceptable, examine the details of the tenders and may disallow them if it takes the view that they are not valid; in that event, if the call for tenders provides that the lowest tender price is the criterion for the award of the contract, the awarding authority is obliged to notify the rejection of the tenders, together with its reasons for doing so, to the Ministry of Public Works, which is responsible for forwarding the information to the Advisory Committee for Public Works Contracts of the European Economic Community within the period laid down by the first paragraph of Article 6 of this Law."

5   Subsequently, in 1987, the Italian Government adopted three decree laws in succession which provisionally amended the third paragraph of Article 24 of Law No. 584 (Decree Law No. 206 of 25 May 1987, Gazzetta Ufficiale No. 120 of 26 May 1987, p. 5; Decree Law No. 302 of 27 July 1987, Gazzetta Ufficiale No. 174 of 28 July 1987, p. 3; and Decree Law No. 393 of 25 September 1987, Gazetta Ufficiale No. 225 of 26 September 1987, p. 3).

6   The three decree laws each contain an Article 4 worded identical terms, as follows:

"In order to speed up the procedures for the award of public works contracts, for a period of two years from the date on which this decree enters into force tenders with a percentage discount greater than the average percentage divergence of the tenders admitted, increased by a percentage which must be stated in the call for tenders, shall be considered abnormal for the purposes of the third paragraph of Article 24 of Law No. 584 of 8 August 1977 and shall be excluded from the tendering procedure."

7   The decree laws lapsed because they were not converted into laws within the period prescribed by the Italian constitution. However, a subsequent law provided that the effects of legal measures adopted pursuant to them e=were to remain valid (Article 1 (2) of Law No. 478 of 25 November 1987, Gazzetta Ufficiale No. 277 of 26 November 1987, p. 3).

8   In preparation for the 1990 World Cup for football, to be held in Italy, the Comune di Milano issued a restricted call for tenders for alteration work

on a football stadium. The criterion chosen for awarding the contract was that of the lowest price.

9 The call for tenders stated that in accordance with Article 4 of Decree Law No. 206 of May 1987 tenders which exceeded the basic amount fixed for the price of the work by a percentage more than ten points below the average percentage by which the tenders admitted exceeded that amount would be considered anomalous and consequently eliminated.

1 0 The tenders admitted to the procedure exceeded the basic amount fixed for the price of the work by an average of 19.48%. In accordance with the call for tenders any tender which did not exceed the basic amount by at least 9.48% was to be automatically eliminated.

1 1 The tender submitted by Costanzo was less than the basic amount. Accordingly, on 6 October 1987 the Giunta Municipale, on the basis of Article 4 of Decree Law No. 393 of 25 September 1987, which in the meantime had replaced the decree law cited in the call for tenders, decided to exclude Constanzo's bid from the tendering procedure and to award the contract to Lodigiani, which had submitted the lowest tender of those which fulfilled the condition set out in the call for tenders.

1 2 Costanzo challenged that decision in proceedings before the Tribunale Amministativo Regionale per la Lombardia, claiming inter alia that it was illegal on the ground that it was based on a decree law which was itself incompatible with Article 29 (5) of Council Directive 71/305.

1 3 The national court therefore referred the following questions to the Court of Justice for a preliminary ruling:

"a. Given that, under Article 189 of the EEC Treaty, the provisions contained in a directive may relate to the 'result to be achieved' (hereinafter referred to as 'provisions as to results') or else be concerned with the 'form and methods' required to achieve a given result (hereinafter referred to as 'provisions as to form and methods'), is the rule contained in Article 29 (5) of Council Directive 71/305/EEC of 26 July 1971 (where it provides that - should a tender be obviously abnormally low - the authority must 'examine the details' of the tender and request the tenderer to furnish the necessary explanations, indicating where appropriate which parts it finds unacceptable) a 'provision as to results' and therefore of such a nature that the Italian Republic was obliged to 'transpose' it without any amendment of substance (as indeed it did, by the third paragraph of Article 24 of Law No. 584 of 8 August 1977) or is it a 'provision as to form and methods', with the result that the Italian Republic could derogate from it by providing that where a tender is abnormally low the tenderer must automatically be eliminated from the tendering procedure, without any 'examination of the details' and without any request to the tenderer to furnish 'explanations' for the 'abnormal tender'?

b   If the reply to Question (a) is negative (in the sense that Article 29 (5) of Council Directive 71/305/EEC is to be held to be a 'provision as to form and methods'):

b 1 If the Italian Republic (after "transposing" the aforesaid provision by way of Law No. 577 of 5 August 1977 without introducing any amendment of substance regarding the procedure to be followed in cases where a tender is abnormally low) retain the power to amend the domestic implementing provision? In particular, could Article 4 of Decree Law No. 206 of 25 May 1987,.Decree Law No. 302 of 27 July 1987 and Decree Law No. 393 of 25 September 1987 (whose wording is identical) amend Article 24 of Law No. 584 of 8 August 1977?

b.2   Could the (identically worded) Articles 4 of the decree laws mentioned above amend Article 29 (5) of Council Directive 71/305/EEC, as implemented by Law No. 584 of 5 April 1977, without stating adequate reasons therefore,regard being had to the fact that a statement of reasons - which is necessary for Community legislation (cf. Article 190 of the Treaty) - appears also to be necessary for domestic legislation introduced to give effect to Community provisions (which is therefore 'sub-primary' legislation and, in the absence of indication to the contrary, must also be subject to the rule which requires 'primary' legislation to state reasons)?

c.   Is there, in any event, a conflict between Article 29 (5) of Council Directive 71/305/EEC and the following provisions:

(a) the third paragraph of Article 24 of Law No. 584 of 8 August 1977 (which refers to 'abnormally low' tenders, whereas the directive is concerned with tenders which are 'obviously' abnormally low and provides for examination of the details only in cases of 'obvious' abnormality):

(b) Article 4 of Decree Laws Nos. 206 of 25 May 1987, 302 of 27 July 1987 and 393 of 25 September 1987 (which make no allowance for preliminary examination of the details or a request for clarification to the party concerned, contrary to Article 29 (5) of the Directive; furthermore, the decree laws mentioned above do not refer to 'obviously' abnormal tenders and to that extent appear to be invalid, as does Law No. 584 of 8 August 1977)?

d.   If the Court of Justice rules that the aforesaid Italian legislative provisions conflict with Article 29 (5) of Council Directive 71/305/EEC, was the municipal authority empowered, or obliged, to disregard the domestic provisions which conflicted with the aforesaid Community provision (consulting the central authorities if necessary), or does that power or obligation vest solely in the national courts?"

1 4 Reference is made to the Report for the Hearing for a fuller account of the facts of the case before the national court, the application legislation, the course of the procedure, and the written observations submitted to the Court, which are mentioned or discussed hereinafter only in so far as is necessary for the reasoning of the Court.

The second part of the third question and the first question

15 In the second part of the third question the Tribunale Amministrativo Regionale seeks in essence to establish whether Article 29 (5) of Council Directive 71/305 prohibits Member States from introducing provisions which require the automatic exclusion from procedures for the award of public works contracts of certain tenders determined according to a mathematical criterion, instead of obliging the awarding authority to apply the examination procedure laid down in the directive, giving the tenderer an opportunity to furnish explanations. In its first question it asks whether the Member States may, when implementing Council Directive 71/305, depart to any material extent from Article 29 (5) thereof.

16 With regard to the second part of the third question it should be noted that Article 29 (5) of Directive 71/305 requires the awarding authority to examine the details of tenders which are obviously abnormally low, and for that purpose obliges the authority to request the tenderer to furnish the necessary explanations. Article 29 (5) further requires the awarding authority, where appropriate, to indicate which parts of those explanations it finds unacceptable. Finally, if the criterion adopted for the award of the contract is the lowest price tendered, the awarding authority must justify to the Advisory Committee set up by the Council Decision of 26 July 1971 (Official Journal, English Special Edition 1971 (II), p. 693) the rejection of tenders which it considers to be too low.

17 The Comune di Milano and the Italian Government maintain that it is in keeping with the aim of Article 29 (5) to replace the examination procedure which it envisages, giving the tenderer an opportunity to state its views, with a mathematical criterion for exclusion. They point out that the aim of that provision is, as the Court ruled in its judgment of 10 February 1982 in Case 76/81 (Transporoute v Minister of Public Works [1982] ECR 417, at p. 428), to protect tenderers against arbitrariness on the part of the authority awarding the contract. A mathematical criterion for exclusion affords an absolute safeguard. It has the further advantage of being faster in its application than the procedure laid down by the directive.

18 That argument cannot be upheld. A mathematical criterion for exclusion deprives who have submitted exceptionally low renders of the opportunity of demonstrating that those tenders are genuine ones. The application of such a criterion is contrary to the aim of Directive 71/305, namely to promote the development of effective competition in the field of public contracts.

19 The answer to the second part of the third question must therefore be
that Article 29 (5) of Council Directive 71/305 prohibits Member States
from introducing provisions which require the automatic exclusion from
procedures for the award of public works contracts of certain tenders
determined according to a mathematical criterion, instead of obliging the
awarding authority to apply the examination procedure laid down in the
directive, giving the tenderer an opportunity to furnish explanations.

20 With regard to the first question, it should be observed that it was in
order to enable tenders submitting exceptionally low tenders to demonstrate
that those tenders are genuine ones that the Council, in Article 29 (5) of
Directive 71/305, laid down a precise, detailed procedure for the
examinations of tenders which appear to be abnormally low. That aim
would be jeopardized if Member States were able, when implementing
Article 29 (5) of the Directive, to depart from it to any material extent.

21 The answer to the first question must therefore be that when
implementing Council Directive 71/305 Member States may not depart to
any material extent from the provisions of Article 29 (5) thereof.

The second question

22 In its second question the national court asks whether, after
implementing Article 29 (5) of Council Directive 71/305 without departing
from it to any material extent, Member States may subsequently amend the
domestic implementing provision, and if so whether they must give reasons
for doing so.

23 The national court raised this question only in the event that the answer
to the first question should be that Member States could, when
implementing Article 29 (5) of Directive 71/305, depart materially from it.

24 In the light of the answer given to the first question the second question
is devoid of purpose.

The first part of the third question

25 In the first part of its third question the national court seeks to establish
whether Article 29 (5) of Council Directive 71/305 allows Member States
to require the examination of tenders whenever they appear to be abnormally
low, and not only when they are obviously abnormally low.

26 The examination procedure must be applied whenever the awarding
authority is contemplating the elimination of tenders because they are
abnormally low in relation to the transaction. Consequently, whatever the
threshold for the commencement of that procedure may be, tenderers can be
sure that they will not be disqualified from the award of the contract without

first having the opportunity of furnishing explanations regarding the genuine nature of their tenders.

2 7 It follows that the answer to be given to the first part of the third question is that Article 29 (5) of Council Directive 71/305 allows Member States to require that tenders be examined when those tenders appear to be abnormally low, and not only when they are obviously abnormally low.

The fourth question

2 8 In the fourth question the national court asks whether administrative authorities, are under the same obligations as a national court to apply the provisions of Article 29 (5) of Council Directive 71/305 and to refrain from applying provisions of national law which conflict with them.

2 9 In its judgments of 19 January 1982 in Case 8/81 (*Becker v Finanzamt Münster - Innenstadt* [1982] ECR 53, at p. 71) and 26 February 1986 in Case 152/84 (*Marshall v Southampton and South West Hampshire Area Health Authority* [1986] ECR 723, at p. 748) the Court held that wherever the provisions of a directive appear, as far as their subject-matter is concerned, to be unconditional and sufficiently precise, those provisions may be relied upon by an individual against the State where that State has failed to implement the directive in national law by the end of the period prescribed or where it has failed to implement the directive correctly.

3 0 It is important to note that the reason for which an individual may, in the circumstances described above, rely on the provisions of a directive in proceedings before the national courts is that the obligations arising under those provisions are binding upon all the authorities of the Member States.

3 1 It would, moreover, be contradictory to rule that an individual may rely upon the provisions of a directive which fulfil the conditions defined above in proceedings before the national courts seeking an order against the administrative authorities, and yet to hold that those authorities are under no obligations to apply the provisions of the directive and refrain from applying provisions of national law which conflict with them. It follows that when the conditions under which the Court has held that individuals may rely on the provisions of a directive before the national courts are met, all organs of the administration, including decentralized authorities such as municipalities, are obliged to apply those provisions.

3 2 With specific regard to Article 29 (5) of Directive 71/305, it is apparent from the discussion of the first question that it is unconditional and sufficiently precise to be relied upon by an individual against the State. An individual may therefore plead that provision before the national courts and, as is clear from the foregoing, all organs of the administration, including decentralized authorities such as municipalities, are obliged to apply it.

3 3 The answer to the fourth question must therefore be that administrative authorities, including municipal authorities, are under the same obligation as a national court to apply the provisions of Article 29 (5) of Council Directive 71/305/EEC and to refrain from applying provisions of national law which conflict with them.

Costs

3 4 The costs incurred by the Spanish Government, the Italian Government and the Commission of the European Communities, which have submitted observations to the Court, are not recoverable. As these proceedings are, in so far as the parties to the main proceedings are concerned, in the nature of a step in the action before the national court, the decision on costs is a matter for that court.

On those grounds,

THE COURT

in answer to the questions referred to it by the Tribunale Amministrativo Regionale per la Lombardia by order of 16 December 1987, hereby rules:

1. Article 29 (5) of Council Directive 71/305 prohibits Member States from introducing provisions which require the automatic exclusion from procedures for the award of public works contracts of certain tenders determined according to a mathematical criterion, instead of obliging the awarding authority to apply the examination procedure laid down in the directive, giving the tenderer an opportunity to furnish explanations.

When implementing Council Directive 71/305/EEC, Member States may not depart to any material extent from the provisions of Article 29(5) thereof.

Article 29 (5) of Council Directive 71/305 allows Member States to require that tenders be examined when those tenders appear to be abnormally low, and not only when they are obviously abnormally low.

Administrative authorities, including municipal Authorities, are under the same obligation as a national court to apply the provisions of Article 29 (5) of Council Directive 71/305/EEC and to refrain from applying provisions of national law conflict with them.

Due,   Joliet,   Grévisse,   Slynn,   Mancini,

Schockweiler,   Moitinho de Almedia

Delivered in open court in Luxembourg on 22 June 1989

J.G. Giraud   O. Due
Registrar   President

Case 194/88R, Commission of the European Communities v Italy

20th July 1988 and 27th September 1988

(for discussion see 12. above)

ORDER (20th July 1988)

1   As to the facts of the case, reference is made to the application made on 18 July 1988 in which the Commission requested the Court to order, by way of interim relief in accordance with Article 84 (2) of the Rules of Procedure, the suspension of the award of a public-works contract by the 'Consorzio per la costruzione e la gestione di un impianto per l'incenerimento e la trasformazione dei rifiuti solidi urbani'.

2   On the basis that the Commission's assertions may, at this stage of the proceedings, be regarded as true, it appears that the adoption of interim measures is necessary.

3   It is necessary to enable the Court to be sufficiently informed and in a position to judge a complex situation.

On those grounds,

THE PRESIDENT

by way of interlocutory decision,

hereby orders:

(1) The Italian Republic shall adopt all the necessary measures to suspend the award of a public-works contract by the Consorzio per la costruzione e la gestione di un impianto per l'incenerimento e la trasformazione dei rifiuti solidi urbani, whose headquarters are at the offices of the City of La Spezia, until 15 September 1988 or such other date as may be fixed by a subsequent order of the Court;

(2) The Italian Republic shall lodge its observations on the Commission's application before 5 September 1988;

(3) Costs are reserved.

Luxembourg, 20 July 1988.

J. G. Giraud   A. J. Mackenzie Stuart
Registrar   President

ORDER (27th September 1988)

1   By an application lodged at the Court Registry on 18 July 1988, the Commission of the European Communities brought an action before the Court under Article 169 of the EEC Treaty for a declaration that as a result of the failure of the Consorzio per la Costruzione e la Gestione di un Impianto per l'Incenerimento e Trasformazione dei Rifiuti Solidi Urbani (hereinafter referred to as "the Consortium"), whose headquarters are at the Town Hall of La Spezia, to publish in the Official Journal of the European Communities a notice concerning the award of a contract for works connected with the Consortium's incinerator, the Italian Republic had failed to fulfil its obligations under Council Directive 71/305/EEC of July 1971 concerning the co-ordination of procedures for the award of public works contracts (Official Journal, English Special Edition 1971 (II), p. 682).

2   By an application lodged at the Court Registry on the same date, the Commission also applied, under Article 186 of the EEC Treaty and Article 83 of the Rules of Procedure, for an interim order requiring the Italian Republic to adopt all the necessary measures to suspend the award of the contract in question in this case until the Court has given judgment in the main action. In the alternative, should the contract already have been awarded, the Court is requested to order the Italian Republic to adopt all the measures which are appropriate in order to cancel the award of the contract or, at the very least, to preserve the status quo until final judgment is given.

3   By an order of 20 July 1988, the President of the Court, by way of an interlocutory decision, provisionally ordered that the Italian Republic should

adopt all the necessary measures to suspend the award of the public works contract in question until 15 September 1988 or such other date as might be fixed by a subsequent order of the court. By an order of 13 September 1988, the President of the Court, by way of an interlocutory decision, extended those protective measures until the date of the final order in these interlocutory proceedings.

4   The Italian Republic submitted its written observations on 2 September 1988. The parties' oral submissions were on 23 September 1983.

5   The Consortium is an association of municipalities situated in the province of La Spezia, in Liguria, which is responsible for the disposal of solid urban waste. For that purpose, it operates an incinerator in Boscalino di Arcola. On 31 December 1986, the Pretore (Magistrate) of La Spezia ordered the incinerator to be closed down and made its re-opening subject to its renovation. The dispute contract relates to the carrying out of that renovation work.

6   The burden of the Commission's charge against the Italian Republic is that in the course of awarding the contract the Consortium infringed the advertising rules laid down in Directive 71/305/EEC by failing to publish a contract notice in the Official Journal of the European Communities, without providing evidence of circumstances of such a nature as to justify a derogation under the provisions of the Directive, in particular Article 9 thereof. It requests that the award of the contract be suspended immediately in order to prevent it causing immediate and serious damage to the Commission, as protector of the Community's interests, and to the undertakings which would have been able to take part in the tendering procedure had a contract notice been published in accordance with the Directive.

7   It is an established and undisputed fact that no notice of the contract in question was published in the Official Journal if the European Communities.

8   Article 186 of the Treaty provides that the Court may prescribe any interim measures requested in cases before it. In order for such a measure to be granted, an application for interim measures must, according to Article 83 (2) of the Rules of Procedure, state the circumstances giving rise to urgency and the factual and legal grounds establishing a prima facie case for the interim measure applied for.

9   First of all, the Italian Government takes the view that there is no prima facie case for granting the interim measure sought, since Directive No. 71/305/EEC does not apply to the contract in question. In the first place, the contract is only exploratory and does not come within the definition of public works contracts laid down in Article 1 of the Directive. Secondly, should that not be the case, the Directive itself states in Article 9 (d) that the provisions relating to advertising do not apply when extreme

urgency prevents the time-limit from being adhered to. The Italian Government goes on to dispute the urgency of the interim measure applied for, since in its view the start of renovation work on the incinerator is much more urgent that any compliance with the formal requirements laid down by the Directive. Finally, the balance of interests tilts in favour of having a rapid start made on the works, given the public health interests at stake when solid refuse can no longer be satisfactorily disposed of.

1 0 The argument that the contested invitation to tender was exploratory must be rejected straight away. The Italian Government explained in this respect that, under Italian legislation, works contracts may be awarded on the basis of exploratory invitations to tender intended to identify the economically and technically most advantageous tender, in accordance with predetermined conditions; in such a case, the public authorities are not in fact required to award the contracts so that the invitation to tender cannot be regarded as relating to a "public works contract" within the meaning of the Directive. This argument must be rejected since, as the Commission has rightly stated, the Directive governs the procedure for awarding contracts for certain works whenever such contracts are awarded by public authorities; the scope of the Directive does not, and cannot, depend on the particular rules laid down by national legislation as regards the duties of the awarding authorities.

1 1 Consequently, the Italian Government's other arguments should be examined together; they are all based on the urgency of the renovation works on the incinerator in question and on the emergency situation which the Consortium was in at the time the invitation to tender was issued. In order to weigh the importance of these arguments for the purposes of these interlocutory proceedings, they must be considered with reference to the chronological order of the facts underlying the dispute in the main proceedings.

1 2 The documents and oral explanations provided by both parties enable the Court to regard the following facts as agreed for the purpose of the interlocutory proceedings:

(a) On 15 December 1982, a Presidential Decree was brought into force relating to waste disposal; the Consortium was aware of the fact that the incinerator at Boscalino di Arcola did not comply with the technical specifications laid down in that decree;

(b) In May and June 1986, the Consortium approved plans for renovating the incinerator;

(c) Meanwhile, the Regional Council of Liguria gave its authorization, on 26 April 1984, for the opening of a dump at Vallescura, in the municipality of Ricco del Golfo, for the disposal of solid urban refuse from a number of municipalities in the province of La Spezia;

(d) In December 1986, the Pretore of La Spezia ordered the incinerator at Boscalino di Arcola to be closed down, making its reopening subject to renovation; in July 1987, the Pretore states that the technical requirements had to be met in full;

(e) During the first few months of 1987, the Ligurian regional authorities found that the dumping of waste in Vallescura had led to seepage into a stream situated below the tip; in July, the Vallescura dump was closed; an old dump in Saturnia was temporarily used, but with great hygiene problems and dangers to public health; a second tip in Vallescura was brought into use, at first for a few months;

(f) On 27 November 1987, the Consortium applied for a loan from the Cassa Depositi e Prestiti in order to finance the works for renovation the incinerator;

(g) In December 1987, the Consortium decided to issue an exploratory invitation to tender for the award of a contract for the renovating work; the award was subject to the grant of a loan by the Cassa; the Consortium expressly stated that shortness of time did not allow another system of awarding contracts to be used, which would necessarily have taken longer; the Consortium sent a letter to seven Italian undertakings, appearing on national lists of specialised construction companies, and invited them to submit tenders;

(h) In February 1988, work was started on a third dump at Vallescura;

(i) On 2 June 1988, a ministerial decree was adopted which included the renovation of the incinerator in Boscalino di Arcola among the 17 priority projects for which the Cassa Depositi e Prestiti was authorised to grant loans

(j) On 15 July 1988, an order made by the Ligurian a regional authorities laid down the conditions for the tipping of refuse on the second and third dumps at Vallescura; the limits set for the use of the second dump were almost reached.

13 To complete this summary of the facts, it should be added that, on the day of the hearing, the loan for the financing of the renovation work on the incinerator had still not been granted by the Cassa Depositi e Prestiti.

14 The chronology of the facts shows first that, however urgent the works to be undertaken may be, that urgency is not due to unforseeable events, since the Consortium has known since 1982 that the renovation of the incinerator was necessary. In order that the exception provided for in Article 9 (d) of Directive 71/305/EEC may be relied on, the "extreme urgency" brought about by events unforeseen by the authorities awarding contracts must prevent the time-limit laid down for the application of the Directive from being kept. There are, therefore, sufficient factual and legal elements for assuming that, prima facie, the Directive applies.

15 At the interlocutory hearing, the argument between the parties in fact concentrating mainly on the urgency relied on by the Commission, on the one hand, and the urgent need to complete the renovation of the incinerator quickly, on the other. The Commission argued that the length of time needed to comply with the advertising requirements of the Directive was quite relative, since compliance with the advertising rules laid down in Article 12 et seq. of the Directive requires a period of only about forty days, and in urgent cases 25 days, whereas the invitation to tender itself dated from December 1987. The Italian Government emphasised the serious risks to public health which additional delays would entail, particularly in view of the uncertainty about the future possibility of using the tip at Vallescura.

16 Given those arguments, it must be recognised that the observance of further time-limits in the completion of the renovation works on the incinerator might entail serious risks for public health and the environment. However, it should also be borne in mind that the Consortium, which is responsible for the work, brought about this situation itself by its slowness in meeting the new technical requirements. Furthermore, the Commission's argument that a failure to comply with the Directive constitutes a serious breach of Community law, particularly since a declaration of illegality by the Court obtained under Article 169 of the Treaty cannot make good the damage suffered by undertakings established in other Member States which were excluded from the tendering procedure, must be accepted.

17 Whilst being aware of the difficulties in which the Consortium now finds itself, the Court considers that the Commission has established the urgency of the interim measure applied for and that in the final analysis the balance of interests tilts in its favour. In this regard, the Court has taken into account in particular the fact that the dumping of refuse at Vallescura must continue for quite a considerable period in any case. In fact, the Italian legislation laying down urgent provisions governing the disposal of waste, which is applicable in this case, allows a period of 120 days between the grant of the loan and the beginning of the works, which must be completed within the ensuing 18 months. In comparison with those periods, those entailed in complying with the Directive appear to be negligible.

1 8 Consequently, the suspension already ordered must be extended until the date of delivery of the judgment in the main action.

On those grounds,

Judge Koopmans, replacing the President of the Court in accordance with the second paragraph of Article 85 (2) and Article 11 of the Rules of Procedure,

by way of interlocutory decision,

hereby orders as follows:

1. The Italian Republic shall adopt all the necessary measures to suspend the award of a public works contract by the Consorzio per la Costruzione e la Gestione di un Impianto per l'Incenerimento e Trasformazione dei Rifiuti Solidi Urbani, whose headquarters are at the offices of the City of La Spezia, until the date of delivery of the judgement determining the main action;

2. Costs are reserved.

Luxembourg, 27 September 1988

J.G. Giraud   T. Koopmans,
Registrar   acting for the President

Case 295/89, Impresa Donà Alfonso di Donà Alfonso & Figli S.N.C. v Consortzio per lo sviluppo industriale del Commune di Monafalcone.

18th June 1991.

(for discussion see 13. above)

Note: the following is an unofficial translation.

JUDGMENT

1   By order of 7 April 1989 received at the Court on 26 September of the
same year the Tribunale Amministrativo Regionale del Friuli-Venezia
Giulia referred to the Court for a preliminary ruling under Article 177 of the
EEC Treaty three questions in relation to the interpretation of Article 29,
para. 5 of Council Directive 71/305/EEC of 26 July 1971, concerning the
co-ordination of procedures for the award of public works contracts (O.J. L
185, p.5)

2   These questions were raised in the context of a dispute in which the
S.N.C. Impresa Donà Alfonso di Donà Alfonso & Figli (hereafter "Donà"),
the applicant in the main action, is seeking the annulment of a decision by
which the tender it had submitted in a procedure for the award of public
works contracts was excluded by the contracting authority the Consorzio per
lo sviluppo industriale de la commune de montfalcone (hereafter "the
consorzio") the defendant in the main action, which awarded the contract in
question to the temporary association of undertakings bringing together the
S.P.A. Impresa Luigi Tacchino and the S.R.L. Impresa Carlutti
Construtrori (hereafter "Tacchino & Carlutti").

3   Article 29, para. 5 of Council Directive 71/305, quoted above, in the
version which was in force at the time of the contentious award procedure
provided that:

"If, for a given contract, tenders are obviously abnormally low in relation to the transaction, the authority awarding contracts shall examine the details of the tenders before deciding to whom it will award the contract. The result of this examination shall be taken into account.

For this purpose it shall request the tenderer to furnish the necessary explanations and, where appropriate, it shall indicate which parts it finds unacceptable.

If the documents relating to the contract provide for its award at the lowest price tendered, the authority awarding contracts must justify to the Advisory Committee set up by the Council decision of 26 July 1971 the rejection of tenders which it considers to be too low."

4   Article 29, para. 5 of Directive 71/305 was implemented in Italy by Article 24, para 3 of the law No 584 of 8 August 1977, concerning provisions for the adaptation of the procedures for the award of public works contracts to the European Economic Community Directives (GURI No 232 of 28 August 1977, p. 6272). That provision reads as follows

"If, for a given contract, tenders appear to be adnormally low in relation to the transaction, the contracting authority, after having requested the tenderer to supply details of the constituent elements of the tender which it considers relevant and having indicated those considered unacceptable, shall verify those constituent elements and can exclude them if it considers that they are invalid; in this situation, if the documents relating to the contract provide for its award at the lowest price the contracting authority must communicate the rejection of tenders as well as the reason pertaining to it to the Ministry for Public Works which, in turn, is responsible for communicating this to the Advisory Committee for Public Works Contracts of the European Economic Community within the period laid down by Article 6, para. 2 of this law."

5   Subsequently, in 1987, the Italian Government successively adopted three decree-laws which contained provisional amendments of Article 24, para. 3 of the law No 584 (decree-law no 206, of 25 May 1987, GURI no 120 of 26 May 1987, p. 5; decree-law no 302 of 27 July 1987, GURI no 174, of 28 July 1987, p. 3; decree-law no 393 of 25 September.1987, GURI no 225 of 26 September 1987, p. 3).

6   Each of these decree-laws contains an identically worded fourth article the terms of which are as follows:

"In order to speed up the procedures for the award of public works contracts, for a period of two years from the date on which this decree enters into force tenders with a percentage discount greater than the average percentage divergence of the tenders admitted, increased by a percentage which must be stated in the call for tenders, shall be considered abnormal for the purposes of the third paragraph of Article 24 of law no 584 of 8 August 1977, and shall be excluded from the tendering procedure."

7 These decree-laws lapsed because they were not converted into Laws within the period prescribed by the Italian constitution. However, a subsequent Law provided that the effects of legal measures adopted pursuant to then were to remain valid. (Art. 1, para. 2 of the law no 478, of 25 November 1987, GURI no 277, of 20 November 1987, p. 3).

8 With a view to realising the works of primary urbanisation and technical equipment of the industrial zone of Schiavetti-Brancolo, the Consorzio conducted a restricted call for tenders. The criterion for awarding the contract was the lowest price resulting from the biggest discount in relation to the basic price.

9 It appears from the contract notice that, in accordance with Article.4 of the decree-law no 393, of 25 September. 1987, quoted above, tenders would be considered abnormally low and would, therefore, be excluded from the award procedure if they showed a percentage reduction exceeding the average rebate shown in the admitted tenders by more than 3%.

1 0 The tenders admitted to adjudication showed an average reduction of 10.098%. In accordance with the contract notice, all tenders which were more than 13.098% lower than the basic price were required to be automatically excluded from the award procedure.

1 1 Donà proposed a rebate of 26.62%. Accordingly, on 22 and 28 March 1988 the Consorzio decided to exclude Donà's tender from the award procedure on the basis of Article 4 of the decree-law no 393 and to award the contract to Tacchino and Carlutti, who had submitted the lowest tender of those which satisfied the condition expressed in the contract notice.

1 2 Donà challenged this decision before the Tribunale Amministrativo Regionale del Friuli-Venezio Giulia claiming, in particular, that it was illegal because it was founded on a decree-law which was itself incompatible with Article 29, para. 5 of Council Directive 71/305.

1 3 That tribunal consequently put the following questions to the Court for preliminary rulings:

1) Is Article 29, para. 5 of Community Directive 305 of 20 July 1971 (which provides that where a tender shows itself to be abnormally low in relation to the transaction the administration must confirm its constituent elements and is under an obligation to request the tenderer to provide

explanations and to indicate those which it considers to be unacceptable) a "provision as to results" and therefore is it in all eventualities of such a nature that it must be implemented by the Italian State without any substantial amendment (as in the case of Article 24, para. 3 of the Law no 584 of 8 August 1977) or does it merely constitute a provision "as to form and methods" which can consequently be partly derogated from at the time of its implementation, by providing for an automatic system rather than an individualised one for dealing with abnormally low tenders and one which, most importantly, leads to the exclusion of the said tenders without the need to precede it with a confirmation of their constituent elements and a request for explanations to this end?

2)   In this second case, having implemented the Community provision quoted above by Article 24, para. 3 of the Law no 584 of 1977 without amending it substantially as far as the procedure of individualisation and exclusion of abnormally low tenders is concerned, can the Italian Republic then amend this national provision by the identically worded Article 4 of each of the decree-laws nos 206 of 25 May 1987, 302 of 25 July 1987 and 393 of 25 Sept. 1987; can these Laws, in turn, effect amendments to Article 29, para. 5 of the directive in question such as it had already been implemented by the Law no 584 of 1987 (Article 24, para. 3) mentioned above?

3)   In any event, is there a conflict between the Community provision quoted (Article 29, para. 5 of Directive no 305 of 1971)and Article.24, para.3 of the Law no 584 of 1977 which refers to "abnormally low tenders" whereas the directive refers to tenders which are "obviously"abnormally low, or with Articles 4 of the decree-laws no 206, 302, and 393 of 1987 which, besides the fact that they do not refer to tenders which are obviously abnormally low provide for an automatic system for tailoring and excluding tenders, without requiring a preliminary confirmation of their constituent elements in relation to the transaction or a request for clarification by the tenderer?

1 4   For a fuller account of the facts of the main dispute, the applicable legislation, the proceedings and the written observations submitted to the court it is necessary to refer to the report for the hearing. Those matters are only referred to here to the extent that they are necessary to the reasoning of the court.

1 5   In the case of 22 June 1989, *Fratelli Costanzo* (Case 103/88) the court replied to questions of identical scope to the ones put to it in the present case for a preliminary ruling.

1 6   In that case the Court came to the conclusion that Article 29, para.5 of Council Directive 71/305 prohibited Member States from introducing laws

providing for the automatic exclusion from public works contracts of certain specified tenders according to a mathematical criterion, instead of obliging the contracting authority to apply the examination procedure laid down in the Directive, giving the tenderer an opportunity to furnish explanations.
1 7 The Court added that in implementing Council Directive 71/305, Member States cannot depart to any material extent from the provisions of Article 29, para. 5 of that Directive.
1 8 Finally, the Court was of the opinion that Article 29, para.5 of Council Directive 71/305 allows Member States to require tenders to be examined when those tenders appear to be abnormally low and not just when they are obviously abnormally low.
1 9 In view of the fact that the instant case presents no factual or legal elements which could require different answers, reference must be made to the text of that judgment of 22 June 1989 for the answers to be given to the Tribunale Administrativo del Friuli-Venezia Giulia, and for the reasoning which leads to those answers.

Costs

2 0 The costs incurred by the Spanish government and the Commission which submitted observations to the Court are not recoverable. As these proceedings are, in so far as the parties to the main action are concerned, in the nature of a step in the action pending before the national court, costs are a matter for that court.

For these reasons,

The Court (first chapter) replying to questions put to it by the Tribunale Amministrativo Regionale del Friuli-Venezia Giulia by an order of 7 April 1989 hereby rules:

1) Article 29, para. 5 of Council Directive 71/305 of 20 July 1971 concerning the co-ordination of procedures for the award of public works contracts prohibits Member States from introducing laws which provide for the automatic exclusion of certain specified tenders from public works contracts according to a mathematical criterion, instead of requiring the contracting authority to apply the examination procedure laid down in the Directive, giving the tenderer an opportunity to furnish explanations.

2) **In implementing Council Directive 71/305, Member States may not depart to any material extent from the provisions of Article 29, para. 5 of that Directive.**

3) **Article 29, para. 5 of Council Directive 71/305 allows Member States to require confirmation of tenders to be examined when those tenders appear to be appear to be abnormally low; and not just when they are obviously abnormally low**

Case C-247/89, Commission of the European Communities v Portugal.

11th July 1991.

(for discussion see 14. above)

Note: the following is an unofficial translation.

JUDGMENT

1   By an application submitted to the Court Registry on 4 August 1991, the Commission of the European Communities instituted an action under Article 169 of the EEC Treaty seeking a declaration that, in having omitting to send a notice of a call for tenders issued by the Aeroportas Navegaçao Aeréa company in relation to the supply and installation of a telephone exchange at Lisbon airport, to the official publications office of the European Communities in order for it to be published in the Official Journal of the European Communities, the Portugese Republic failed to fulfil its obligations under Council Directive 77/62 of 21 December 1976 concerning co-ordination of the procedures for the award of public supply contracts (O.J. 1977, L 13, p.1) and in particular its obligations under Article 9 of the Directive.

2   Article 1(a) of Directive 77/62, quoted above, defines public supply contracts as contracts for consideration concluded in writing between a supplier (a natural or legal person) and a contracting authority concerning the delivery of products. According to Article 1(b) there shall be considered as contracting authorities the state, regional or local authorities and legal persons governed by public law or, in Member States where the latter are unknown, bodies corresponding thereto as specified in Annex 1 of the Directive.

3   The combined provisions of Article 26 and Annex 1(ix) (d) of the Act concerning the conditions of accession of the Kingdom of Spain and the Portugese Republic and the adjustments to the Treaties (O.J. 1985, L 302, p.21 and p.139, hereafter the"Act of Accession") added to the list of legal persons governed by public law and entities envisaged by Article 1(b), and mentioned in Annex 1 of Directive 77/62:"

... xiii In Portugal: legal persons governed by public law whose award of public supply contracts is subject to State control "

4   According to Article 9 of Directive 77/62, quoted above, contracting authorities wishing to award a public contract are obliged to send the notice by which they make known their intention as soon as possible and by the most appropriate routes to the official publications office of the European Communities with a view to its publication in the Official Journal.

5   Article 2, para. 2(a) of Directive 77/62 excludes supply contracts awarded by organisations which administer transport services from the sphere of application of the directive.

6   By virtue of Articles 392 and 395 of the Act of Accession, Directive 77/62 was required to be implemented into the law of the Portuguese State by 1 January 1986.

7   The public undertaking Aeroportos e Navegaçao Aeréa (hereafter the "ANA-EP") is a legal person governed by public law which was established by the decree-law no 246/79 of 25 July 1979 (Diarioda Republica, no 170, series I). According to that decree-law and to the constitution of the ANA-EP annexed to it, that body is responsible for the operation and development of support activities for civil aviation with the aim of orientating, directing and controlling air traffic, ensuring the departure and arrival of planes as well as freight, embarkation, disembarkation and routing of passengers and post. The ANA-EP also undertakes the activities and services which are inherent to airport infrastructures and aerial navigation among others at Lisbon Airport. Finally it is responsible for the study, planning, construction and development of new civil airport infrastructures and for aerial navigation.

8   In 1987, the ANA-EP conducted a call for tenders with a view to the supply and installation of a telephone exchange at Lisbon airport. To this end it placed an advertisement in the Portuguese weekly O Expresso of 29 August 1987.

9   Having become aware of that advertisement the Commission noted that all the conditions for the application of Directive 77/62, quoted above, were satisfied and that none of the derogations in relation to its sphere of application were applicable.

1 0   Having noted that, in its capacity as a contracting authority, the ANA-EP had not conformed to the obligation to send the notice of the call for tenders to the official publications office of the European Communities as provided for by Article 9 of Directive 77/62, the Commission addressed a letter of infringement to the Portuguese government on 28 September 1987.

1 1   In its reply dated 20 October 1987, the Portuguese government disputed the applicability of Directive 77/62.

1 2   Considering that the Portuguese government could not justify the failure to publish the notice of a call for tenders in the Official Journal of the European Communities, the Commission sent a reasoned opinion under Article 169 of the Treaty on 21 November 1988, inviting the Portuguese government to take the necessary measures to comply within one month from the date of notification.

13 In its reply to the reasoned opinion, the Portuguese government expressed its intention to amend the Portuguese legislation. The Commission decided to institute the present action feeling that that stance was not satisfactory.

14 For a fuller account of the legal context and of the background to the litigation as well as of the grounds and arguments of the parties reference must be made to the report for the hearing. These matters are referred to below only to the extent necessary for the reasoning of the court.

I - Admissibility

15 The Portuguese government claims that the action is inadmissible. In this respect it invokes several arguments based, on the one hand, on the non-attributability of the alleged breach to the Portuguese Republic and, on the other hand, on the contradiction between the grounds of the reasoned opinion and those put forward in the application as well as the ambiguous position of the Commission and the insufficiency of the time limit fixed in the reasoned opinion.

16 Concerning the non-attributability of the alleged breach, the Portuguese government holds that Article 9 of Directive 77/62, quoted above, only obliges the State to publish notices of calls for tenders in the Official Journal when it is the contracting authority. But the ANA-EP is a legal person distinct from the State and consequently the absence of publication of its notices of calls for tenders ought not to be attributed to the latter. The Portuguese government adds that as the directive has not yet been implemented into the domestic legal system, the ANA-EP is not subject to the obligation of publication of the notice of its public supply contracts.

17 On its part, the Commission emphasises that the ANA-EP is a contracting authority within the meaning of Directive 77/62 in the light of the control exercised by the Portuguese State over the award of its public contracts. It considers that, in these circumstances, the responsibility for the fact of the omission by the ANA-EP to publish its calls for tenders falls on the Portuguese State. It adds that this interpretation of the directive ought not to be invalidated by the fact that it has not yet been implemented into domestic law.

18 In this respect it suffices to state that the question whether the behaviour of the ANA-EP can be attributed to the Portuguese State involves an assessment of facts which falls under the examination of the merits of the action for breach and not the admissibility of that action.

19 This question must therefore be attached to the examination of the substance of the case.

20 Concerning the contradiction between the grounds in the reasoned opinion and those put forward in the application, the Portuguese government points out that, in the reasoned opinion the Commission categorised the ANA-EP as a contracting authority within the meaning of Directive 77/62, quoted above, because the award of public contracts by it was subordinate to an approval or authorisation of the Portuguese government whereas in the application it declared that the removal of this procedure for the approval or authorisation of public contracts did not affect the ANA-EP's quality as a contracting authority within the meaning of the directive. They also hold that the Commission's position was ambiguous to the extent that it never specified the nature of the measures to be taken to put an end to the breach. They emphasise in this respect that the Commission did not object to their intention to abrogate the obligation of approval or authorisation of the State for certain public contracts. Finally the Portuguese government points out that the time limit fixed in the reasoned opinion was insufficient to undertake an amendment of the legislation.

21 According to the Commission, all of those arguments are unfounded. The definition of the behaviour for which the Portuguese state is criticised was never amended. That criticism envisaged, equally the reasoned opinion as according to the application, the notice of a call for tenders made by the ANA-EP. The Commission points out that it never requested an amendment of the Portuguese legislation. It also disputes the existence of an obligation to specify in the reasoned opinion the measures to be taken with a view to eliminating the criticised behaviour. Finally it points out that the time limit fixed in the reasoned opinion was reasonable and sufficient, given the fact that the first communication from the Commission to the Portuguese State, namely the letter of infringement, was sent on 28 September 1987.

22 In this respect it must be borne in mind firstly that according to the case law of the court, the reasoned opinion must contain a detailed and comprehensive account of the reasons which led the Commission to believe that the State concerned failed in one of its obligations under the Treaty (case of 28 March 1985, *Commission v Italy* 274/83). However, the Commission ought not to be obliged to indicate in the reasoned opinion the measures which would permit the elimination of the criticised failure.

23 It appears from the terms of the reasoned opinion attached to the file that it satisfies the requirements of the case law. In effect the Commission specified in it, in a sufficiently detailed manner, the context, the facts, the legal context and the arguments which laid it to believe that the Portuguese Republic has failed in the obligation laid down by Article 9 of Directive 77/62, quoted above. The Commission never, either in the course of the

precontentious phase or the contentious phase of the litigation, changed this argument which ought not, therefore, to be considered ambiguous.

2 4 It must then be stated that the argument contained in the reasoned opinion and in the application is identical in substance and envisages the same ground for complaint namely the violation of Article 9 of Directive 77/62 cited above.

2 5 With regard to the time limit fixed in the reasoned opinion, it must be emphasised that the failure complained of to the Portuguese government was brought to the notice of the latter by the letter of infringement of 28 September 1987, or more than one year before the reasoned opinion delivered on 21 November 1988. It must also be pointed out that as soon as the administrative procedure was begun the Portuguese government disputed the alleged failure by invoking at the same time the inapplicability to the case in question of Directive 77/62 and the non-attributability of the breach to the Portuguese State. In these conditions, the time limit of 1 month fixed in the reasoned opinion to enable the Portuguese government to comply with its obligations must be considered as reasonable and sufficient.

2 6 It appears from the foregoing considerations that the arguments based on the inadmissibility of the action must be rejected.

II - Merits

2 7 The Commission holds that the ANA-EP was obliged by virtue of Article 9 of Directive 77/62, quoted above, to send notice of the call the for tenders in question to the official publications office of the European Communities for publication in the Official Journal, on the ground that all the conditions of application of that provision are satisfied in this case and the situation envisaged does not come under any of the derogations provided for by that directive.

2 8 On the other hand the Portuguese government considers that the provisions of Directive 77/62 were not applicable to the award of the contract in question.

2 9 In support of this ground, the Portuguese government points out first that the activities of the ANA-EP as defined by the decree-law no 246/79, quoted above, and its constitution, on the one hand and aerial transport services, on the other hand, are complementary and cannot be dissociated. It follows that the ANA-EP must be considered as an organisation which manages transport services within the meaning of Article 2, para. 2(a) of Directive 77/62 whose award of public supply contracts does not fall within the sphere of application of that directive.

3 0 The Portuguese government then refers to Council Directive 90/531/EEC of 17 September 1990 concerning the procedures for the award of contracts in the water, energy, transport and communications sectors (O.

J. L 297, p.1). That directive envisages, among others, public contracts in those sectors as largely excluded from the sphere of application of Directive 77/62, quoted above, as last amended by Council Directive 88/295/EEC of 22 March 1988 (O. J..L 127, p.1). The fact that the ANA-EP expressly figures among the organisations subject to Directive 90/531, quoted above, proves, according to the Portuguese government, that the ANA-EP does not come within the sphere of application of Directive 77/62.

31 The Portuguese government also emphasises that Article 2, para. 2(a) of Directive 77/62 which excludes from its sphere of application "organisations which manage transport services" has a wider meaning than the new wording of that article resulting from Article 3 of Directive 88/295, quoted above. In effect, this last provision only excludes from the sphere of application of Directive 77/62 "Carriers by land, air, sea or inland waterway." This difference demonstrates that Article 2, para. 2(a) of Directive 77/62 includes in the version which was in force at the date of the call for tenders in question, organisations which, like the ANA-EP, manage ground services.

32 On its part, the Commission considers that the ANA-EP is not an organisation which manages transport services within the meaning of Directive 77/62. Referring to the Community guidebook on public contracts (O.J. 1987, C358, p.1) the Commission points out that Article 2, para. 2(a) of the directive, which must be restrictively interpreted, only envisages organisations which undertake the transport of persons or goods from one point to another. It adds that the new wording of Article 2, para. 2(a) resulting from Directive 88/295, quoted above, has the aim of clarifying but not amending the scope of that provision. Finally the Commission points out that the mention of the ANA-EP in the terms of Directive 90/531, quoted above, is an expression of the aim pursued by that directive which is to place public undertakings and private organisations which manage airports on an equal footing.

33 It must be emphasised first that, according to Article 2, para. 2(a) of Directive 77/62 in the version in force when the call for tenders in question was sent out, that Directive does not apply to public supply contracts awarded by organisations which manage transport services.

34 This exclusion is justified by the sixth and seventh preambles to Directive 77/62 under the terms of which

"... whereas the bodies currently administering transport services in the Member States are governed in some cases by public law, in others by private law; ... in accordance with the objectives of the common transport policy equality of treatment should be ensured not only between separate undertakings concerned with the same mode of transport but also between such undertakings and undertakings concerned with other modes of transport;

... pending the drafting of measures for coordinating the procedures applicable to transport bodies and in view of the said special circumstances, those authorities referred to above, which by reason of their legal status would fall within it, should be excluded from the scope of the Directive."

3 5 It must then be observed that the notion of an organisation which manages transport services to which Article 2, para. 2(a) of Directive 77/62, quoted above, refers in the version applicable in this instance, envisages the transport services sector in its entirety.

3 6 The activities pursued by the ANA-EP by virtue of the decree-law no 246/79, quoted above, and of its constitution are closely linked to the aerial transport of persons and goods in the sense that that transport cannot be realised without the necessary infrastructure and airport services.

3 7 It must also be emphasised that the common transport policy to which the preambles quoted above in point 34 refer includes activities linked to the functioning of the infrastructure necessary to transport and that the requirement of equality of treatment mentioned in them also envisages that organisations which are undertaking services and activities which are inherent to airport infrastructures and to aerial navigation in the Member States are sometimes governed by public law and sometimes by private law.

3 8 It follows from the foregoing considerations that an entity like the ANA-EP which undertakes such activities and services must be considered to be an organisation which manages transport services within the meaning of the version of Article 2, para. 2(a) of Directive 77/62, quoted above, which was in force on the date of the call for tenders in question.

3 9 This statement is confirmed by the provisions and the scope of Directive 90/531, quoted above, on the procurement procedures for entities operating in the water, energy, transport and telecommunications sectors which the Council issued on 17 September 1990.

4 0 It must be pointed out in this respect that, by virtue of Article 2, para. 2(b)(ii) of that directive, which envisages among other things the regulation of procedures for the award of contracts in the transport sector, applies to the use of a geographical area with the aim of making airports available to air carriers and that the ANA-EP figures in Annex VIII of that directive as a contracting entity which satisfies the criteria expressed in Article 2, para. 6 of that same directive.

4 1 It clearly appears from the sixth and seventh preambles of Directive 90/531 that the transport sector falls under the sectors excluded from the sphere of application of Directive 77/62, as last modified by Directive 88/295, quoted above.

4 2 Consequently, the argument in favour of a restrictive interpretation of the notion of an organisation which manages transport services, drawn by the Commission from the terms of Article 2, para. 2(a) of Directive 77/62 ought not to be upheld.

43 In view of all the foregoing considerations and without the need to rule on the other grounds of defence raised by the Portuguese government it must be stated that the ANA-EP as an organisation which manages transport services within the meaning of Article 2, para. 2(a) of Directive 77/62 did not at the time of the call for tenders in question come within the sphere of application of that Directive and that the action for breach is therefore unfounded.

Costs

44 Within the terms of Article 69, para. 2 of the Rules of Procedure the party against whom judgement is given undertakes costs. The Commission having failed in its grounds is ordered to pay costs.

For these reasons the Court declares and lays down that

1. **The application is dismissed**

2. **The Commission is ordered to pay costs.**

Case C-351/88, Laboratori Bruneau Srl v Unità Sanitaria Locale RM/24 de Monterondo

Judgment of 11 July 1991

(for discussion see 15. above)

Note: the following is an unofficial translation.

JUDGMENT

1   By an Order of 30 May 1988, received by the Court on 6 December 1988, the Tribunale Amministrativo Regionale del Lazio (Italy) referred to the Court for a preliminary ruling under Article 177 of the EEC Treaty a question in relation to the interpretation of Articles 30 and 92 of the EEC Treaty, with a view to assessing the compatibility with these provisions of Italian legislation which reserved a percentage of public supply contracts to undertakings established in the Mezzogiorno area.

2   This question was raised in the context of a dispute between the Unità Laboratori Bruneau company and the l'Unità Sanitaria Locale RM/24 de Monterotondo (Rome) (hereafter "U.S.L.") following the former's exclusion from the procedure for a contract for the supply of suture equipment.

3   By virtue of Article 17, para. 16 and 17 of the Law no 64 of 1 March 1986 (Disciplina organica dell' intervento straordinario nel Mezzogiorno) the Italian state imposed an obligation on all public bodies and authorities as well as on companies in which the state has a shareholding including the local health authorities situated on national territory, to obtain at least 30% of their supplies from industrial and agricultural undertakings and small businesses established in Southern Italy, in which the products concerned undergo processing.

4   In accordance with that legislation, the U.S.L. fixed the conditions for a restricted tendering procedure for the contract for the supply of suture equipment. The Laboratori Bruneau company challenged this decision before the Tribunale Amministativo Regionale del Lazio putting forward as a reason the fact that it had been excluded from the procedure for the award of the contract on the ground that it was not established in Southern Italy.

5   In the context of considering that action the national tribunal decided to refer to the court for a preliminary ruling the question whether:

"Articles 30 and 92 of the EEC Treaty must be interpreted in the sense that national legislation which reserves a percentage of public supply contracts to undertakings established in certain regions of the national territory must be considered as constituting "measures equivalent to quantitative restrictions" or "aids" and whether they conflict with the said provisions?"

6   For a fuller account of the provisions of national law in question, the facts of the dispute in the main action, the proceedings as well as the written observations submitted to the Court, reference must be made to the report for the hearing.

7   In its decision of 20 March 1990, *Du Pont de Nemours* (case C-21/88), the Court replied to questions of identical scope which were referred for a preliminary ruling by the Tribunale Amministrativo Regionale della Toscana, that Article 30 of the Treaty must be interpreted in the sense that it is inconsistent with national rules which reserves a proportion of public supply contracts to undertakings established in certain regions of the national territory, and that the possibility of qualifying national rules as aid within the meaning of Article 92 of the Treaty could not exempt them from the prohibition in Article 30 of the Treaty.

8   Given the fact that no factual or legal element appears from the observations submitted to the Court which could lead to a different answer, the answer given in the case of 20 March 1990, *Du Pont de Nemours* (C-21/88, quoted above) must be followed.

Costs

9   The costs incurred by the Italian government and by the Commission of the European Communities, which have submitted observations to the Court, are not recoverable. As these proceedings are, in so far as the parties to the main action are concerned, in the nature of a step in the action pending before the national court, costs are a matter for that court.

For these reasons,

Ruling on a question referred to it by the Tribunale Amministrativo Regionale del Lazio, by an Order of 30 May 1988, hereby rules:

1.   Article 30 EEC must be interpreted as precluding national rules which reserve undertakings established in particular

regions of the national territory a proportion of public supply contracts.

2. The possibility of qualifying a national regulation as an aid within the meaning of Article 92 of the Treaty cannot exempt it from the prohibition set out in Article 30 of the Treaty.

Case C-272/91R, Commission of the European Communities v Italy

31st January 1992

(for discussion see 16. above)

Note: the following is an unoficial translation.

ORDER

1 By an application lodged with the Court Registry on 18 October 1991, the Commission of the European Communities instituted proceedings under Article 169 of the EEC Treaty aimed at obtaining a declaration that the Italian Republic, in omitting to communicate for the purposes of publication in the Official Journal of the E.C., firstly, at the beginning of 1990, a notice indicating the total amount of contracts which the Italian Finance Ministry envisaged awarding during the course of that same year, then during the month of November 1990, a notice in relation to a call for tenders for the concession contract for the automation of the lottery, and by limiting participation in the contract exclusively to bodies, companies, consortiums or groupings whose registered capital taken in isolation or in its entirety is in the majority in public ownership, failed in its obligations under Articles 30, 52 and 59 of the EEC Treaty and Articles 9 and 17 to 25 of Council Directive 77/62 of 21 December 1976, concerning the coordination of procedures for the award of public supply contracts (O.J. 1977 L13 p.1) as amended by Council Directive 88/295 of 22 March 1988 (O.J. L127 p.1).

2 By a separate act lodged with the Clerk of the Court on the same day, the Commission instituted an application for interim measures by virtue of Article 186 of the EEC Treaty and Article 83 of the Rules of Procedure with the aim of requiring the Italian Republic to take the necessary measures to suspend the legal effects of the Finance Minister's decree of 14 June 1991, awarding the contract in question, or any possible contract concluded as a result of it.

3 The defendant made written observations on the application on 31 October 1991 and the oral submissions of the parties were heard on 2 December 1991.

4   During the hearing, the defendant submitted two documents and the parties were invited to make additional observations which the documents rendered necessary. The Commission made observations on 9 December and the defendant did so on 16 December 1991.

5   Before examining the merits of the application for interim measures, it is necessary to briefly recall the previous history of the dispute.

6   On 13 November 1990 the Italian Finance Minister undertook the publication in the Italian press of a contract notice concerning a call for tenders for a concession contract for the automatisation of the lottery system.

7   It appears from the file that the lottery is a game administered by an administrative entity answerable to the Finance Ministry. In this game, players bet on one or several numbers with a weekly draw in mind. The taking of bets is carried out at agreed recording outlets (mainly tobacconist shops) and a draw takes place every Saturday in each of the 10 draw zones ("ruote") into which the Italian territory is subdivided. A bet can be in relation either to the draw in the zone in which the recording outlet is situated or the draws in the whole of the zones. Winnings, the amounts of which are determined mainly according to the stake following a calculation method fixed by Italian legislation, are payable at the recording outlet or, for winnings exceeding a certain sum, at the premises of the Finance Ministry.

8   The concession for the automisation of the game which is envisaged by the contract, is, according to the contract notice, made up of the premises, supplies, installation, maintenance, running, transmission of data and all other aspects of the operation of the lottery game service.

9   According to the contract notice, the duration of the concession is limited to 9 years and upon its expiration the whole of the automated system, including the premises, appliances, terminals of the recording outlets, fittings, fixtures, programmes, records and all other necessary elements of the operation, administration and running of the system must be handed over to the administration free of charge.

1 0   It is specified that the concession is made up of three phases : an initial phase of supply, installation and trials carried out simultaneously with the manual system which is achieved by putting the automated system into operation in one draw zone; a second phase comprising the extension of the system to all the zones; and, finally, a third phase of total operation involving a progressive increase in the number of recording outlets. The tenders must indicate the length of time required to complete each phase.

1 1   The concessionaire for the system will have no right to remuneration during the first phase but during the second and third phases will collect a percentage of the gross returns on bets automatically recorded. Tenders must indicate the relevant percentage.

1 2   The contract notice further specified the economic and technical criteria according to which the bodies or undertakings wishing to be invited to make submissions will be selected.

1 3   According to the contract notice, however, participation in the contract was reserved to bodies, companies or consortiums as well as groupings whose registered capital taken in isolation or its entirety is for the most part held by the public sector, the Finance Ministry having to take into account the particular nature and size of the automatic operation of the lottery game which, administered in the context of fiscal monopolies to obtain maximum return, requires special guarantees as well as absolute security and confidence in the setting up and the operation of the system.

1 4   Three bodies or undertakings were invited to take part in the award procedure. By a decree of the Finance Ministry dated 14 June 1991, the concession was awarded to the Lottomatica Consortium formed by the Olivetti company among others.

1 5   As early as 8 April 1991 the Commission sent a formal notice to the Italian authorities, followed on 2 September 1991 by a reasoned opinion. In it the Commission points out primarily that the exclusive reservation of the contract in question to companies or entities the majority of whose capital is held by the public sector constitutes a breach of Articles 52 and 59 of the EEC Treaty, to the extent that it favours Italian companies, as well as amounting to a measure having an equivalent effect to a restriction on imports as prohibited by Article 30 of the Treaty. In this respect, the Commission reminds the Italian authorities that in the case of 5 December 1989, *Commission v Italy* (C-3/88) the Court considered that an Italian regulation exclusively reserving the possibility of concluding contracts for the development of computer systems for the public administration to companies with a majority of their shareholding in public ownership was contrary to Articles 52 and 59 of the EEC Treaty and gave judgment against Italy for failing to fulfil its obligations. The Italian authorities have not yet taken the measures required to comply with that judgment and the Commission has, because of this, instituted proceedings for failure under Article 171 of the EEC Treaty.

1 6   In their reply to the reasoned opinion the Italian authorities point out primarily that the contract in question is not of the type envisaged in the judgment of the Court quoted above. The contracts in that case concern, in effect, the supply of computer systems of which the supplier must equally undertake the administration but in the capacity of a service performed for the administration, whereas the contract here concerns a concession by which the administration entrusts the exercise of a public authority activity to a third party, that is, the recording of bets under the lottery system. But, in accordance with Article 55 of the EEC Treaty the provisions of Articles

52 and 59 do not apply to activities in the Member States involving the exercise of public authority.

1 7 It must be borne in mind that, by virtue of Article 186 of the EEC Treaty, the Court has competence to order necessary interim measures in cases which come before it.

1 8 According to Article 83, para. 2 of the Rules of Procedure, a decision ordering interim measures such as the ones being sought here requires the existence of circumstances establishing urgency as well as legal and factual grounds which, prima facie, justify their award. In accordance with established case law, the urgent nature of a request for provisional measures must be established in relation to the need to make an interim order with a view to avoiding serious and irreparable harm being caused to the party seeking the interim measures.

1 9 It must be examined whether these conditions are satisfied in the present case.

2 0 First, as regards the condition of fumus bon juris, the Commission points out that the violation of Articles 52 and 59 of the EEC Treaty is manifest and that the instant case is perfectly identical to the one which led to the judgement quoted above of 5 December 1989. The concession in question for the automated system ought not to be considered as involving the exercise of public authority within the meaning of Article 55, para. 1 of the Treaty. This same argument was advanced by the Italian government in relation to the contracts in question in the case of 5 December 1989 for the development of data processing systems for the public administration. In this respect, the Court reiterated that the exception to freedom of establishment and freedom to provide services provided for in Article 55 of the Treaty must be limited to activities which in themselves constitute direct and specific involvement in the exercise of public authority and stated that that was not the case in relation to activities concerning the creation, application and administration of data-processing systems which are activities of a technical nature.

2 1 The defendant points out that the concession for the automated lottery system involves a genuine transfer of public powers to the concessionaire and cannot be assimilated to a contract for the supply of goods and services. The remuneration of the concessionaire by a percentage of returns cannot be reconciled with such an assimilation. The lottery game is strictly reserved to the State by virtue of Italian legislation and every operation in relation to the game thus involves the exercise of public powers which, within the meaning of Article 55, para. 1 of the Treaty can be not only decision-making powers but also powers of organisation, inspection or certification. The technical programme submitted by the defendant in relation to the call for tenders during the hearing evidences the powers which the state transfers to the concessionaire. It mainly concerns the taking of bets as the lottery tickets, in order to be valid, must be issued by the concessionaire's terminals which are installed at the recording outlets, and the determination of winning tickets effected by the development centres of the concessionaire in each draw zone.

2 2 In the first place, it must be pointed out that the introduction of the automatic system in question does not appear at first glance to bring about any change in the different operations which are inherent to the lottery game, as they take place at the moment according to the description which is given of it in the technical programme submitted by the defendant. At first glance the responsibility for none of those operations is transferred to the concessionaire. In this way, the recording outlets remain responsible for the taking of bets, the function of the concessionaire's terminal being restricted to the recording by automatic confirmation and to the transmission of data resulting from its use by the person responsible for the recording outlet who, according to the technical programme, must in the event of an error, be in a position to correct the recording and even cancel a ticket issued by the terminal. The same applies to the determination of winning tickets, the zone commission, which is an administrative body, remaining responsible for the control and validation of those tickets.

2 3 In the second place it must be pointed out that the obligations which are incumbent upon the concessionaire of the automatic systems of the lottery game do not appear at first glance to be different from the obligations arising from the contracts for the development of data processing systems for the public administration, which were the subject of the case quoted above of 5 December 1989. In both cases the contract concerns the creation of computerised systems, the supply of necessary material and application programmes as well as the management of the system. It is true that the automatic system of the lotto game does not become the property of the State until the expiration of the concession's fixed time limit and that the remuneration of the concessionaire consists of an interest in the returns attributable to the use of the system but these circumstances appear, at first glance, to be irrelevant, as regards the Community legal rules in question.

2 4 It follows that it can be stated, regard being had to the case quoted above of 5 December 1989, that the action of the Commission does not at this stage seem to be unfounded and the fumus bon juris condition is satisfied.

2 5 Regarding the condition of urgency, the Commission points out that by waiting for the decision in the main action it will suffer serious and irreparable damage in its capacity as guardian of the application of the Treaty. While the Court is deciding that action, the automatic system for the lottery game will long since have been in place and the Commission will have to accept this fait accompli despite a flagrant breach of Community law. In order that the intervening decision of the Court can be effective it is necessary to award interim measures.

2 6 The defendant makes the observation in this respect that the concession contract with the Lotto Matrica Consortium was signed on 22 November 1991 and that the first phase of the concession must end on 1 April 1992, the second phase on 31 December 1992. They point out that the introduction of the automatic system represents a considerable improvement on the game which is the only means of putting an end to the significant clandestine games which are currently being run. The loss of returns for the State in the event of the system's not being put into operation could be estimated at 500 000 million lire per annum. The removal of the clandestine games and the very significant fiscal returns resulting from the automation of the game should therefore be balanced against the Commission's interest in ensuring the respect of the formal rules of the Treaty.

2 7 In this respect it must be stated, as the Commission points out, that if it is successful in the main action the decision will be of no useful effect in the absence of interim measures.

2 8 Concerning the balance of interests it must be pointed out that the interest which the defendant has in achieving a quick automation of the lottery game must be weighed against the interest the Commission has in its capacity as guardian of the Treaties in preventing a breach of their fundamental rules. Regard being had particularly to the decision of the Court of 5 December 1989, the Commission's interest must prevail over that of the Member State in question.

2 9 The condition in relation to urgency thus being satisfied, the requested provisional measures must be ordered.

For these reasons,
The President orders that

1. The Italian Republic take the necessary measures to annul the decree of the Finance Minister of 14 June 1991 awarding the concession of the automatic system of the lottery game and the execution of the contract concluded to this effect with the Lotto Matrica Consortium.

2. The decision on costs is reserved.

Index to text